WALKS OF
NEW ENGLAND
GARY FERGUSON

Illustrated by Kent Humphries
Research Coordinated by Jane Ferguson

PRENTICE
HALL
PRESS

New York London Toronto Sydney Tokyo

PRENTICE HALL PRESS
15 Columbus Circle
New York, New York 10023

PRENTICE HALL PRESS and colophon are registered
trademarks of Simon & Schuster Inc.

Library of Congress Cataloging-in-Publication Data

Ferguson, Gary, 1956–
Walks of New England / by Gary Ferguson; illustrated by Kent
Humphries; research coordinator, Jane Ferguson.—1st ed.
        p.   cm.
ISBN 0-13-944372-X
1. Hiking—New England—Guide-books.   2. New England—Description
and travel—1981— Guide-books.   I. Title.
GV199.42.N38F47   1989
917.4—dc19   88-36992
                                                          CIP

Designed by Irving Perkins Associates
Manufactured in the United States of America

10   9   8   7   6   5   4   3   2

To Chuck, who taught me that the best views
come to those farthest out on the limb.

Thanks

Contents

THE MOUNTAINS   73

Vermont

New Hampshire

Maine

The Walks by State

Introduction

Follow any of a thousand threads in the cultural tapestry of America, and sooner or later you'll find yourself in New England. Held in the short swell of ground that rises from the north shore of Long Island Sound to the chilly blue waters of Passamaquoddy Bay—less than 2 percent of the nation's total land area—are the underpinnings of much of our religion, our economic structure, our politics, our art, and our literature. As historian Bernard De Voto wrote in 1932, New England was "the first old civilization, the first permanent civilization in America."

What's not so apparent, however, is the amount of that civilization's ideology that was fueled by the landscape—the roll of the Atlantic, the hush of primeval forests, the swell of broad-shouldered mountains. Though it's true that the stern, somber religion of the Puritans gave them no higher purpose than to subdue this nature, there can be no question that they were dazzled by its abundance. John Josselyn was astounded by the great flocks of migrating passenger pigeons in colonial America, which he tells us "had neither beginning or ending, length nor breadth, and so thick that I could see no sun." In 1630, Reverend Higginson confesses that "the abundance of Sea-Fish are almost beyond believing." There were also geese, ducks, and turkey too numerous to count, as well as deer, elk, fox, beaver, otter, martin, and moose. And even though colonial writer Thomas Morton was measuring this plenty according to how it filled basic human needs (in particular, a warm fire and a full belly), his comments about the place were hardly uninspired. "If this land be not riche," he said, "then is the whole world poore."

As New England's struggling population stabilized, and then blossomed through the revolution, the relationship of some of her people to their natural surroundings began to blossom as well. Ralph Waldo Emerson, one of the most influential literary figures of the nineteenth century, spent much of his life cultivating the notion that we should establish not just pragmatic but spiritual ties to the American landscape. Emerson was quick to embrace the transcendental essays of University of Vermont president John Marsh, and wasted no time in building from them his own special set of lessons about the worth of the wilds. He concluded, "The lover of nature is he whose inward and outward senses are still truly adjusted to each other; who has retained the spirit of infancy even into the era of manhood."

Not far away lived a friend and protégé of Emerson's, a man named Henry David Thoreau. Eccentric as Thoreau may have seemed to his neighbors, he minced no words when writing about the profound opportunity for personal satisfaction that awaited him in the forests surrounding Concord. "I went to the woods because I wished to live deliberately, to front only the essential facts of life, and see if I could not learn what it had to teach, and not, when I came to die, discover that I had not lived."

Both Emerson and Thoreau traveled widely through the natural areas of New England—to Mount Monadnock and the summits of the White Mountains, to the thick, dark forests of Maine, to the shimmering waters of Lake Champlain. But they were hardly the only ones embarking on such quests, deliberately seeking personal and creative vision from the landscape. Also making pilgrimages through New England were Henry Wadsworth Longfellow, William Cullen Bryant, Rudyard Kipling, Thornton Wilder, Francis Parkman, Herman Melville, Robert Frost, and even Mark Twain. Nathaniel Hawthorne absolutely fell in love with the mountains of New Hampshire, roaming them time and time again to glean material for such works as "The Great Stone Face," "The Ambitious Guest," and "Canterbury Pilgrims." Appropriately, Hawthorne died at the edge of the high country in 1864, in a small inn on the banks of the Pemigewasset River.

The grandeur of New England also caught the attention of the art world. It was the great work of landscape painter Thomas Cole in New Hampshire's White Mountains, in fact, that launched the famous Hudson River School. After a grueling climb to the top of Mount Chocorua in 1928, Cole made a telling note in his diary: "With all its beauty the scene was too extended and maplike for the canvas," he wrote. "It was not for sketches that I ascended Chocorua but for thoughts; and for these this was truly the region." Also to the mountains came Frederick Church, Albert Bierstadt, Godfrey Frankenstein, Thomas Doughty, and Asher Durand, to name but a very, very few.

But perhaps the real excitement of New England is that, despite sometimes crushing growth, you will still find here a rich braid of quiet forests, dancing rivers, and untrammeled mountain paths. It's important to keep in mind that the walks in this book were chosen not for the destinations they offered as much as for the weave of life they hold along the way. I fully hope that there will be at least a few of you who get so sidetracked in some nook or cranny that you never do reach the turnaround point. Throw your lunch, a pair of binoculars, and a set of guide books into your day pack and hit the trail. What happens after that is best left to chance.

To strengthen his case about the virtues of walking, Thoreau once related an anecdote about the English Romantic poet William Wordsworth, a man nearly as dedicated to rambling across the countryside by foot as was Thoreau himself. A traveler, so the story goes, stopped by Wordsworth's house when he was not at home and asked his servant if he could see the poet's study. "Here is his library," she answered, "but his study is out of doors."

As it was in Thoreau's time, the landscape of New England remains one of the finest studies in the world. Abandon the desk and the easy chair, and come see for yourself.

THE FOREST

Why should not we, who have renounced the king's authority, have our national preserves, where no villages need be destroyed, in which the bear and panther, and some even of the hunter race, may still exist, and not be "civilized off the face of the earth," . . . not for idle sport or food, but for inspiration and our own true recreation? or shall we, like the villains, grub them all up, poaching on our own national domains?

HENRY DAVID THOREAU
The Maine Woods

Nowhere will you find a more profound testimony to the powerful healing mechanisms of nature than in the forests of New England. Despite nearly three hundred years of hard use and abuse, today these woodlands still weave an enchanting tapestry of life across the landscape, from the hush of pitch pine groves at Cape Cod to the flutter of sugarbush in the windswept valleys of northern Vermont. The New England forests are in many places, in fact, more beautiful than they have been in a long, long time.

Long before the pilgrims landed in Massachusetts in 1620, explorers from an increasingly wood-poor Europe stood in awe of the trees of the American Northeast. When Verrazano arrived at Narragansett Bay in 1524, he found not tangled thickets of useless, impenetrable wilderness, as is commonly believed, but an open patchwork of robust, towering oaks, hickories, chestnuts, and scattered pines—a blend that extended throughout eastern Massachusetts, Rhode Island, and Connecticut. Besides providing good

3

habitat for game, there was abundant high-grade timber for building lumber, shingles, and firewood, with more than enough left over to export across the Atlantic. Indeed, the first commercial shipment the pilgrims made to England the year following their arrival was a ship's hull nearly full of clean, strong clapboard.

The forests in the more northern reaches of New England, on the other hand, were thicker and denser, comprised primarily of conifers, beech, birch, and maple. While these were less appealing lands for settlement, their commercial possibilities seemed endless. There were gargantuan white pines from which could be fashioned highly prized one-piece masts for the ships of the Royal Navy. Sassafras could be shipped to Europe not only for tea and tonic but as a highly touted treatment for syphilis. Sugar maples were there too, not only for sugar but for use in crafting tool handles and fine furniture. Due to their high resistance to rot, cedar groves were especially prized. And even beyond the wood products themselves, the forests of New England supported an abundance of beaver, fox, lynx, otter, mink, and marten, all of which provided a strong base for the development of a European fur trade.

Unfortunately, too often this remarkable forest was treated as if there were absolutely no end to it. Virtually all colonial construction (even roof shingles!) was completed using sections of only the very largest trees without a single blemish. Smaller, or slightly imperfect, wood was simply gathered into enormous piles and burned. Agriculture was even more devastating, as farmers cleared every beech-maple grove they could in order to get at the moist, rich soils that lay beneath. Taken together, the sawmill and the plow changed the face of both northern and southern New England in remarkably little time. By 1835, 75 percent of the forested lands of southern and central New England had been cleared. The vast majority of the commercially valuable timber even in the remote mountains of New Hampshire and Vermont was gone by 1875. Perhaps even more amazing was the fact that by about the same time, the once plentiful beaver, turkey, and even the white-tailed deer had completely vanished.

And so it seems rather amazing that today, even though human tinkering has greatly altered the basic composition of the New England forest, it is still a vital, beautiful place, a natural haven that each year draws literally millions of people to its twisted braids of back roads and trails.

To better understand the composition of the New England forest, we must follow its development back about ten thousand or twelve thousand years. This period was the close of the ice age, when the mammoth slabs of ice that had bulldozed their way southward out of Canada, grinding down jagged mountain peaks and scooping out tremendous U-shaped valleys, at last began to retreat. Under the warm fingers of the sun they fell back, inch by inch, into the colder regions of the north.

For a long time the thin, cold soils that were left in the wake of the glaciers would support nothing but arctic vegetation. Indeed, had you been able to don your wool underwear and saunter around the landscape a bit, you would have found the scene to look a great deal like the Arctic tundra looks today. But as temperatures increased, spruce and then fir began creeping northward through the valleys, ever so slowly pushing the arctic vegetation higher and higher until it remained only on the tops of the highest northern New England peaks, where you will still find it today. It was much later that hardwoods like aspen and birch were able to gain a roothold, again beginning in the warmer, more protected valleys, and then working their way upslope. These were then followed by even warmer-climate species, such as maple, oak, and white pine.

In those early days of forest "migration," there was a kind of jostling for position that took place among the various tree species, which eventually resulted in a fairly stable patchwork of oak and hickory in the south, and yellow birch, beech, and sugar maple, along with large pockets of spruce, hemlock, and white pine, in the north. Of course, even today the distribution of these trees follows no distinct line. The rise and fall of the mountains, the highly variant soils, and the twisted maze of shaded valleys and ravines that cut across this landscape have created a mix of forest that defies easy categorization.

But no matter what the exact blend of trees you happen to be talking about, there can be no argument that the depth of beauty these forests bring to the six New England states is immeasurable. Many find this beauty to be especially evident in autumn, when great clatters of birds can be seen hopscotching along the flyways, and the long, lovely swells of leaf canopies begin to shimmer with splashes of color so vibrant they seem almost lit from within. October in New England, in fact, is almost as much a feeling as it is a visual sensation—a time when, as the poet Humbert Wolfe once described it, "the air is wild with leaves."

That dazzling flush of color, by the way, is triggered each fall by the combination of shorter days and cooler temperatures. When this mix reaches a certain point, cells are activated in the tissues that connect the leaf to the stem. Gradually, the moisture and nutrients that flowed into the leaf all summer long are choked off. When this happens, the chlorophyll, with its overpowering green pigment, begins to break down, revealing other color pigments that have been there all along. Yellows and oranges, for example, are the result of carotene and xanthophyll pigments becoming visible.

The magnificent reds, pinks, and even purples, however, are fashioned from a slightly different process. These shades are found only in trees that have large amounts of carbohydrates in their leaves. It's the breaking down of these carbohydrates in the presence of bright sunlight that forms a special red pigment known as anthocyanin. (That bright sunlight, incidentally, is an important ingredient in the color equation. Overcast, rainy days just before the time of peak color will diminish the intensity of the show.) Do a little pigment mixing, especially of anthocyanin and carotene, and maples, white oak, and sumac let loose with their deepest, most dazzling blush. Sooner or later, of course, the dried leaf stem breaks loose from the branch and floats to the forest floor, where it will be broken down to provide nutrients for other plants in springs to come. How many leaves actually fall during a New England autumn? One estimate placed the number at a cool 72 billion bushels.

While fall is a time when deciduous trees shut down for the winter, when those juices do start flowing again after the first March thaw, another event begins to draw special attention—maple "sugarin'." When a sugar maple reaches maturity, usually in about forty years, taps are inserted into the tree's trunk through which sap flows drip by drip into attached buckets. This rather watery liquid is then heated to high temperatures in a large steel evaporator pan. Within this pan are a series of compartments, through which the sap flows toward a special draw-off valve. Then, at just the right moment, it's poured off as maple syrup. The amount of sap you collect, unfortunately, is hardly the amount of syrup you end up pouring off. In fact, it takes about forty gallons of sap to make a single gallon of syrup. Today Vermont continues to lead in the production of maple syrup, tapping roughly a million trees in order to produce about five hundred thousand gallons. (When the Indians showed New Englanders how to tap the sap from maple trees, the newcomers began regular harvesting of it in order to produce sugar, not syrup.)

There was a time in many Vermont villages when the annual sugaring-off was a common social event. Neighbors would all gather round, while a quantity of syrup was poured off and then simmered in a special pan until it formed a thick, gooey sugar. This sugar was eaten as is, or sometimes dribbled onto pans of packed snow and then wound onto forks or wooden paddles. A tub of sour pickles was always on hand, standing by as an antidote to the incredible sweetness of the main course.

Although there is little left in New England of Longfellow's "forest primeval," the enchantment remains. It's scattered across the breadth of the land in a thousand secret nooks and crannies, waiting to be discovered yet again by the next passerby. Certainly there could be no greater priority than the preservation of these woods—both for the sake of the life forms they embrace, as well as for the spirit they spark in the human heart.

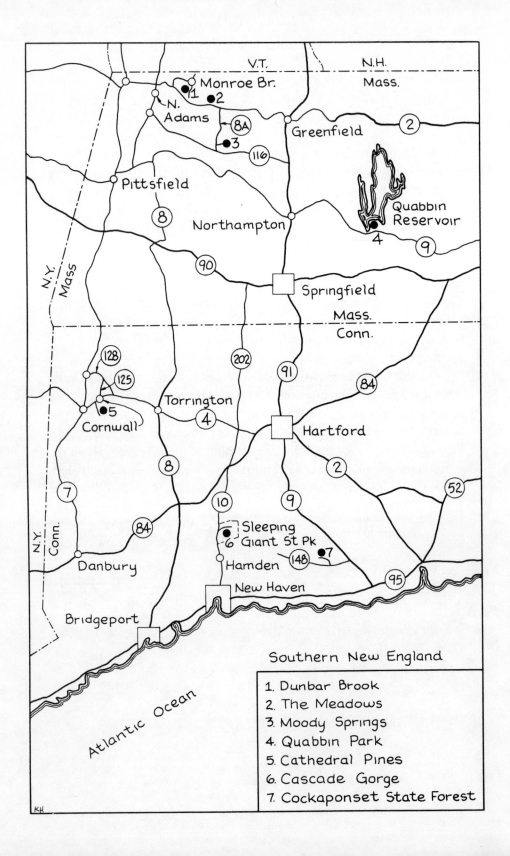

Southern New England

1. Dunbar Brook
2. The Meadows
3. Moody Springs
4. Quabbin Park
5. Cathedral Pines
6. Cascade Gorge
7. Cockaponset State Forest

Southern New England

DUNBAR BROOK

Distance: 1.8 miles
Location: Monroe State Forest. From the intersection of Massachusetts highways 8 and 2 in the town of North Adams, head east on Route 2 for approximately 5.6 miles to Tilda Hill Road, and turn left (north). (This turn will be just east of the Florida Fire Station.) Proceed northward on Tilda Hill Road for 6.3 miles to Kingsley Hill Road, and turn right. In approximately 1.4 miles you'll reach a T intersection in the village of Monroe Bridge. Turn right. The trailhead parking area will be on your right in 1.75 miles, across from a New England Power Company picnic area.
Note: To find the trail from the parking area, you must walk roughly 20 yards south up a two-track road that parallels a power line; at the top of a small hill, you'll see our pathway taking off into the forest toward the west.

While the steely web of power lines woven across the Deerfield River Valley is hardly the kind of scenery that inspires one to plunge feet first into nature, beautiful Dunbar Brook, protected from development by a thick veil of state forest, is most certainly worth a closer look. The blend of cool stream waters dancing through shady slices of mature maple, hemlock, and yellow birch forest creates a very serene, almost cathedrallike atmosphere here, delightful in nearly any kind of weather.

Straddling the lovely Hoosac Range, meeting place of the Berkshire and Green mountains, here is a medley of soft, round-shouldered plateaus and steep, dizzy plunges through the forest, all dissected by a braid of dark, forested valleys lined with ribbons of running water. Three centuries ago this line of mountains marked the end of New England and the beginning of the wilderness frontier, the boundary held in check largely through the tenacious efforts of a few small towns to the east. (In Deerfield's Memorial Hall Museum you can inspect the front door of settler John Sheldon's house, much of it laced with gashes from flying tomahawks, courtesy of angry Indians in 1704.)

Yet these mountains proved a formidable barrier to those wishing to push westward long after the threat of Indian attacks was over. Unable to find a practical overland railroad route, in the 1870s, with the help of a marvelous new explosive known as nitroglycerin, the 5-mile-long Hoosac Tunnel was blasted through the rocky underpinnings of the range, just south of where you now stand. This engineering feat was truly one of incredible proportions. Unfortunately, by the time it was completed in the fall of 1873, the great tunnel had claimed more than two hundred lives.

Our path begins in a beautiful hemlock forest, with branches woven into a dark green lace that all but blocks out the warm fingers of the sun. Hemlocks are quite common throughout much of the Berkshire Plateau, a region that was among the last of the New

Eastern Hemlock

10

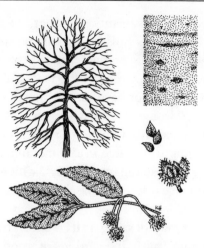

American Beech

England lands to be populated. Many of those who did settle in this area did so with an eye toward harvesting the forest. To this end hemlock was cut in great quantities and the bark was sold for tannin, which was used in the production of leather. The nearby town of North Adams, in fact, was a leading producer of manufactured leather.

Where there is hemlock, there is usually beech, and a beautiful example of this latter tree is found 0.1 mile into the walk on the right side of the trail, its smooth "elephant trunk" bark lending color and texture to the forest. Both hemlock and beech grow and reproduce best in shaded areas, with their feet planted in very acidic soil. Interestingly, you'll find that most of the beech-hemlock forests you come across in New England are located in moist areas, even though both trees are capable of growing on drier sites. This location may have to do with the fires that for centuries licked across much of the New England landscape. Since neither hemlock nor beech is capable of sprouting new growth from burned trunks, these lowland areas at one time may have been the only safe refuges for either tree. As we continue to suppress fires, these fellows may well get their chance to venture out into drier horizons.

By 0.25 mile, yellow birch has come on the scene, along with maple, witch-hazel, bluebead lily, and whorled wood aster—all crowded into a narrow corridor framed on the south by a steep, forested hillside, and on the north by the delightful rills and pools of

11

Dunbar Brook. Notice the beautiful carpets of apron and white-tipped moss growing on this hillside. In this particular instance the old adage about moss growing on the north side of trees and hills, out of reach of the drying rays of the sun, is true. (If you're lost in the woods, however, you'd better have more chips of wood lore up your sleeve than this one. Moss will grow wherever it's damp and shady—east, west, south, or north.) Growing on these massive boulders, moss serves as the front-line force in the manufacture of soil. Tiny, tiny pieces of rock are loosened by the moss, which, when combined with its own dead leaves, forms a base for other plants, even some trees, to take root and grow.

Continue past mats of sarsaparilla, violets, partridgeberry, and Indian cucumber, along with fine gardens of wood, hayscented, and Christmas fern. (The hollylike evergreen leaflets of this latter fern have made it a popular holiday decoration for centuries; hence its common name.) At 0.5 mile, on a small hill just before reaching a small streamside campsite, is a wonderful view into the shaded depths of the forest. The dark green of hemlocks is broken here and there by the shimmering, ghostly trunks of white and yellow birch. Young striped maples lean their supple trunks into the light of the trail, while overhead are magnificent eastern cottonwoods, their high-flying canopies all but lost to sight in a tangle of lesser trees. Pause here for a moment and listen. You may hear the lovely flute music of the wood thrush, the sleepy song of the warbling vireo, or, if you're lucky, the rich, haunting song of the veery.

From this small forest perch the trail again descends toward the creek, and soon passes clumps of wild oats, false Solomon's seal, tall meadow rue, blue violets, shinleaf, baneberry, and foamflower. Our turnaround point is at a wooden footbridge across Dunbar Brook, which is reached in 0.9 mile, just after taking a right turn at a fork in the trail. Those not yet ready to turn around can continue up the path for several more miles to Main Road, much of the route cheek to cheek with this delightful stream.

THE MEADOWS

Distance: 3.5 miles

Location: Mohawk Trail State Forest. Located on the north side of Massachusetts Highway 2, 14.2 miles east of the intersection of Massachusetts highways 8 and 2, in the town of North Adams. Cross the bridge and turn left, parking just outside of the entrance station to the campgrounds. The walk begins along the main campground entrance road.

This forested ravine, sliced down to bedrock by the tumbling waters of the Cold River, is one of the more beautiful sections of the old Indian path known as the Mohawk Trail. The Mohawk Trail was likely blazed in the middle of the seventeenth century, not by the Mohawks but by the Pocumtucks of the Connecticut River Valley. The Pocumtucks punched this path westward through the wilderness in order to gain better raiding access to their archenemies the Mohawks, who at the time were located in what is now extreme eastern New York State. The early Dutch settlers in the area found themselves in the middle of this game of pillage that for years flew back and forth across the Hoosac and Teconic mountains.

The diplomatic Dutch prodded and cajoled the two tribes to stop their mutual slaughter, and were ultimately able to formulate a peace treaty that would allow everyone concerned to save face. Alas, a couple of Pocumtuck warriors could not behave themselves, and murdered Mohawk prince Saheda, even as he was traveling along this trail to put his mark on the Dutch treaty. That did it. The Mohawks were outraged and set out on the warpath once again. This time, however, fueled by a burning drive for revenge, it took them less than two days to, for all practical purposes, wipe the Pocumtucks from the face of the earth.

Of course, this Mohawk victory was, in the grand scheme of things, hardly a winning of the territorial war. For that was ultimately fought against an even more zealous tribe from across the Atlantic Ocean, whose battle cries were fueled with the fire of a Christian god. "The blasphemy, and insolence, and prodigious barbarity of the savages," wrote Cotton Mather in 1702 about the snuffing of the Indians, "was come to a sufficient heighth for the 'Lord God of Zaboath' to interpose his own revenges." Indeed, the taking of many

13

Indian lands throughout New England was at least in part justified by the notion that the natives were not subduing their lands as instructed by the biblical book of Genesis, and therefore should forfeit any claim to the lands. Under this notion, then, lands that the Indians had cultivated were, for a time, at least, protected under the law. "What landes any of the Indians . . . have by possession or improvement, by subduing of the same," the Massachusetts court ruled, "they have just right thereunto, accordinge to that Gen: 1:28, chap: 9:1, Psa 115,16." Unfortunately, the Indians in northern New England for the most part did not farm, and therefore had no rights whatsoever.

Although the first portion of this walk is along the campground road system, it would be hard to find a finer route through a coniferous forest. Just to the north of where you parked you'll see a fine stand of planted Norway spruce. This beautiful import is the conifer commonly found throughout much of northern Europe, and holds the distinction of producing the largest cones of any spruce in the world. As you make your way up the entrance road you'll also see the first of many large hemlocks, which in a few places hover over beautiful patches of mountain laurel, as well as an occasional clump of closed gentian. The genus name for this latter plant, whose lavender flowers are held in tight, bottle-shaped clusters, comes from a second-century B.C. king of Illyria named Gentius, who is often credited with discovering the healing powers of the gentians. (In fact, records indicate that the Egyptians were using gentians in their medicine a thousand years before the good king came to throne on the shores of the Adriatic Sea.)

By 0.3 mile the road will have plunged into a corridor of towering white pine, their nearly branchless trunks rising into the sun like a battalion of soldiers snapped to attention. Looking at these beautiful giants, actually small compared to what they will one day become, it's easy to see why England's Royal Navy coveted them for use as ships' masts. It was for just such a purpose that when Massachusetts received its charter in 1691, settlers were forbidden to cut any public tree "of the diameter of twenty-four inches and upwards at twelve inches from the ground."

Take a right at 0.4 mile, following the signs to the group camping area. The broken trees you see just past this junction are from a tornado that roared through the campground in the summer of 1988, snapping massive hemlocks and white pines as if they were matchsticks. Soon you'll come to a dirt road taking off to the right, which we'll follow past the group campground and into the more untrodden forest lying just beyond. Past the campground are still more white pine and hemlock, as well as an occasional maple, beech, and yellow birch. Watch the ground for starflowers, bracken fern, and both white wood and whorled wood asters. The blooming of these asters is, by the way, a sure sign that summer is coming to a close.

A short way past a faint road taking off to the left at about 1 mile, you'll see our blue-blazed trail, also taking off to the left. Along this quiet stretch of needle-lined pathway are some of the most extensive mats of clubmoss you'll ever see. Like ferns, clubmosses also reproduce by releasing millions of spore into the air early each autumn. In fact, if you're here in September, a pass of your hand through one of these carpets is likely to launch a veritable cloud of yellow spore. Each of these very tiny spores is extremely uniform in both size and shape, a trait that led to their being used for everything from coating pills so that they would be easier to swallow to providing a measuring standard for looking at objects through microscopes. What's more, clubmoss spore also tends to burn very rapidly, leading not only to the spore's widespread use in fireworks but also to its use as a prime ingredient in the famous "poof!" flash system employed by early photographers.

Whorled Wood Aster

At 1.4 miles you'll intersect a small road at the edge of a wonderful meadow, the first of two such clearings on this walk. At the time of this writing there was not an easy-to-follow path connecting this meadow with the one just below it, so I recommend that you simply walk to the end of the upper meadow and then return to the road the way you came. Then resume the loop walk by heading east on this road. (Facing the meadow, turn right at the point where the trail first intersects the road.) In 0.1 mile further, this road will take you to the southern edge of the lower meadow, which can be explored in a similar manner.

Spend some time in the arms of these lovely clearings, fringed on the near edge by huddles of conifers, and beyond that, by a swell of uplands covered in a thick weave of northern hardwood forest. In spring these meadows blaze with magnificent carpets of wildflowers, the various species bursting with the warm roll of the season like the carefully orchestrated movements of a symphony. This show will continue on a more subdued note throughout the entire summer, as the land quietly fades into sprinkles of milkweed, bindweed, yarrow, rough-fruited cinquefoil, orange hawkweed, and pokeweed.

At the edge of the lower meadow our road turns to the right along the bold, fast run of the Deerfield River. Just past the grave site of Revolutionary War soldier John Wheeler and his wife Susannah, you'll come to a Y intersection where you'll turn right. Wrapped once again in the hush of the conifer forest, this road will lead you back to the parking area in 1.2 miles.

MOODY SPRINGS

Distance: 0.8 mile
Location: Kenneth Dubuque Memorial State Forest. From the intersection of Massachusetts highways 2 and 8 in the town of North Adams, head east on Highway 2 for 18.1 miles, and turn right onto Massachusetts Highway 8A. Follow southward for 8.7 miles, and make a sharp left onto Hallockville Road, a dirt road that climbs through the forest toward the northeast. (This intersection is near the north shore of Hallockville Pond.) Down this road 1.3 miles, turn left, just past a small pond on the right. There will be a Y intersection 0.4 mile from this turn, where you'll stay to the left, following Moody Springs Road. Our parking area and trailhead will be on your right next to a camping shelter, 0.7 mile from this last Y intersection.

For anyone heading into the western hills of Massachusetts intent on wrapping themselves in a thick blanket of peace and quiet, Kenneth Dubuque Memorial State Forest is unquestionably the place to go. Here is a wide, twisted maze of dirt roads and trails, many of the latter overgrown to the point where following them any distance at all can be an exercise in woodsmanship. Yet on those paths that are still navigable there is very little to distract you from the pleasures at hand: watching the crimson flash of a scarlet tanager, or the bold stripes of a black and white warbler as it circles tree trunks looking for insects; listening to the "teacher! teacher!" cry of the ovenbird, or the staccato rap of a northern flicker announcing its territory.

Scarlet Tanager

But first things first. Walk down to the outflow of Moody Spring and help yourself to a big swig of cold, fresh water. As the nearby sign verifies, people long have drunk water from this spring to treat various physical disorders. And besides, even if this earthen brew doesn't solve all that's ailing you, you can bet it will more than cure a case of thirst on a hot Massachusetts day. With your back to the spring (facing downhill), you'll see a small trail to the left, marked by a series of blazed trees. This trail is our walking path. Be forewarned that there are a few places where the trail itself is a little hard to see, but never is the next blaze very far away. The route will basically take you on a very short but sweet romp through a variety of northern hardwood nooks and crannies—moist ravines, patches of violets, orchids, Canada mayflower, and sarsaparilla, and hauntingly beautiful clumps of white birch in the distance, their shimmering trunks seeming to draw you into the cool, deep shadows of the forest.

One of the creatures to be especially on the lookout for on this walk is the beautiful white-tailed deer. While deer are plentiful in this area, they nonetheless can be difficult to see. They not only have excellent hearing (you can watch their ears constantly scanning the surroundings) but also, though color blind, are thought to be able to detect movement down to the blinking of a man's eye. What's more, few large animals know their surroundings better than a deer. An eastern white-tail typically has a range of only about a square mile, which it knows like the back of its hoof. Deer that have been tagged and moved to other areas, perhaps a dozen or more miles away, have quickly found their way back to their home turf.

The female white-tail bears her fawns in the spring. If it's her first birth she may have only one youngster, but in succeeding years twins will be the rule. A fawn can stand just ten minutes after birth, is gulping milk by the cupful in less than a minute, and can walk in less than an hour—a fact that mom takes advantage of by prodding the fawn away from its birth spot in case the scent of the birthing activity should attract a predator. (The fawn itself has so little smell during the first days of life that even hunting dogs walking nearby may fail to detect it.) Because very young fawns are so defenseless, they tend to lie very quietly for the first few days after birth, letting the spots on their coats camouflage them from sight. During this time the mother will keep away from the fawn except to nurse it, since her own scent might otherwise give the youngster's location away. Should

White-tailed Deer

the fawn wander, the mother will be able to track it by following a scent trail left behind by a special gland on the hoof.

The fact that a surprised white-tail can career through a crowded forest at 35 miles per hour in 20-foot leaps is testimony not only to her swiftness but to her grace. It's a downright humbling experience to watch a mature doe calmly leap over an 8-foot-high fence from standing position.

Would-be deer watchers should keep in mind that a feeding white-tail will often shake its tail immediately before it looks up to survey its surroundings. If you're trying to get close for a better look at one of these beautiful creatures, advance quietly, and stop as soon as you see the tail move. Also, since deer relish many different types of nuts, plan to take a few evening walks in the fall through forests of oak, beech, and hickory.

At just over 0.4 mile the blazed trail will come out on Moody Springs Road. Turn left here, and walk through a fine slice of hard-wood forest back to the Moody Springs shelter. If it's late in the evening, wait to walk this final stretch until a flush of darkness has covered the land. Slow your pace, and listen for the first faint stirrings of the night crew. This time of day, after all, is when the curtain goes up, when the real magic of nature begins to stir. Authors who write about their experiences in the dark woods seem to do so at a deeper, more profound level of imagery, as if in losing clear sight, they gain a sixth, more mystical sense of perception. Thoreau walked along a moonlit lake in Maine and later wrote about seeing "the shores of a new world" that "left such an impression of stern, yet gentle wildness on my memory as will not soon be effaced." Henry Beston, author of *The Outermost House,* cautioned that "with the banishment of night from the experience of man, there vanishes as well a religious emotion, a poetic mood, which gives depth to the adventure of humanity." Even the rather matter-of-fact Americana grass-roots poet Stephen Vincent Benét got a bit mysterious when writing about certain happenings under the cloak of darkness:

> When Daniel Boone goes by at night
> The phantom deer arise
> And all lost, wild America
> is burning in their eyes.

QUABBIN PARK

Distance: 2.7 miles
Location: From Belchertown, head east on Massachusetts Route 9 for 2 miles to the west entrance to Quabbin Park. (This is the first of several park entrances.) Proceed past the Metropolitan District Commission headquarters, across the dam, and turn left. Continue on this road past the Enfield Lookout and a picnic area on the north side of the road to a trail along the south side of the highway marked by a number 8. You can park directly across the highway from this trail. (This walk ends at marker 11, on the same road you parked on. Turn left at the highway and walk 2 miles to return to your car, increasing the walk to 4.7 miles.)

Quabbin, a Nipmuc Indian word meaning many waters, has in the twentieth century come to mean just one—the more than 400 billion gallons of Swift River and Beaver Brook waters held back in the form of Quabbin Reservoir, built by the Massachusetts Metropolitan District Commission a half century ago to feed the hungry faucets of Boston. Beneath these shimmering waters lie the remains of four small communities: Dana, Prescott, Greenwich, and Enfield. Yet largely because of a tidal wave of industrialization rolling across the land that brought new opportunities in the cities, these small towns were dancing to the tune of big brother Boston long before Windsor Dam stilled the tumbling waters of the Swift. Long gone were the heydays of these towns, which had been fueled by the cotton and woolen textile mills. In fact, when the waters of Quabbin finally began to rise, there were 7,500 dead pulled from the valley's 34 cemeteries and moved to Quabbin Park Cemetery just to the south— three times the number of living residents that had to pack up their memories and head for higher ground.

Ironically, from nature's point of view it was the drowning of the Swift River Valley beneath the still waters of Quabbin that gave the best possible protection to this 55,000-acre watershed. The land here is fairly well managed, and has long served as an expansive field laboratory for researching wildlife, acid rain, and watershed productivity. It's here at Quabbin that you'll have the best chance of seeing bald eagles. It's in these woods that you'll find wild turkeys, bobcat, red fox, fisher, coyote, and perhaps even eastern mountain lion. Though it can seem a contradiction of sorts to want a dam while also wanting local wildlife, in this case there's no question that there would be far less species diversity were it not here.

Major Quabbin Park trails are blazed by circles of yellow paint on the trees, while most starting points and junctions are marked by numbered posts. (You should plan to get a park trail map from the visitor center, which you passed on the way in.) Our trek begins at marker post number 8, which is on the south side of the peninsula circle drive, just east of a developed picnic area. It ends on the east side of the park, about 0.5 mile north of Massachusetts Highway 9.

The pathway begins in a fairly young mixed forest of spruce, hemlock, red oak, black oak, beech, birch, red maple, and white pine. Especially common here are the ferns, which in places form a tight weave of feathery fronds that sprawl across the forest floor as far as the eye can see. You should see bracken, hayscented, and New York ferns, as well as beautiful mats of large cinnamon ferns, this latter plant named for the lovely cinnamon-colored fertile leaves visible in late spring. Cinnamon fern and the somewhat drier soil interrupted fern, incidentally, are the most common ferns you'll see on most of your treks through the Northeast.

Red Fox

Through the forest, to your left at 0.5 mile, you'll see a marsh area in the last stages of succession. What was once open water has felt the inevitable turn of nature. As plant debris accumulated at the edges of this water pocket, they formed fertile layers for even more plants to take hold—sedges, rushes, cattails, and arrowhead. This rush of life from the shore squeezed the open water into a smaller and smaller pool until one day there was no longer any visible water left; ferns, grasses, shrubs, and even trees took over. Such is the fate of all ponds. The rate of fill depends on the initial size of the pond, the water supply, and the climate of the area.

If you need more convincing that this place was at one time much different looking, just after passing over a stone wall and making a right turn, look to your left at the collection of beaver-gnawed trees along the trail. The descendents of these dedicated engineers, who were likely responsible for the existence of the pond in the first place, have long since moved to much wetter pastures. In fact, there are currently more than fifteen hundred acres of marshes and ponds in the Quabbin watershed that have been created entirely by the engineering efforts of resident beavers.

Wind your way through nice stands of red pine at 0.7 mile, followed once again at 0.8 by a more deciduous mix. Through here you'll find more ferns, as well as clumps of twisted stalk, huckleberry, round-leaved dogwood, and Japanese barberry. Common barberry, incidentally, a relative of the Japanese version you see here,

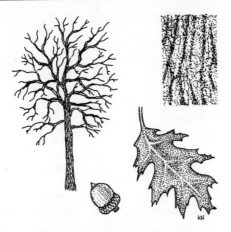

Northern Red Oak

was once widely used by the Egyptians as an ingredient in a formula they employed against plagues. (Barberry does in fact have antibacterial qualities that may have helped protect people against such disease.) It was also used in more modern times for treating irritated eyes. In fact, the next time you're trying to "get the red out," look and see if the solution you're using contains berberine. If so, it may well have been extracted from common barberry.

At 1.2 miles you'll reach a V junction with a trail over your right shoulder. Make the sharp turn onto this much fainter path, following the yellow circles carefully as they drift through a forest of red, black, and white oak, spruce, red maple, and white pine, later peppered with occasional gardens of maidenhair fern, interrupted fern, and sweet fern. Soon after this junction, all visible signs of a pathway dribble out entirely. From here, for a distance of roughly 1.5 miles, you will be ambling through an open forest guided only by a line of marks on the distant trees. The feel of hiking like this through a deep forest, especially over such distances, is absolutely uncanny. What was before just another slice of woodland is suddenly a kind of heartland of unspoiled, untrammeled nature. You find yourself going much slower, not just because you have to look for the next blaze but because you begin to focus on choosing a route to that point that will best touch the blooms and sprouts that most pique your curiosity. The end point of the walk along the highway at marker number 11 came much too quickly for me. That initial rush of a car flying over the blacktop was startling—too abrupt an end to the deep, restive hush of a Quabbin woodland.

CATHEDRAL PINES

Distance: 0.9 mile

Location: From the intersection of Connecticut state roads 4 and 25 at the town of Cornwall, turn south onto Pine Street. Continue south to the end of Pine Street, and turn left on Valley Road. In approximately 0.25 mile you'll reach Essex Hill Road, forking to the left. Take this road for 0.2 mile to a small parking area on the left, beside a large boulder. The trail takes off behind this boulder.

Of all the tree species in New England, few have been prized more than the white pine—once solely for its commercial value, and today for the striking, almost ethereal beauty its few remaining mature stands lend to the land. Because England, and indeed, much of Europe, was already tree poor by the time colonists began arriving in the New World, the timber of New England was a welcome sight to early merchants. Oak, white pine, and pitch pine were felled as fast as men could swing their axes, loaded into the hulls of ships, and sent east across the Atlantic. So valuable was the white pine, in fact, that the English constructed special ships so that whole tree trunks could be transported.

One of the main reasons that the white pine was so attractive was that it proved perfect for creating masts for the Royal Navy. (In most of Europe there were no trees of sufficient length to create a mast in one piece; instead, several pieces had to be spliced together.)

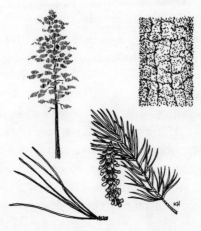

Eastern White Pine

War with the Dutch in the middle of the seventeenth century cut off the navy's supply of Scotch pine, which made the white pines of New England even more important to the English. By the 1690s, the English had become so dependent on the great white pines of New England that the Crown issued a set of regulations to the colonies that prohibited the cutting of any potential mast tree from nonprivate lands. Lest there be any question about which was a mast tree, royal surveyors tramped through the forest, cutting wide, arrow-shaped blazes on all trees in question. These "broad arrow laws," as they became known, carried stiff fines for violators. Yet the shortage of any kind of police force, along with a general disregard by colonial merchants for much of anything the Crown had to say, meant that most white pines still fell to colonial axes.

The trail for this walk begins behind a large boulder located immediately adjacent to the parking area. The path climbs rather sharply upward, meandering first past tangles of bramble, rose, and elderberry, and then into the shady recesses of white pine and hemlock. Most of the greenery here occurs not at ground level but in a tight weave of white pine branches suspended more than a hundred feet in the air. What little sunlight drips onto the forest floor is not enough to support much else. Other than shaggy carpets of shade-loving ferns, ground covers are scarce. Here and there a small hemlock stands patiently, biding its time until a white pine topples over, and enough sunlight finally streams in for it to get down to serious growth.

When a tornado felled a number of white pines here during the summer of 1980, researchers studied the fallen giants in an effort to get a better idea of the age of this forest. Surprisingly, several proved to be over three hundred years old—a full century older than previously thought. These trees were saplings soaking in the New England sunshine at the time when apples were falling on Sir Isaac Newton's head! Though most of the large trees you'll see along this trail are younger, they are by no means spring chickens. Consider that when they were just youngsters fighting for their place in the sun, German trees were being processed into the paper that would hold the musical notions of a young prodigy named Beethoven.

Continue to follow the blue-blazed trail, past an occasional maple and birch. In 0.4 mile you'll reach a thick wall of laurel, and

25

Red-eyed Vireo

then, as the canopy suddenly opens, an explosion of shrubs, ground covers, and young deciduous trees.

In 0.6 mile the trail joins Essex Hill Road. Turn here, and follow Birdseye Brook back to the parking area. Cock an ear toward the more open deciduous forest on the left, and you may hear the choruses of scarlet tanagers, red-eyed vireos, and wood thrushes. Watch along the roadside for blooms of geraniums and bedstraw, as well as the soft green fronds of sensitive ferns, which are especially common on the right side of the road near the parking area.

CASCADE GORGE

Distance: 1.7 miles
Location: Sleeping Giant State Park. From Connecticut Route 10, or Whitney Avenue, north of Hamden, proceed past Mt. Carmel Avenue (this is the southern entrance to Sleeping Giant), and turn right 0.55 mile later, onto Tuttle Avenue. Our parking area and trailhead is 1.1 miles down Tuttle Avenue, on the right.

To the Indians of this area, the giant called Hobbomock was no pleasant fellow. His name was synonymous with death and disease, and he was thought of as representing not only the color black but the cold, angry fury of the north wind. Some young warriors would go through great rituals of physical abuse and endurance for this devil god, including the drinking of false white hellebore juice (also used to poison arrow tips), in an effort to make a kind of covenant with Hobbomock whereby he would protect them from death by the arrows and knives of their enemies.

It was after Hobbomock had gone on a particularly nasty rampage against his human subjects, during which he thundered his foot down upon the earth 14 miles northeast of here and changed the entire course of the Connecticut River, that the good spirit of Kietan came to the rescue. She placed a special spell on Hobbomock that caused him to grow very, very tired, and finally collapse into a deep sleep. Thus the name, and the profile, of the sleeping giant. On this walk we'll be climbing to the old boy's left thigh, where, since the time he first lay down here, a beautiful tumble of hemlock, beech, and maple has taken root. The high point of the park occurs at the giant's left hip, which rises to an elevation of 739 feet, and is located approximately 0.75 mile southwest of our turnaround point.

Throughout this walk we'll be following a north-south trail blazed with red circles, which winds along a forest floor sprinkled with tufts of mountain laurel, white wood asters, Canada mayflower, violets, false Solomon's seal, sarsaparilla, trillium, and jewelweed. If you've visited the other side of the park, near the main entrance and campground, you may recall that it contained fewer ground plants. The south-facing slopes there receive more sunlight, which tends to leave less moisture in the soil to support the growth of ground plants. Some plants, though, such as the hickories, actually prefer their feet to be a bit drier. You'll find more of them, therefore, on the other side of the park.

By 0.2 mile you'll have gained a high ledge from which you can look down into a wonderful gorge. In many places this shady, twisted ravine is lined with beautiful huddles of hemlock, the dark green lace of their branches lending an almost mystical quality to the scene. You'll find in the park several variations of the Canadian hemlocks that cradle this gorge. In fact, botanists have identified nearly one hundred varieties of this tree throughout North America, many of which show up as dwarf, shrub-looking plants, or as braids of thin branches running across the forest floor.

We'll cross a flat section of pathway at 0.55 mile that runs through an open, sunlit hollow with chestnut oaks, red maple, Christmas fern, round-lobed hepatica, wood sorrel, beech, and ground cedar. From here the path climbs again, though much more gently, to a great talus pile. This massive jumble of gray rocks contains pieces of a large slab of igneous basalt, a material that was forced up as molten liquid through cracks in the layers of sandstone some 200 million years ago. Unlike sandstone, however, this basalt is quite hard and hearty, having easily survived a thorough scouring by ice, wind, and rain. Among the rocks look for clumps of the delightful little plant known as herb Robert, which produces very attractive pink flowers from May through October. Who the "Robert" is in herb Robert is much in question. Popular candidates, however, include a twelfth-century duke of Normandy, a French monk, and Robert Goodfellow, also known as Robin Hood. The plant was long used to treat a severe skin disease known as erysipelas, and, thanks in large part to its tannin content, made a very effective compress to stop bleeding.

Just past this talus pile, in a garden of jewelweed, violets, wood aster, and Christmas fern, our path first crosses a lavender trail, and, a few yards later, a blue trail. If you continue straight for another hundred yards the path will make a left turn into a sheltered nook that cradles a quiet slice of swamp habitat. Although there's little

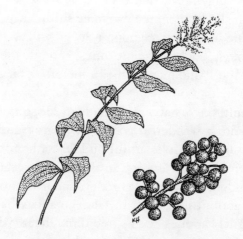

False Solomon's Seal

28

water visible here, the variety and density of plant life is remarkable. You'll find clumps of sweet pepperbush, chestnut, sassafras, and sweet birch, to name but a very few. It's the oil of sweet birch, incidentally, obtained from a distillation of the twigs and bark of young trees, that once gave the wintergreen flavor to hundreds of candies and medicines. Unfortunately, the fact that it took nearly a hundred trees to produce one quart of wintergreen oil did not bode well for the survival of the species. (Wintergreen oil is now synthesized from wood alcohol and salicylic acid.) In addition, it was the sap of the sweet birch, gathered with taps in early spring, that was fermented and turned into birch beer.

Also here are delightful pockets of cinnamon ferns, sensitive ferns, and royal ferns. This latter plant, often growing 4 feet to 6 feet tall and looking somewhat like a locust tree, is considered by many to be the loveliest of all the ferns.

COCKAPONSET STATE FOREST

Distance: 2.4 miles

Location: From Connecticut Highway 9, head west on Connecticut Highway 148 for 1.6 miles, and turn right. Follow this road for another 1.6 miles and turn left, into the Pataconk Lake State Recreation Area. Proceed for 0.4 mile, past the southern end of the reservoir, to a set of parking areas, one on either side of the road. You'll find our blue-blazed Cockaponset Trail just past these lots, heading to the right (northwest).

Walking a quiet slice of New England woodland often lulls me into aimless, ambling thoughts about all kinds of subjects. On the back side of this particular loop, amid the quiet groves of beech, red maple, hickory, and yellow poplar, I happened to end up mulling over how a small state like Connecticut could possibly have been responsible for such a long, long line of significant world "firsts," many of which are understandably a source of pride for state historians and residents alike. These range from the somewhat trivial, such as the first Graham cracker, frisbee, can opener, corkscrew, and lollipop (which was named, by the way, for a winning racehorse), to others that are rather profound. Not only was the planet Mars officially discovered by Connecticut professor Asaph Hall in 1877 but the first documented meteor in the United States hit the dirt in Weston. The man behind the cotton gin, Eli Whitney, was from New Haven. Likewise the first model of the steamboat, the first American bicycle, the first helicopter, nuclear submarine, commercial gramophone, and FM radio station came from the minds of Connecticut.

Yet there were also a few somewhat less than wonderful firsts to rise from the Constitution State, especially with regard to the strict Puritan ethics that once ruled here. The first witch to be executed, for instance, met her maker at the end of a rope in Hartford. Even the first blue law was enacted here, consisting of a 1647 prohibition against "social smoking."

As our dear witch found out, breeches of mandated behavior were not taken lightly in Connecticut. Consider these items from the Code of 1650, which is thought to have been prepared by attorney Roger Ludlow: First-time burglars had a letter *B* branded on their foreheads. (Unless, of course, you robbed on the Sabbath, in which case you got your ear cut off to boot.) If caught cursing, you were required to hand over 10 shillings, or, if short the cash, off you went for a couple of hours in the stocks. As of 1650, you could also no longer play that wild and crazy game known as shuffleboard, during which "much precious time is spent unfruitfully and much waste of wind and beer occasioned." Getting caught would cost you 5 shillings, or if you owned the public house where the game was being played, 20 shillings. Shuffleboard, then, was quite an evil, seeing that it cost some men twice as much as a good curse.

But on with our walk. While you're hardly about to be the first to traverse this popular trail along the Pataconk Reservoir, hitting it on a cool morning in late autumn will offer you a few stretches where it might seem that way. Just over 0.1 mile down the path the Cockaponset Trail meets our path, the Pataconk Trail, which takes off to the right along the lakeshore, marked by a series of blue blazes with red dots in the middle. Once past a string of picnic tables things quiet down considerably, the waterside trail coursing along jumbles of rocks and clumps of beech, maple, highbush blueberry, and clubmoss. At 0.4 mile is a small inlet, which you may see peppered with a blanket of yellow pond lilies. The seeds of this beautiful plant were

Highbush Blueberry

once toasted like popcorn, while the tubers can be roasted or boiled in a couple of changes of water for a food that tastes rather like a potato. (An odd, and in no way appetizing, addendum to this bit of folklore claims that the roots of yellow pond lily can be steeped in milk and set out to kill cockroaches, while the smoke from burning them will send crickets off to new chirping grounds.)

In 0.55 mile you'll cross a very quiet, brackish-looking brook sprinkled with water striders. These amazing water walkers stay afloat on six legs, each of which is covered with water-repellent hairs. Only four of these legs are out to the side of the insect; two other long ones are underneath the front of the body, and serve both for grabbing onto things and as oars for paddling. Some researchers maintain that water striders can communicate with each other by tapping out messages with their legs. If you're tempted to submerge a strider to see what happens, don't. The poor fellow will likely be unable to break through the surface again, and will quickly drown.

You'll reach Pataconk Brook in 1.2 miles, an absolutely delightful forest stream that seems to utter a light chuckle as it tumbles head over heels across a braid of rocks. It's here that you'll find our blue-blazed path, the Cockaponset Trail, coming from the left. This is the path we'll take back to the parking area, a quiet but rather sublime route that crosses the wooded crown of a 500-foot hummock. The latter part of this stretch, traversing a lowland where the beech and maples have attained significant size, is especially lovely—a cathedral that on summer mornings is filled with an impressive outburst of birdsong.

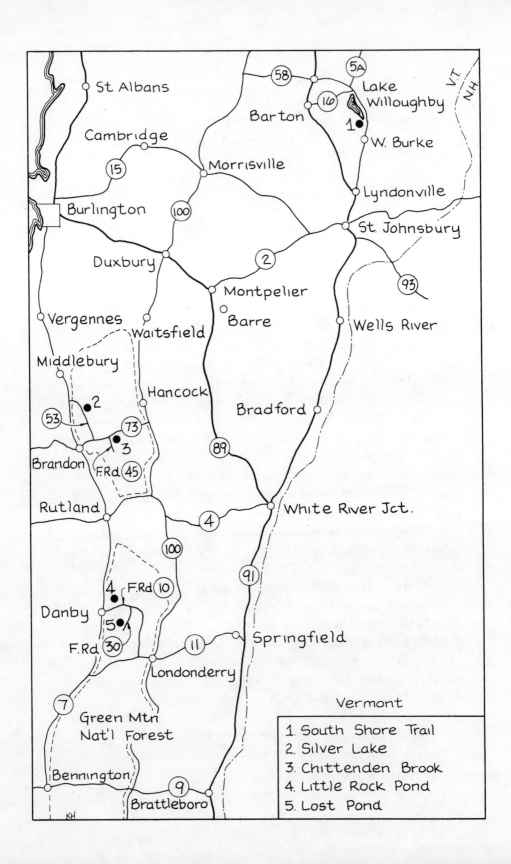

St Albans

Cambridge

(15)

Burlington

(100)

Duxbury

Vergennes

Waitsfield

Middlebury

(53)

Hancock

(73)

2

3

Brandon

F.Rd (45)

Rutland

(100)

Danby

4   F.Rd (10)

5

F.Rd (30)

(11)

Londonderry

(7)

Green Mtn
Nat'l Forest

Bennington

(9)

Brattleboro

KH

(58)

(5A)

Barton

(16)

Lake
Willoughby

1

W. Burke

Morrisville

Lyndonville

St. Johnsbury

(2)

(93)

Montpelier

Barre

Wells River

Bradford

(89)

White River Jct.

(4)

(91)

Springfield

Vermont

1. South Shore Trail
2. Silver Lake
3. Chittenden Brook
4. Little Rock Pond
5. Lost Pond

V.T.
N.H.

Vermont

SOUTH SHORE TRAIL

Distance: 2.4 miles
Location: Willoughby State Forest. From the junction of Vermont highways 16 and 5A, head south on Highway 5A to the south end of Lake Willoughby. Past the beach 40 yards, turn right into a small parking area. The trail begins on the north side of the parking lot.

This walk is a gentle meander, ideal for younger children, through the mixed deciduous forest that blankets the steep southwestern flanks of Lake Willoughby. Here you'll find small streams dancing down dimly lit, boulder-choked ravines, and hear the lilting chanty of warblers raining down from the trees. This relatively young forest grows thick and healthy here, nourished by rich beds of lime that were laid down 500 million years ago. In many places along the trail the leaf canopy is woven so tightly that the great lake below is barely visible, no more than a faint shimmer through the slender branches of the sugar maples. This trail is perhaps best enjoyed by slow and deliberate walkers—those who revel in bright splashes of spring wildflowers, those who like the soft, cool brush of ferns against their bare legs.

Once the sole domain of the St. Francis Indians, the shores of Lake Willoughby had by the middle 1700s felt the restless feet of the

Europeans. At first they came in small trickles, pouring over the upper drainages of the Connecticut River looking for furs and fish. By the 1780s, however, they were arriving with a determination to wrest settlements from these remote, wild lands, which had recently been made available to them by the "Independent State of Vermont."

After working their proverbial fingers to the bone to clear this land and farm it (under the grant laws of the time, at least five acres had to be cultivated), tensions with the British again began to rise, culminating in the War of 1812. The people of the village of Westmore, located on the northeastern side of the lake, were well aware of the danger they were in due to their extreme isolation from other Americans, and their close proximity to the British troops to the north. The writing on the wall could not have been clearer. Almost all the residents packed up their belongings and headed for larger population centers to the south. The shores of Willoughby grew quiet—quiet, that is, but for the occasional smuggler who hid in this maze of forest and twisted ravines.

The smugglers of northeastern Vermont were hardly wild-eyed pirates with evil, toothless grins—rogues who defined a bad day as one without murder and pillage. Because of the isolation of this part of Vermont—only a few bad roads connected it to cities of the south—the economic survival of early settlers here was tightly bound to Canadian population centers such as Montreal. When President Jefferson issued the Embargo Act, which forbade trade with England and any of her colonies, it was a terrible economic blow to the people of this region. Some residents took to smuggling cattle across the Canadian line, where they brought fat prices from the British. The major route for these little operations was just west of here in the Barton Valley. The Lake Willoughby area is thought to have been a popular place for these renegade cowboys to catch their breath during dogged pursuits by federal marshals.

From the parking area 0.1 mile, you'll pass through an open campsite. Our walk continues down a small slope, and, in about 40 yards, takes off to the right on a small footpath. Along this stretch in June you'll see early blooms of purple-flowering raspberry, as well as the last, lovely blossoms of the purple trillium. This latter plant is as foul in odor as it is beautiful in blossom. The smell, in fact, is so

Purple Trillium

reminiscent of decaying flesh that early herbal medicine doctrine, which said that a plant's characteristics defined its appropriate use in humans, prescribed an ointment made from the roots as a treatment for gangrene. You may hear various nicknames for purple trillium, including stinking Benjamin, Wake-robin, and birthroot. The reason for stinking Benjamin is obvious. Wake-robin, however, refers to the fact that this is one of spring's first wildflowers. Birthroot, on the other hand, comes from the days when women were given tea made from the roots of the plant to ease childbirth.

The trail continues through stands of sugar maple, hobblebush, and striped maple. Striped maple, incidentally, especially when young, is easily recognized by its bright green bark striped with white lines. (As the tree matures, the bark will turn a red-brown color, with light vertical lines.) Deer relish the bark of the striped maple, as do moose, a fact that has given rise to a very common New England nickname for the tree—"moosewood."

Between 0.4 and 0.5 mile into the walk you'll pass several ravines, some of which have clear, cold braids of water pouring down their rocky throats. One of these, located at 0.45 mile, is choked with giant boulders, or "glacial erratics," which were carried here on the great sheets of ice that flowed south out of Canada thousands of years ago. Over many, many years, the action of ice and rain, as well as the patient fingers of mosses, have broken down the upper surfaces of these rocks into layers of soil. On the tops of many boulders you'll see beautiful collections of ferns and even young striped maples—island gardens that appear to be squeezing life out of solid stone.

At 0.9 mile you'll pass a large jumble of boulders cloaked in a thick green quilt of ferns. Notice the small protected hollows that lie along the base of some of these stones. On a hot summer day these wet, earthen pockets remain remarkably cool, like outlet ducts to some great subterranean air conditioning system.

Shortly after the boulders you'll spot the great ice-scoured cliffs of Mount Hor rising high above the trail. Just before our turn-around point in a rocky ravine at 1.2 miles, you'll catch fine views of Lake Willoughby, framed to the east by the soaring cliffs of Mount Pisgah.

SILVER LAKE

Distance: 3.2 miles
Location: Green Mountain National Forest. This walk leaves from a parking area located along Vermont Highway 53, 0.1 mile south of Branbury State Park. Our walk does not start here, but rather along a dirt road heading to the left of Highway 53, 0.1 mile south of the parking area.

This walk climbs gently through a mixed deciduous forest, coming out in 1.6 miles at an absolutely delightful lake, cradled by shimmering white birch and the feathery evergreen branches of white pine. Although you'll see a trail leading off from the parking area that would eventually lead you to the same place, instead walk south on Vermont State Highway 53 for 0.1 mile and turn left onto a gated dirt road. This route is far less cluttered, and the walking is a great deal more pleasant.

Once away from the rush of wheels on Highway 53, take a moment to notice some of the more common members of this forest community. On the ground, for instance, are beautiful clusters of Christmas fern. This fern is indeed green at Christmastime, and was once commonly used as a holiday decoration. Because it likes rocky soil, you'll often see it growing along the rock walls that snake their way across so much of the New England landscape.

Common trees along the first 0.3 mile of the walk include beech, striped maple (sometimes called moosewood, since moose enjoy eating the bark), birch, sugar maple, white pine, hemlock, and witch-hazel. Witch-hazel, incidentally, whose medicinal values were introduced to us by the Indians, remains one of the most commonly used natural healing plants. Leaves and twigs of the witch-hazel are typically mixed with rubbing alcohol and used as a liniment for treating strains and bruises. (The aftershave lotion you're using, in fact, may well have an extract of witch-hazel in it.) Settlers from Great Britain used forked branches of the tree as divining rods to locate underground water. There's some argument as to whether or not the expression "to witch for water" is a leftover tag from the sixteenth century, when religious leaders thought such activities to be the work of the devil, or if "witch" is simply derived from a word that once meant "to bend."

Also common here is the American beech, a lovely tree with smooth, gray bark and alternate toothed leaves. Beech was a welcome sight to settlers in this area, since it was usually an indication of rich loam soils lying beneath—the best kind for producing crops. The roasted nuts of the beech served as a substitute for coffee, and, in some parts of the East and Southeast, it was common to extract oil from them for use in cooking. As for its medicinal value, various Indians and European settlers alike used the beech in concoctions designed to treat poison ivy, burns, and even ulcers.

As you continue to climb, notice how the road cut you're following has allowed enough sunlight to pour through to support

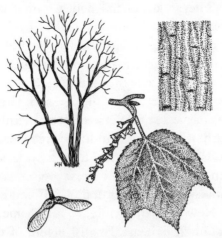

Striped Maple

37

Partridgeberry

many ground plants that could not survive further back in the more shaded forest. An event so simple as a tree falling and tearing a hole in the tree canopy can have far-reaching effects on the kind of plants that will sprout in the surrounding area.

At 0.5 mile pass beneath an electric line and water flume (carrying water from Silver Lake) to a point just south of the Falls of Lana. As the interpretive sign here will tell you, the name of the falls was changed by a group of passing army men from what they considered to be a distasteful name—"Sucker Brook Falls"—to its current tag, which was meant to honor their fearless leader at the time, General Wool. (The good general had a tour of duty in Mexico, where he was known as "llana," which is the Spanish word for wool.)

Soon our road makes a switchback to the right up a hill. At 1.2 miles, about the time that the road begins to level, are thick carpets of wood nettle along the side of the road. Even though cooked nettles are edible, don't touch one with your bare skin in the wild, as their stinging hairs can cause a severe case of dermatitis. Shortly after this prickly nettle garden is a delightful little stream whispering its way through the woods, with a beautiful little twin-leaved ground cover called partridgeberry nearby. This forest ground cover is one of the loveliest, its leathery green leaves and cheery red berries persisting even through a New England winter. Though not much of a food supply for either human or beast, English colonial women once drank a tea made from partridgeberry leaves to ease menstrual cramps.

At 1.6 miles you'll reach Silver Lake. Stay right, on a path that winds along the east side of the lake first to the picnic area, and then to the beach. If it's too busy here to suit your tastes, a small footpath circles the lake, offering the solitude seeker plenty of quiet nooks and crannies among the birch and pine.

CHITTENDEN BROOK

Distance: 2.5 miles

Location: Green Mountain National Forest. From the intersection of Vermont state highways 53 and 73, head east on Route 73 for just over 9 miles; then turn right (south) onto the entrance road to Chittenden Brook Campground (Forest Road 45). Follow this road to the campground entrance, where you'll see a small two-track road to the left, marked by a sign that reads Campground Loop Trail. Park here, out of the way of campground traffic, and begin your walk along this path.

There's a lot packed into these 2.5 miles of pathway, from meadows splashed with wildflowers to cool, tumbling streams, from beaver ponds to thick blankets of rich, green forest. A few walkers will be fortunate enough to see moose along the latter stretches of trail, and nearly everyone will be audience for the splendid singing of red-eyed vireos, chestnut-sided warblers, and, one of Thoreau's personal favorites, the wood thrush.

Both the campground and the lovely brook that will accompany you throughout much of this walk take their names from a colorful farmer and barkeep who was to become Vermont's first governor, Thomas Chittenden. Chittenden, whose one eye gave him a rather formidable appearance, served nearly continuously as governor of the Vermont republic and state for nearly twenty years, from 1778 to 1797. It was in large measure Chittenden who had helped hold this fledgling republic together during Ethan Allen's imprisonment during the late 1770s—no small feat, considering the packs of land-hungry New Yorkers and various others that stood by the door waiting to lay into the lands of the Green Mountain Boys. Royall Tyler, a lawyer who eventually gained appointment to the Vermont Supreme Court, once wrote a rousing little ditty about Governor Chittenden:

> Talk not of your Washingtons,
> Hancocks and Sullivans,
>   And all the wild crew;
> Our Tom set on high
> With his single eye
> Can more espy
>   Than they can with two.

The first part of this walk climbs along a wide, grassy path fringed with sugar maples, yellow birch, and striped maple. Black-eyed Susans nod their sunny yellow heads in the breeze, while patches of red clover (Vermont's state flower) and fireweed lend striking touches of pink and lavender to the broad strokes of grassy green. Fireweed, a tall plant sporting spikes of bright purple blossoms, is not only beautiful to look at but is considered by many to be quite tasty. The stem has a sweet inner pith, and the leaves are often used both for making teas and as a cooked green. For that matter, the red clover here is hardly without some rather unexpected virtues of its own. Herbalists in Europe have long prescribed a tea made from clover blossoms to aid in constipation, while clover poultices are used even today in treating athlete's foot.

As you continue to climb gently, watch the edges of this pathway for ruffed grouse, which may flush very suddenly. When a female is with her chicks, as you approach she'll likely run off through the brush feigning a broken wing, all the while making the most amazing whimpering noises—all of which is a well-orchestrated ruse to distract you away from her young. In 0.75 mile the path will make a sharp turn to the right, nuzzling to a fine thicket of hobblebush. This viburnum, easily recognized by its large, round opposite leaves displaying prominent veins, is so named because its low-slung branches often take root, forming trip lines that catch, or "hobble," those wandering through the forest. Hobblebush is one of the first shrubs to flower in May, displaying flat clusters of tiny white blossoms that are encircled by much larger white blooms. (These outer blossoms are actually sterile.) Later in the summer the smaller flowers produce berries that turn from red to blue-black. These are very sweet, and so much like a raisin that many people actually refer to hobblebush as "wild raisin."

Soon the grass pathway meets Chittenden Brook. As of this writing it was necessary to take a left here and cross the water a short distance upstream. A new bridge was being considered, however, which would take you directly across Chittenden Brook in a straight line. At any rate, when you reach the other side of the water, turn right, following the Campground Loop Trail as it follows the brook downstream through the forest.

Notice the difference in the plants that grow in this slice of cool, green forest compared to what thrived in the open, drier grassy patches you just traversed. Suddenly there's a riot of trilliums, blue-bead lilies, and wood sorrel, as well as Indian cucumber, partridgeberry, and hair cap moss. As you gain a high bench overlooking the brook below, the walk becomes a gentle amble through a myriad of soft shadows, muted summer light dripping like honey into the deep ravines of the forest.

At 1.5 miles you'll intersect the Chittenden Brook Trail. Follow the signed pathway to the beaver ponds, which you'll find at the end of an easy 0.2 mile walk to the west. The beaver activity in this area varies from year to year, but late in the evening, those who

Wood Thrush

41

Chestnut-sided Warbler

would brave the bugs and thickets may well see these furry engineers taking care of business. If you're ever close enough to a beaver to get a really good look, you'll notice that the animal's rear feet, which lie at the end of short, powerful legs, are webbed between the toes to aid in swimming. (For "high-speed" water travel—perhaps 2.5 miles per hour—the beaver alternates use of these feet with strokes of its large, flat tail.) A beaver's front feet are without webs, and shaped like small hands. With these it can drag sticks, dig holes, comb fur, and a host of other tasks.

A beaver family will vary in number, but typically consists of an adult female, male, yearlings, and kits—generally five to seven animals in all. Adult females call the shots in beaverland, but on the whole the family is extremely sociable. In late evening they can be seen grooming each other and generally frolicking together before they all settle back into their large, conical-shaped lodges. In the spring of their second year—the age of sexual maturity—teenagers either volunteer or are persuaded by their parents to set up house somewhere else, often many miles away from where they were born.

While you're tromping around these wet areas, watch the muddy ground for tracks of another common visitor here—the moose. When you're ready, return to the Campground Loop Trail the same way you came. Turn left, and in just over 0.25 mile, after a delightful walk along the stream, you'll find yourself on the far side of Chittenden Brook Campground.

LITTLE ROCK POND

Distance: 4 miles
Location: Green Mountain National Forest. Head south out of
Rutland, Vermont, on U.S. Highway 7 to the little village of
Danby. From here head east on Forest Road 10 for approximately
3.1 miles to a parking lot on the right. Our trail (which is a
section of the Long and Appalachian Trail system) takes off on
the other side of the road from this parking area.

It's been 80 years since Vermont Academy assistant headmaster
James Paddock Taylor, a man who swore by the virtues of tromping
the open countryside, began to daydream about building a hiking
trail that would connect the long line of summits that form the rocky
backbone of the Green Mountain State. At the time of Taylor's dream
there were, much to his chagrin, few mountains in Vermont that
could even be climbed without the blustery art of bushwhacking.

There is no question that, as far as the general population was
concerned, Taylor was either ahead of his time or simply outside of it
altogether. The average New Englander of the day tended to view
mountains as much more of a liability than an asset. Hiking to the top
of a high peak for the fun of it was something that only a few crazy
tourists would do. (To place the timing of Taylor's plan in perspective
for you, consider that Benton McKaye's notion of a trail running from
Georgia to Maine along the spine of the Appalachian Mountains—
what would become the famous Appalachian Trail—was still more
than a decade away.)

After initially receiving little encouragement from Boston's
Appalachian Mountain Club, which apparently was under the opin-
ion that the topography of Vermont was rather like western Kansas,
Taylor decided that the support he needed to pull off such a project
could only be garnered from certain influential people in Vermont.
On March 11, 1910, a group of 21 people, most of whom were
powerful men in the state, called the first meeting of the now famous
Green Mountain Club to order. Their motto, "To make the Vermont
mountains play a larger role in the life of the people," was as open and
optimistic as their first president, James P. Taylor himself. A couple of
decades and 255 miles of trail later, after a turbulent set of arguments
that ranged from whether or not grades should be limited to 15

percent (quickly nixed) to what colors the blazes should be, Taylor's dream of the Long Trail came true at last.

This particular slice of the Long Trail to Little Rock Pond contains none of the ambitious climbs of other sections of the foot-path. Instead, this is a gentle amble, often cheek to cheek with a stream flowing through a beautiful northern hardwood forest of birch, beech, and maple. In many places the trail is fringed by delicate ground covers, which through the year offer unexpected splashes of color against the thick wash of Green Mountain green.

In the first few yards of trail you'll pass selfheal (a favorite with herbalists for treating sore throats), tall meadow rue, false Solomon's seal, bluebead lily, and hobblebush, and in 0.1 mile, a nice blanket of whorled wood aster. Almost without your noticing it the path soon eases into one of those deep, soothing slices of mature hardwood forest so common to the Green Mountains. No matter what the weather, there is a haunting beauty to this kind of woodland. Beech trees tower above you, their smooth, gray "elephant trunks" disappearing in a vast dome of fluttering leaves. Occasionally clumps of white birch can be seen far off through the forest, each trunk in the cluster leaning back from the base, like a huddle of sailors trying to steady their boat in a stiff breeze.

Watch the ground at 0.5 mile for Indian cucumber, as well as patches of wood sorrel, with its distinct shamrock-shaped leaves. (There are some who claim this common wood sorrel was the original Irish shamrock, made famous by St. Patrick himself.) Sorrels, the leaves of which can be nibbled in small amounts to quench thirst, do best in partially shaded environments. In fact, if you see sorrel growing in the sun (probably yellow sorrel), you may find it has dropped its leaves to a more vertical position in order to reduce the drying effects of direct light.

By 1 mile into the walk you will have also passed several fine fern gardens. In this area you'll find cinnamon ferns, hayscented ferns, and sensitive ferns, the latter so named because it withers with the first frost. Soon you'll reach the first of a series of wooden plank walkways. Surrounding the first of these are fine collections of tall meadow rue, which, during its flowering season, will no doubt be attended to by a number of hard-working bees and butterflies.

At 1.8 miles into the walk you'll pass by a short signed trail taking off to the right to Lula Tye Shelter. Lula Tye, incidentally, was secretary and treasurer of the Green Mountain Club for 29 years, beginning in 1926. Her ability to organize the increasingly complex matters of the fledgling club were legendary—a feat for which she was eventually paid a whopping $375 per year.

In another 0.2 mile you'll reach the shore of Little Rock Pond. This pocket of water is lovely, surrounded by a quilt of deciduous trees laced with the dark greens of spruce and balsam fir. In fall you may see small flocks of mallards or Canada geese, which often pause here for a rest and for refueling on their long flights from winter. If you'd like to add a little extra distance to this walk, set your feet adrift on the easy, meandering loop trail that circles Rocky Pond.

Sensitive Fern

LOST POND

Distance: 6.1 miles
Location: Green Mountain National Forest. From Rutland, Vermont, head south on U.S. Highway 7 to the small village of Danby. From here head east on Forest Road 10 for 6.75 miles, and turn right onto Forest Road 30. Our parking area and trailhead are at the end of Forest Road 30, 2.3 miles from this last turn. Begin by following the closed roadway west across the bridge.

Although longer than most of our walks, this pleasant loop is an easily managed trek through some especially lovely Green Mountain scenery. There are both the riots of grasses and wildflowers typical of lands lying bare to the sun, as well as the rich, shady silences of the mature hardwood forest. The back side of the walk follows beautiful streams, the tempo of their rushing, rocky dances winding slowly down as the days drift further into summer.

The walk begins on a roadway now closed to motorized vehicles, climbing slowly in various grades toward its intersection with the Appalachian and Long trails. Once you pass the dirt mound across the road at 0.5 mile, you'll be able to get a wonderful sense of how tenacious nature can be in reclaiming a landscape altered by human hands. This road was closed in 1984, and already, young striped maples and pin cherries are working their way out of the forest cover, the advance guard for the more shade-tolerant yellow birch, sugar maple, and beech, which are following close behind.

This initial stretch of roadway is an especially fine place to study the kinds of plants that thrive in open areas. While the gardener tends to lump many of these species into the catchall category of "weeds," I find that they tend to cast their own kind of beauty here in the wild, blooming far and free from our notions of what, in cultivation, is either useful or sublime. Indeed, most of our current pronouncements about what is and isn't a worthless weed are simply current fashion. Lamb's quarter and curly dock, for instance, were as recently as 50 years ago a regular part of many people's diets. Drift back further in time and our "worthless weeds" list shrinks more.

Lying beneath your feet will be a diverse enough mat of vegetation to tatter the pages of your identification books. You'll find horsetail, yarrow, wild indigo, and selfheal, as well as tall meadow rue, bladder campion, cow vetch, milkweed, and sweet and hop clovers. Purple-flowered raspberries splash lavender along the trail, while buttercups and golden Alexander add touches of gold. Cutleaf and red-banded sedges tickle your thighs; sensitive ferns peek out from the roadside under a light cover of striped maples.

Be prepared along the wooded edges of this tall grass to be surprised by sudden explosions of ruffed grouse, who seem especially prone to scaring humans by not launching themselves out of their nests until the last minute. When young chicks are present, the mother, if she feels it is necessary, will put on a bit of acting to which Siskel and Ebert would unhesitatingly give two thumbs up. This is a "near-death" scene, and it plays to the tendency of nearly all predators to go after a sick or injured animal. A broken wing is almost always part of the show, and if that doesn't work, she may emit a series of mournful, high-pitched squeals. Finally, in the case of humans too stupid to be lured by even that, she may lie on her back and beat the ground with her wings! Once she has lured the threat away, she'll circle back and gather her chicks. By autumn the young grouse are able to fly, at which time the birds will roost in the safety of trees.

At 2.6 miles, after a stretch of moderate climbing, you'll reach the intersection with the Long and Appalachian trails, where you'll turn right toward the Lost Pond Shelter. (Lost Pond seems the perfect name. During my visit, which was during a rather dry year, it

False Nettle

Fireweed

was nowhere to be found.) A stark change awaits you as you leave the open, sunlit road cut into a hushed forest of hemlock, beech, and yellow birch. No longer is the path lined with composites, vetches, and milkweeds, but rather with the shade-tolerant, more moisture-loving bluebead lily, clearstem, wood sorrel, Indian cucumber, and false nettle, as well as the increasingly rare Jack-in-the-pulpit.

Continue to descend on this pathway for approximately 1.5 miles to the intersection of a trail to Old Job Shelter, and turn right, onto the last leg of our loop. This stretch of the walk is perhaps the loveliest, marked by a gentle, smooth climb beside boulder-choked streams, weaving in and out of a forest exploding with life. This trail, as much as any other you could find, typifies the wet, verdant beauty of the Green Mountains. At 4.9 miles you'll reach Old Job Clearing, which in summer sports huddles of tall, beautiful fireweed spikes, each one practically screaming its purple color to you as you pass.

At Old Job Shelter the trail turns right, into a beautiful forest of yellow birch, beech, and maple. Beside you is Lake Brook, which will, over 0.75 mile, guide you gently home. To help celebrate your return is a beautiful plunge pool at the trailhead, delicious to the touch on any warm summer afternoon.

New Hampshire

POETRY-NATURE TRAIL

Distance: 0.5 mile
Location: The Frost Place. From the intersection of New Hampshire routes 18 and 116 in the town of Franconia, follow 116 south for just under 1 mile. Turn right, following the signs to the Frost Place.
Note: The Frost Place is open limited hours from Memorial Day to Columbus Day. To find out the current schedule, write to the Frost Place at Box F, Franconia, NH 03580, or call the director at 603-823-5510 or 603-823-8038.

Everybody should be free to go very slow. . . . What you want, what you're hanging around in the world waiting for, is for something to occur to you.

ROBERT FROST
March 21, 1954

A great many things "occurred" to Robert Frost during his 5 full years and 18 summers spent at this idyllic Franconia country home. It was here, perched before the long, lovely swell of the Franconia Mountains, that this Pulitzer prize–winning poet would write some of his most beautiful collections of verse: *A Boy's Will*, *North of Boston*, *Mountain Interval*, and *New Hampshire*. "A poem," he once said in a

49

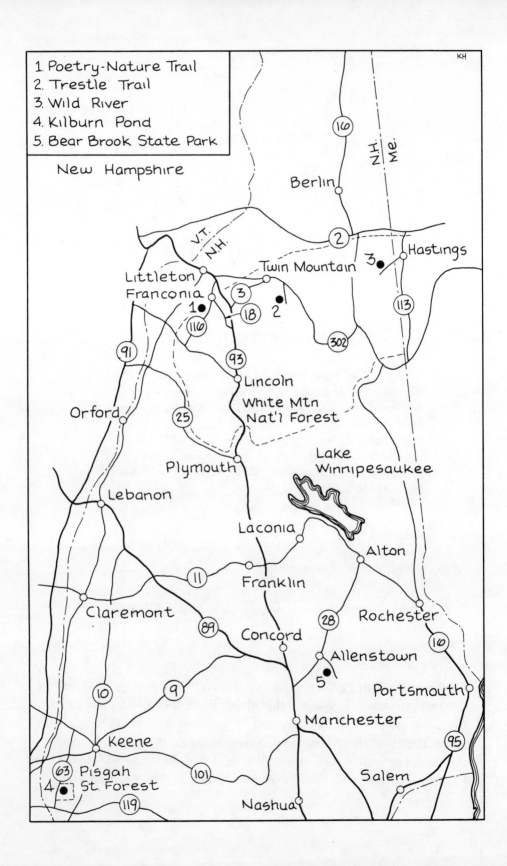

1. Poetry-Nature Trail
2. Trestle Trail
3. Wild River
4. Kilburn Pond
5. Bear Brook State Park

New Hampshire

KH

16

Berlin

N.H. Me.

2

Twin Mountain
3 ● Hastings

Littleton
Franconia
1 ●
3
18   2 ●

V.T.
N.H.

116

91

93

113

302

Lincoln
White Mtn
Nat'l Forest

Orford

25

Plymouth

Lake
Winnipesaukee

Lebanon

Laconia

Alton

11

Franklin

Claremont

89

Concord

28

Rochester

10

Allenstown
5 ●

Portsmouth

10   9

Manchester

95

Keene

63 Pisgah
4 ▢ ● St. Forest

101

Salem

119

Nashua

letter to Louis Untermeyer, "begins as a lump in the throat, a sense of wrong, a homesickness, a lovesickness. It finds the thought and the thought finds the words."

Along this 0.5-mile trail you'll have an opportunity not only to read some of Frost's poetry, which is displayed beside the trail, but also to observe some of the same plants and bird life that kept him company during his years at Franconia. Before setting out, be sure to pick up one of the trail guides.

Our first pathway poem, "The Tuft of Flowers," is a verse about Frost's encounter with a butterfly and a streamside cluster of, appropriately enough, butterfly weed. Butterfly weed is a brilliantly colored relative of the common milkweed, and each summer without fail its orange blooms manage to attract countless butterflies, from monarchs to swallowtails. Indians and European settlers frequently used the plant to treat serious ailments of the respiratory system. Some Indian peoples also crushed the long, fleshy taproot of the butterfly weed and applied it to burns and lesions of the skin.

As you enter the woodland near the very beginning of the walk, keep your eyes out for Jack-in-the-pulpits, tall meadow rue, and purple trillium, the latter plant also once known as birthroot, since a tea prepared from the plant was given to women in order to ease childbirth. Also here are balsam fir and sugar maples, both of which are doing an admirable job of reclaiming the old highway cut that can still be seen coursing through the woods behind Frost's poem "The Road Not Taken."

This wooded stretch of pathway is usually wrapped in a blanket of birdsong, including the melodies of one of Frost's favorite songsters, the hermit thrush. This little bird makes its nest on the floor of the forest or in a low bush, and has the unique habit of flicking its tail up and down several times a minute. Frost was not the only one to embrace the song of the thrush, which for this species consists of a single flutey tone followed by a lilting series of rising and falling notes. Across the Atlantic, English poet Robert Browning was also similarly enchanted:

> That's the wise thrush; he sings each song twice over,
> Lest you should think he could never recapture
> The first fine careless rapture!

Tall Meadow Rue

A short way into the forest you'll reach one of Frost's most memorable works, "Stopping by Woods on a Snowy Evening." Frost is thought to have stopped his horse that snowy night approximately 6 miles west of here, near a small pocket of water known as Pearl Lake. For such a small pond, Pearl Lake has most certainly had its share of attention. First it was known as Bear Pond, for the large population of bear in the area; later this name was changed to Mink Lake for all the mink. Then, in the middle 1800s, a fisherman supposedly found clam shells in the lake that contained sizable pearls. When a man named True Page was reported to have found one gem worth over thirty dollars (and how can you doubt a man named True Page?), the "event" could only result in the name of the place being changed to Pearl Pond. Before long, people were coming by the dozens, spending all daylight hours knee-deep in lukewarm pond water, certain that the big find was just another clam away.

On the back side of the Poetry Trail you'll come to Frost's "The Quest of the Purple-Fringed." The verse refers to the purple-fringed orchid, a plant sporting a fragrant cluster of feathery lavender flowers. This particular orchid holds its pollen in a mass below the anther, to which a sticky disk is attached. Moths sticking their tongues down the bloom catch the pollen ball and inadvertently remove it, taking it with them to the next flower, which is thereby pollinated.

In the next poem, "Hyla Brook," Frost mentions jewelweed. Jewelweed is common throughout much of New England, and has for centuries provided relief from the painful itching of both stinging nettle and poison ivy. Scientists have documented that the plant also has significant fungicidal qualities, which explains one of its other common uses—a treatment for athlete's foot.

Finish the trail past milkweed, selfheal, yarrow, orange hawk-weed, and wild lupine. As you come off the path, take a moment to drink in a bit of the sweeping view that Frost had of the Franconia Mountains, a slice of the White Mountains that took their name from a resemblance to the Franconian Alps of Germany. They are an absolutely beautiful sight from winter to fall, an inspiration that was never lost to Robert Frost. It's easy to understand his drive to end up on the front porch of this particular house, an aspiration he relates rather matter-of-factly in a stanza from the poem "New Hampshire":

> The farm I made my home on in the mountains
> I had to take by force rather than buy.
> I caught the owner outdoors by himself
> Raking up after winter, and I said
> "I'm going to put you off this farm: I want it."
> "Where are you going to put me? In the road?"
> "I'm going to put you on the farm next to it."
> "Why won't the farm next to it do for you?"
> "I like this better." It was really better.

And that is exactly what happened. And if the poetry he created here is any indication, then this place must have really been the better place, after all.

TRESTLE TRAIL

Distance: 1.1 miles

Location: From the town of Twin Mountain, New Hampshire, head east for 3 miles on U.S. Route 302 to Zealand Road. Turn right (south), and proceed for 0.6 mile to a trailhead parking area on the right. Both the Trestle Trail and the Sugarloaf Trail leave a short distance south of this parking area, on the other side of a bridge crossing the Zealand River.

The cool, shaded twists and turns of the Trestle Trail make it the perfect respite for weary highway potatoes. Dozens of quiet nooks and crannies along this path will delight anyone who simply slows down enough to notice them. In the best tradition of nature rambling, it makes little difference here whether you do the entire 1.1-

mile loop, or simply park yourself on a flat rock by the river for a soak in the sunshine. All such moments will put the same broad smile on your face.

Our walk begins in a mix of maples, birches, and fir, with smatterings of wild sarsaparilla, bunchberry, bracken, bluebead lily, and Canada mayflower. If you spend much time at all in the woods, you might enjoy watching a few common plants to see the kinds of changes that each goes through from spring to fall. In time you'll come to see the woods as a kind of intricate timepiece, whose ever-changing face can reflect with surprising precision the slow, deliberate roll of the seasons.

Let's take a closer look, for instance, at the Canada mayflower, whose shiny, pointed leaves are visible throughout much of this walk. The leaves of this ground cover appear in middle spring, pushing up their way from the forest floor in tightly rolled, inch-long projections. These will slowly uncurl to reveal plants with one, two, or three leaves. Only those with two or three, however, actually produce flowers in May—clusters of ivory-colored, star-shaped blooms that exude a rich fragrance not unlike that of lily of the valley. Four to six weeks after the blooms appear, toward the end of June, you'll be able to see the beginnings of fruits on the lower portions of the flower stalks. At first these are a speckled white-green color, but later, nearer to autumn, they will turn a beautiful ruby red. These berries may remain on the plants well into winter, providing side dishes for many a hungry grouse.

Canada Mayflower

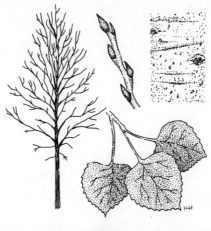

Aspen

In 0.2 mile you'll reach the intersection with the Middle Sugarloaf Trail, which takes off to the left. Stay right, continuing along the froth and spray of the Zealand River. In another 0.3 mile you'll cross a north-south trail, and shortly afterward, you'll come to an enormous boulder. This boulder is a glacial erratic, so named because fifteen thousand to twenty thousand years ago a glacier delivered this monster here after having carried it from the uplands, inch by inch, on a thick tongue of ice.

A few yards past this erratic the trail will veer to the left. Look to your left at this point and you'll see a small clump of young quaking aspen, their leaves dancing in the slightest puff of summer breeze. Aspen, by the way, are the most widespread deciduous tree on the entire continent, and are particularly good at being the first to grow on areas that have been disturbed by fire or logging. They achieve this temporary dominance both by growing very quickly— most aspen will already be two feet tall by the time they reach their second year of growth—and also from being able to sprout young trees from existing root systems. (Bigtooth aspen can also sprout new trees from stumps.) A single root system may create a forest of thousands of trees that will cover more than a hundred acres, though most such clone groups are not nearly that large.

Three quarters of a century ago, when this entire valley stood bare and ravaged from the saws and fires of timber mogul J. E. Henry's logging operations, aspen sprouts would have been a very common sight. Like other "pioneer" species, however, most of these groves eventually yielded their ground to more shade-tolerant trees.

Speaking of J. E. Henry, at 0.65 mile you'll reach a Zealand River footbridge that sits in almost the exact spot where one of Henry's railroad trestle bridges was located. The Zealand Valley Railroad, sometimes called the most crooked road in New England, began hauling logging cars past this point in 1884. Before long there were five trains a day snaking their way down this valley, each typically hauling at least eight cars of logs. (Interestingly, this valley was originally called New Zealand. Just why the "New" was dropped no one can say for sure, but the most accepted explanation is that the railroad and post office simply found it more convenient to use the edited version.)

On the other side of the bridge stay left, following the yellow-blazed trail to the campground loop road. Take a right on this road, past fine stands of red maple, shadbush, balsam, and aspen. In 0.2 mile you'll see the Trestle Trail taking off to the right. Follow it through blueberries, raspberries, bracken fern, and false violet, reaching the parking area again in 0.1 mile.

WILD RIVER

Distance: 6 miles
Location: White Mountain National Forest. From U.S. High-way 2 in extreme southwestern Maine, head south on Maine Highway 113 for a couple miles to a signed turnoff on the right leading to Wild River Campground, 5.7 miles to the southwest (in New Hampshire). Continue a few yards past the campground entrance station to a small parking area on the left, where both the Basin and Wild River trails meet.

Though labeled as a forest walk, this easy path does indeed rub elbows more than a few times with the beautiful Wild River, a clear, swift stream that does the sprightliest of rocky hopscotches on its journey from Black Mountain to the Androscoggin. (*Androscoggin,* by the way, is a word that first showed up in the journals of Captain John Smith in 1616, and literally means fish-curing place. This name is testimony to the great runs of migratory ocean fish, including shad, alewives, and salmon, that once ran up the cool waters of the Androscoggin to breed.)

This walk is lovely during much of the year, though it takes on a special appeal when the road is dusted with autumn. Leaves, now cut off from nutrients and water, at last lose the green chlorophyll masks that they have worn since spring, revealing colors we could have never guessed were there had we not seen this all before. Especially wonderful on this trail is the carpet of birch leaves that pad your steps, shimmering in the shafts of October sunlight like weathered chips of gold on some mythical roadway to kingdom come. Even Shakespeare was at his best when it came to writing about the melancholy beauty of autumn:

> That time of year thou mayest in me behold
> When yellow leaves, or none, or few do hang
> Upon these boughs which shake against the cold,
> Bare ruined choirs, where late the sweet birds sang.

Looking at this forest today, it's hard to believe that it was ravaged by extremely heavy logging from 1860 to 1917. The tracks of a lumbering railroad twisted not only along the path you're walking but up most of the side-stream ravines as well, hauling out enormous amounts of softwood, and tons of hemlock bark for tanning shoe leather. Though you would never know it today, the place where Maine Highway 113 meets the road to our trailhead was the sight of the boisterous logging town of Hastings, a hodgepodge of boarding house, general store, post office, school, engine house, and mills serving more than a thousand people.

It's difficult to imagine the rate at which our early forefathers used the forests for firewood, fences, and building materials. Construction of utilitarian items from shingles to barrel staves was completed using only the choicest cuts of wood, while much of the timber was, as described in one 1800 Maine diary, "piled and burned on the spot." In eastern Massachusetts 75 percent of the forest was gone by 1825. Thereafter building projects depended on wood being sent by ship from forests like this one in the far north. Yet even these didn't last long. It has been estimated that the vast stands of commercial softwoods in the great White Mountain forests to the west were gone by 1890.

With the trees, of course, went the animals that made their homes there—white-tailed deer, beaver, elk, bear, and various species of game birds. (Again the wildlife situation was far worse in southern New England. Massachusetts closed its first deer-hunting season in 1694. By the end of the eighteenth century, the abundance of game animals that so impressed early colonists had vanished. "Hunting with us," wrote Timothy Dwight in the late 1700s, "exists chiefly in the tales of other times.")

For the first 1.1 miles of trail you'll wind through groves of white and yellow birch, hemlock, sugar and striped maple, oak, alder, and mountain ash, with a few bigtooth aspen thrown in for good measure. Then, at the point where the road ends, the star of the show becomes the Wild River. Take the opportunity during this next 0.5 mile to perch yourself riverside on a big slab of granite and watch this watery world churn by. Especially beautiful here is the jumble of giant boulders that choke the stream, pushing the water into chutes, splitting it into forks, flinging it headlong over high slabs into deep, smooth basins below. You may notice here piles of sticks, grass, and even tree trunks lying in rock crannies six or seven feet above the streambed, testimony to the extraordinary high water levels that occur on the Wild River during spring floods, when rain and snow-melt roar out of the White Mountains like a runaway freight train.

The path will continue to flirt with the river, arriving at its edge and then disappearing again into the forest, now also peppered with spruce and balsam fir. At 3 miles you'll intersect the Black Angel Trail. Turn right here to our turnaround point on a footbridge crossing the Wild River. The upstream view from this bridge is especially beautiful, a fresh toss of high-country river framed on either side by birch and conifers, and in back by the high, sweet swell of 3,303-foot Black Mountain.

On the upper flanks of Black Mountain, where the Wild River first begins its long tumble to the northeast, are stands of conifer that provide excellent habitat for pine martens. Martens are beautiful members of the weasel family, covered with thick coats of rich, silky fur. It was this fur, in fact, that in large part led to the marten's demise in the White Mountains at the hands of trappers, a decline that wasn't helped by the fact that martens seem totally unwary of traps. (Even in the remote wilds of Maine, martens required full protection for 35 years before their numbers stabilized again.) The marten is a tremendous tree climber, and sustains itself on generous

58

Marten

helpings of everything from red squirrels and chipmunks to insects, small birds, and fruits.

KILBURN POND

Distance: 1.5 miles
Location: Pisgah State Forest. The Kilburn Road access to Pisgah State Forest is located on the east side of New Hampshire State Highway 63, 4.5 miles south of the intersection of Highway 63 and State Highway 9. There's a gravel turnoff immediately adjacent to the highway, with a metal gate across Kilburn Road. Park outside the gate and begin your walk on this roadway.

There's a lovely rise and fall to this northwest corner of Pisgah State Forest, a collection of twisted cuts in the woodland that tumble sharply downward from the surrounding highlands—Porter Hill to the south, Bear Mountain to the west, Davis Hill to the north, and 1,303-foot Mount Pisgah, which lends its name to this preserve, to the east. Though like most land in New England this area has been logged time and time again, the tenacious blood flow of the forest has once again brought forth a beautiful blanket of trees, along with ground plants, animals, and birds.

59

Along this 0.7-mile stretch of Kilburn Road are fine stands of birch and beech, as well as striped maple, hemlock, mountain maple, and red oak. If you look carefully you may also see young sprouts of American chestnut, that once grand, very common component of the forest that has been all but wiped from the face of America. The gathering of chestnuts was at one time a great tradition in rural New England. After the husks had been split by heavy frosts, many a youngster would bundle up and head into the forest on some chilly fall morning to gather the nuts by the basketful. As the Christmas crooning of Nat King Cole suggests, "chestnuts roasting on an open fire" was indeed a common way of preparing such harvests, since heat made it much easier to peel away the outer shell and bitter inner husk to reveal the sweet, mealy chestnut inside. You could eat these nuts on the spot, make pudding out of them, or even add them to vegetables. Besides consuming the nuts, New England Indians once made a tea out of the leaves that was reportedly an effective remedy for whooping cough.

From the time that the chestnut blight first arrived in New York from Asia in 1903, not twenty years passed before virtually every tree in New England had been infected. And still the effects of the blight are with us. The beautiful young trees you see here are growing from sprouts, and will only reach heights of 10 to 20 feet before they too will feel the sting of blight in their upper branches, the fungus slowly working its way down until the tree is destroyed. Naturalist John Kieran once called American chestnut saplings the

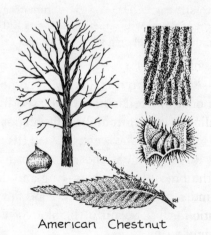

American Chestnut

"Peter Pans of the tree world," since they, like that fictional character, can never grow up.

At 0.2 mile into the walk you'll see some fine stands of mountain laurel growing on both sides of the road. In winter these evergreen leaves stand out in sharp relief against the blankets of snow, and in late spring and early summer they offer delicate splashes of pink and white flowers. Mountain laurel can grow to more than fifteen feet high under ideal conditions, and will occasionally live for more than a hundred years. The genus name of this plant, *Kalmia*, is in honor of Peter Kalm, a European who traveled the United States collecting specimens for the famous Swedish botanist Carolus Linnaeus. It was Linnaeus who, in the first half of the eighteenth century, set as a goal for himself to name every single item in the three kingdoms of the natural world—minerals, plants, and animals! Though of course he fell far short of this mark, his influence on modern botany cannot be understated. The two-part system he devised for labeling plants, one name for genus and one for species, is still used today.

Continue walking down the Kilburn Road. At 0.7 mile, near the bottom of a short hill, turn right onto the Kilburn Loop Trail. This is a 4.3-mile loop walk that heads well south of Kilburn Pond and then returns on the east side. For our walk, however, we'll simply make our way along Kilburn Pond for a few hundred yards, looking for any good cutoff through the trees that will bring us to the edge of the water for a better look. Along this stretch you'll see hobblebush, and in mid- to late summer after a good rain, the almost translucent white stalks of Indian pipe. Indians crushed the juice from this plant and mixed it with water for use as a wash for irritated eyes. There are even some reports of it being given for epilepsy, hence one of its other common names—"convulsion-root."

The edge of Kilburn Pond is a shaggy, convoluted place, an impossible shoreline for getting a clear look at the entire body of water. A thick blanket of both deciduous trees and conifers crowds the water's edge, with pond lilies and islands of sedge and rushes peppering both the bays and open channels. Much of Pisgah State Forest has this kind of wild, soothing flush to it, a welcome respite from the civilization that continues to sprout like summer weeds across the breadth of southern New Hampshire.

BEAR BROOK STATE PARK

Distance: 3 miles

Location: From the intersection of U.S. Highway 3 and New Hampshire 28, proceed north on Highway 28 for 3 miles to the park entrance road, and turn right. Continue east for 3.2 miles, staying to the right at the one Y fork in the road, to a camping area entrance on the right. Turn here and, again keeping to the right, continue for 1.4 miles to our trailhead, which is on the right marked by a letter *D*.

These 3 miles of pathway pass very easily beneath the feet—a flat, wooded meander through stands of conifers and hardwoods of varying ages, with chances along the way to rub elbows with fine slices of both marsh and meadow. The second leg of the trek, however, can have a few muddy spots in early or even mid-summer, so make sure your feet are ready.

The trail takes off on a grassy two-track road, with nice gardens of interrupted, sensitive, and hayscented ferns. There is something very special about ferns, their congregations of soft green fronds braided into a feathery quilt around the feet of the forest. Fern gardens seem to bring a kind of delicate hush to the land, and, as often as not, I'll lighten my step and cock an ear so that I can better hear the sound of honest-to-goodness quiet.

At certain times during your woods walks, most of the ferns

Hayscented Fern

you'll come across will have tiny rust-colored dots or lines on the underside of one or more of their fronds. These are actually tiny clusters of spore cases, many of which are covered by a thin shield that protects them until they are ready to be released. Some ferns produce millions of spores, many so light and durable that some researchers feel they are transported from continent to continent in the jet stream, a notion that got substantial support recently when a fern that grows only in Asia and Europe appeared on the east slope of the Colorado Rockies.

When one of these spores germinates, it first grows into what resembles a very thin thread, and then, if conditions are right, spreads into a tiny heart-shaped unit called a prothallium. (Those willing to put their nose to the ground in a suitable habitat, such as a carpet of moss, can often see dozens of prothallia lying on the surface.) Prothallia are actually independent, self-contained plants, sporting both male and female organs of microscopic proportions. Sliding on a thin film of water, male sperm wriggle into the funnel-shaped female organ and fertilize the egg. Though nursed for a while by nutrients contained in the prothallium case, eventually the plant sends a root into the soil, and begins making its own food. The parent prothallium withers away while the young fern continues to grow, unrolling its fronds from fiddleheads—the only plants, incidentally, to uncoil their leaves in such a manner. The time required for a ripe spore to become a new fern plant can vary according to species and growing conditions from a few weeks to nearly two decades!

Ferns are outnumbered by seed-bearing plants 30 to 1. Yet there are few places in the world where they cannot be found, from the Arctic to the Antarctic, and a million mountain ledges, lakes, ponds, fields, and forests in between. The magical history of ferns is a long and complex one, ranging from an old Irish belief that they were a sign of fertility, to their once being viewed by many religions, including Christianity, as having a kind of strange alliance with the evil doings of serpents. Ferns also had plenty of medicinal applications. Sweet brake was used from the days of the early Greeks to very modern times as a powerful remedy for tapeworm. Polypody has long been used as a laxative, while a tea made from maidenhair fern has been used by herbalists to treat coughs for more than two thousand years.

Continue through a forest of oak, hemlock, white pine, yel-

Interrupted Fern

low birch, and witch-hazel, the trailside flushed with Canada may-flower, wintergreen, sedges, and clubmosses, as well as, on occasion, the lovely spotted orange petals of the wood lily. At 0.9 mile, a short distance after crossing a small stream and a fine huddle of hemlocks, you'll reach marker *B*. Turn right here, and follow the path through a moist forest laced with fern, blueberry, Indian pipe, ground cedar, and bunchberry.

You'll reach marker *A* at 1.5 miles, where you'll once again turn to the right, picking up gray birch and sugar maple, as well as a towering stand of white pine at 1.75 miles. The marsh mentioned earlier—a humanmade water project to encourage wildlife—will be found at marker 4. In this area beaver and even great blue heron can occasionally be seen, although the pond has matured to the point where the latter are, for the most part, now only visitors.

Follow the road along the north side of the marsh, and then, 50 yards past it, turn right onto a small trail taking off through the woods. This trail will soon join another road where you'll take another right. Soon after this turn you'll find yourself cradled by a nice sedge and wildflower meadow on the right, and by bracken fern, oak, white pine, gray birch, aspen, mountain maple, pin cherry, and milkweed on the left. Take a right when you reach the entrance road at the far end of this clearing, and walk 0.3 mile back to your car.

Maine

LITTLE ABOL FALLS

Distance: 2 miles
Location: Baxter State Park. Enter Baxter through Togue Pond
Gate, located at the southeast corner of the park. Once through
the gate, bear to the left, following signs for Abol Campground.
Park across from the campground on the south side of the road
and walk in. At the first branch road in the campground, turn
right. Our trail takes off between camping shelters 8 and 10.

In a region that can truly be defined by superlatives, humble Little
Abol Falls Trail, climbing gently through a regenerating forest, does
not really stand out. It doesn't have the glassy pockets of smooth blue
water that frame nearby Daicey and Grassy Pond pathways, or the
dizzy, breathtaking plunges that hang off the steep, rugged sides of
Abol Trail. What it does present, however, is a long draw of thick
forest wrapped in peace and quiet, a few teasing glimpses of Mount
Katahdin's mighty south face, and in the end, one of the loveliest
white-water dances you may ever see. If you're in the area and in the
mood for a good, easily accessed daydream spot, Little Abol Falls is
hard to beat.

Hardly will you have stepped out of Abol Campground when
you'll cross clear, crisp Abol Stream, making a quick dash toward the
southeast. Immediately after this crossing, our trail makes a sharp

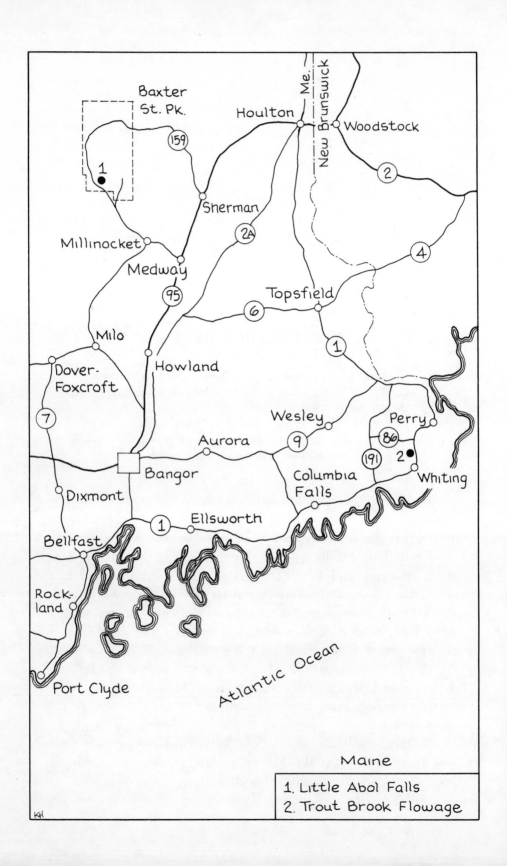

Baxter St. Pk.

Houlton

Me.

New Brunswick

Woodstock

159

2

Sherman

2A

4

Millinocket

Medway

95

Topsfield

6

Milo

1

Dover-Foxcroft

Howland

7

Wesley

Perry

9

86

Aurora

191

2

Bangor

Columbia Falls

Whiting

Dixmont

1

Ellsworth

Bellfast

Rock-land

Atlantic Ocean

Port Clyde

KH

Maine

1. Little Abol Falls
2. Trout Brook Flowage

left turn into a young forest of white birch, balsam fir, red maple, white pine, and spruce. This pathway is a good stretch for making the acquaintance of whorled wood and large leaved asters, bunchberry, and pearly everlasting. Further down the trail, at approximately 0.7 mile, you'll also find some nice examples of striped maple, which in some parts of the country is also known as moosewood.

If you keep your eyes peeled, you should be able to see an occasional glimpse of Katahdin through the forest, its staggering ramparts looming across the northern horizon like a fortress built by a kingdom of giants. (The name *Katahdin*, incidentally, is derived from an Abnaki Indian phrase meaning principle or great mountain.) Any view of this magnificent peak, no matter how brief, tends to make one bless the day that Governor Purcival Baxter took up the banner (and ultimately donated nearly six thousand of these two hundred thousand acres) to protect this "grandest and most beautiful of all the natural attractions of our State" for the people of Maine. Not only did Baxter engineer the creation of the park that bears his name but he also left enough money through his estate—more than 6 million dollars—to ensure proper management of the resource in the years to come.

At 0.9 mile the path descends briefly into a cool, moist hollow, and then rises again to meet the watercourse just a few yards upstream of Little Abol Falls. Notice on the far side of the cascade how clumps of white birch hang from the high, rocky ledges by their

Balsam Fir

toenails, in a heroic effort to grab branches full of sunshine as it pours into the twists and turns of this open gorge.

The Appalachian Trail makes its final ascent up a steep southwest ridge of Mount Katahdin, 2 miles north of where you now stand, ending a magnificent 2,000-mile run from Springer Mountain, Georgia. By the time "end-to-enders" (people walking the entire length of the trail) make it to Katahdin, they have had a level of experience chiseled into their spirits that is virtually unknown in modern society. In 1964, Chuck Ebersole and his son John became the first father-and-son team to traverse the entire Appalachian Trail in a single season. Chuck's recollection of a night spent at Lake-of-the-Clouds Hut in New Hampshire's White Mountains offers a look into the special blend of camaraderie that seems to exist between people who value personal adventure.

When suppertime came the guests sat on long benches while the hut boys served steaming dishes family style on the varnished surfaces of the wooden tables. Grace was said, and then amid laughter and chatter, everyone enjoyed the tasty meal. While the hut boys cleared things away, hiking groups recited poems or sang songs. Darkness settled in, and then the real fun began. Hiking musicians arrived with an accordion, two guitars, a banjo, and an enormous bull fiddle. When the kitchen chores were finished those instruments were tuned up and put to work. All kinds of songs were played, with everyone singing. The hut boys made another huge pot of hot chocolate and served it with cookies. The singing lasted for several hours. One song which tugged at my heart was "This Land is Your Land." A song like that always brings tears to my eyes. I love the green hills, the blue sky, the clean streams, and the good soil of Mother Earth, and that song exemplified what I was trying to find and enjoy by hiking the Appalachian Trail.*

* This is taken from *Hiking the Appalachian Trail*, vol. 1, edited by James R. Hare, 2 vols., Emmaus, PA: Rodale Press, 1975, pp. 426–427.

TROUT BROOK FLOWAGE

Distance: 1.6 miles
Location: South unit of Moosehorn National Wildlife Refuge, near Cobscook Bay State Park. From the intersection of Maine Highway 86 and U.S. Highway 1, head south on Highway 1 for 3 miles, to Weir Road, a small, gated, dirt road on the west side of the highway. Park here and begin walking southwest on Weir Road.
Note: Refuge managers use this road on a regular basis. Do not block the gate.

Moosehorn is noted for its gentle roadway walks through rich coniferous and mixed deciduous forests flushed with deer, black bear, raccoon, coyote, fisher, and moose; for its quiet ponds peppered with ducks, geese, osprey, and beaver. No matter where you are in Moosehorn, in fact, there seems to be another precious pocket of land or water worth exploring just around the bend. Walking Weir Road is a good example. The 0.8-mile path to Trout Brook Flowage provides a quick, easy breath of fresh air for pavement-weary travelers on U.S. Route 1. Those wanting additional air can continue walking another 0.5 mile to Maple Flowage, then another 0.25 mile to Alder Flowage, then another 0.4 mile to Middle Brook Flowage, then . . . well, you get the idea.

Surrounding the gate next to the highway are a few clumps of bigtooth aspen and alder, but these give way quickly to blankets of white and black spruce and balsam fir. Bunchberry makes a good showing along the early stretches of the walk, as does sweet fern, wintergreen, sheep laurel, and that common, unfairly maligned summer weed—goldenrod. It was long assumed that goldenrod released clouds of pollen into the air, which then found their way into people's sinus tracts, where they caused some rather amazing sneezing fits. In fact, goldenrod pollen is not released into the air, but is instead carried by insects. Ragweed, a plant that blooms at the same time as goldenrod, is to be blamed for harassing hay fever sufferers.

Goldenrod flowers produce a beautiful yellow dye, and tea made from the plant's leaves not only tastes good but is a proven remedy for gas. It's even been suggested that when the colonists rebelled against taxes by dumping a shipload of British tea into Boston Harbor, it was the leaves of goldenrod that came to the rescue,

Black Bear

offering a substitute beverage that was quickly dubbed "Liberty Tea."

As you proceed southward along the road, watch for black spruce draped with spindly tufts of "old man's beard," a grizzled green lichen that, given sufficient sunlight, often hangs in profusion in old stands of spruce and fir. Contrary to what appearances may lead you to conclude, lichens such as old man's beard are not parasites simply sponging off their hosts for food. The branches of these trees do, however, allow the lichen to gain access to far more sunlight than they would be able to garner were they to remain on the forest floor. Lichens are actually two organisms—a fungus and an algae—that have gone into business together. Basically, the algae provides manufactured sugars while the fungus offers physical protection to the algae, and, to a limited extent, nutrients from rootlike structures known as hyphae. Lichen is, in fact, one of the most successful partnerships (symbioses) in all of nature. Lichens can not only withstand grueling cold and drought but can eke out a living from the slimmest fare imaginable, including the bare face of solid rock.

Beneath the chatters of red squirrels—who, when not scolding intruders like yourself, are busy consuming everything from conifer seeds and sap to insects, flowers, and fruits—the road winds through lovely stands of white pine and white birch. Near the forest edge are pockets of bracken fern, blueberries, raspberries, wintergreen, and an occasional St. Johnswort. This latter plant, incidentally, because it tends to bloom near the time of the summer solstice, was a major component of pagan sun worship rituals. Though the advancing Christians would have nothing to do with sunshine shenanigans, they hardly wrote off the plant. It was promptly renamed after Saint John the Baptist, whose birthday occurred shortly after the summer solstice, and quickly became a favorite "holy herb" of priests in the Middle Ages, who would use it to assist them in the performance of exorcisms. In a more pragmatic vein, American Indians long used a tea made of St. Johnswort to treat tuberculosis.

Trout Brook Flowage is reached in 0.8 mile, the water fringed by sedges and cattails, with nice mats of hop clover, orange hawkweed, and birdfoot trefoil growing nearby. This pond has a rather lonely look to it, clusters of dead trees making frantic, frozen gestures against the evening sky. If you happen to be here as the last light is fading, it's easy to imagine that a hale gang of old gray ghosts has risen from the puddles, bound for a last little fling among the living timber.

THE MOUNTAINS

*A people who climb the ridges and sleep under the stars in high
mountain meadows, who enter the forest and scale the peaks, who
explore glaciers and walk ridges buried deep in snow—these
people will give their country some of the indomitable spirit of the
mountains.*

WILLIAM O. DOUGLAS
Of Men and Mountains

Although New England's mountains have been pared by ice,
wind, and water to half their former stature, their collective
reaches of rock and timber remain one of the greatest of the
New England magics. There are the smooth, gentle drumlins of the
Windham Hills in eastern Connecticut, and solitary massifs rising
high and lonely above the forested plains of southern New Hampshire. There are the yawning north-south swells of the Green Mountains, the stark profiles of the Taconics, and the complex meta-
morphic mishmash of the White Mountain range.

As far as pleasant destinations go, it would be hard not to be
impressed with any of these uplands. Visitors in the far north nearly
lose their breath at the grandeur of Maine's Mount Katahdin. Indeed,
this peak can look every bit like the Indians saw it—home of the
fierce god Pamola, who, as one 1880s visitor tells it, is so ferocious
"that he can pick up a moose in one of his claws." Trails to the
summit of Katahdin were once so rugged that guides tell of hikers
wearing out the seats of their pants sliding down them.

From Katahdin you could drift through a long tumble of high,
rolling lake country in southwest Maine, finally reaching the shoulder
of 6,288-foot Mount Washington in the White Mountains. The ther-

mometer atop this peak has plunged to 50 degrees below zero, while during certain parts of winter the winds may reach hurricane velocity two out of every three days. It was, in fact, in April of 1934 that gauges on the summit of Washington pegged the wind at a phenomenal 231 miles per hour—the biggest alpine blow ever recorded on Earth.

West of Washington 70 miles is 4,303-foot Mount Mansfield, the crowning jewel of the Green Mountains. The Greens are among the oldest mountain ranges in New England, rising from the earth nearly 450 million years ago. The forces of wind, water, and ice have long been at work on these peaks, removing several miles of rock from them since they were first formed—rounding them, sculpting them into the fairly soft profiles you see today. Though gentler in stature, the Green Mountains still exude a sense of wildness. Ethan Allen, swearing to maintain the independent nation of Vermont, said he would, if necessary, "retire with the hardy Green Mountain Boys to the desolate Caverns of the [Green] Mountains, and from there wage war with human nature at large!" The Greens are also the home of the legendary French-Canadian creature "loup-garou," a man half changed into a wolf as punishment for some past evil. Though impervious to bullets and blades, some think this wolf-man may have finally met his demise. You see, it's been quite a few years since any wild-eyed hunters have come into Green Mountain villages babbling strange tales of having come face to face with a werewolf.

The mountains begin to mellow as they drift toward the northwest corner of Massachusetts, home of the lovely Berkshires. Yet even these hills were once considered to be the wild frontier. Their steep, wooded faces, uncut by a single river, created a formidable barrier to passage during much of the eighteenth century. (The route that did eventually cut through the Berkshires was along an old Indian path known as the Mohawk Trail; this trail would become the gateway through which thousands of easterners would pass on their exodus to the American West.) Though not as dramatic as other New England ranges, there has been many a New Englander who has fallen head over heels in love with this sublime southwest hill country. Among them were some very influential writers, including Oliver Wendell Holmes, Sr., Nathaniel Hawthorne, and Herman Melville, the latter who once claimed that the roll of the Berkshires sparked memories in him of ocean waves—appropriate imagery for someone laboring to capture the salty tale of *Moby Dick*.

The formation of each of New England's mountain regions is remarkably complex; put together the formations can send the most dedicated rock hound into a geological head spin. To give you a better sense for the depth of these tales, let's take a quick look at the formation of the northern Appalachians, which geologists refer to as the Acadian Mountains.

About the time that fish were in the process of becoming fish, there was a great series of collisions between three massive continental plates located thousands of miles to the southeast. The sheer force of this land bashing is on a scale absolutely unknown to us today. On the continental plate we call Laurentia, from which North America would be fashioned, the eastern fringes of sedimentary rock were shoved westward for 10 miles with such force that they folded upon each other layer after layer. The heat and pressure that accompanied these movements were so intense that the very nature of the rocks themselves was changed, as they first melted and then were recast into schist, slate, and gneiss (pronounced "nice").

As the collisions continued, those original rocks were uplifted and squeezed back toward the east again. The uplifting, folding, and oozing of molten rocks marked much of the period, with great domes of semimolten gneiss rising to the surface like bubbles in a boiling pot of molasses. On and on went the great uplifts, until the northern Appalachians finally came to rest 50 million years later. Yet even as great mountains are created, they are being destroyed by the forces of erosion. Grain by grain these rugged, soaring peaks were slowly worn into a flat delta, only to again be uplifted and sliced by erosion.

Following this first great mountain-building episode, those three original landmasses we mentioned earlier fused into a great supercontinent known as Pangaea, which remained intact for nearly 200 million years. Tremendous forces rose yet again within the earth and tore the continents apart, though along slightly different fracture lines than existed originally. (This process is how parts of Europe and Africa welded to our east coast.) And then, ever so slowly, America began to drift to the northwest.

It stretches the imagination to think that great continents could go floating around the surface of the earth. But it becomes slightly more believable when you consider that we are standing on less than 20 miles of solid crust, which in turn rests on nearly 4,000 miles of shifting, unstable rock and magma. Proportionately, our solid footing is only half as thick as an eggshell is to the inner portion of the egg! This movement, in fact, continues to carry us westward at a rate of about 2 inches per year.

So when a geologist says that a mountain is 400 million years old, he's not implying that it was sitting where we see it today for that long, but rather that the rocks that formed the range were created at that time by certain processes within the earth. The actual shaping of the New England peaks into the profiles we see is much more the result of erosion. This erosion ranges from tiny refinements made by falling raindrops to great ravines that have been carved by tumbling streams; from the chiseling of cliff faces by freezing water expanding in the cracks to mammoth glaciers, enough rocks and gravel clutched in their bellies to scour 50,000 square miles of land almost beyond recognition.

Southern New England

SPRUCE HILL

Distance: 3 miles
Location: Savoy Mountain State Forest. From the intersection of
Massachusetts highways 8 and 2 in the town of North Adams,
head east on Massachusetts 2 for 4.5 miles. Turn right, and follow
the signs for just over 3 miles to Savoy Mountain State Forest.
Our walk takes off on the right side of the road, 0.3 mile past the
entrance to the forest, and approximately 75 yards beyond the
forest headquarters. At the fork a few yards into the walk, take a
right.

There is no better way to get a sense for the ruggedness of this slice of
New England than to survey it from a towering, rocky perch like
Spruce Hill, rising 2,566 feet along the extreme western fall line of
the Berkshires. The long rise of uplands created by the marriage of
the Green and Berkshire mountains is unbroken by a single valley for
more than 150 miles. For centuries this area was considered to be the
western wall of the American wilderness, a howling, treacherous land
of wild men and beasts, a region dissected only by the Mohawk Trail
a few miles to the north of where you now stand. It was along this
sinewy, trampled, brown path that Massachusetts Indian tribes made
raids on neighboring tribes in the forested uplands of eastern New
York. The trail also felt the feet of a young man from Boston named

79

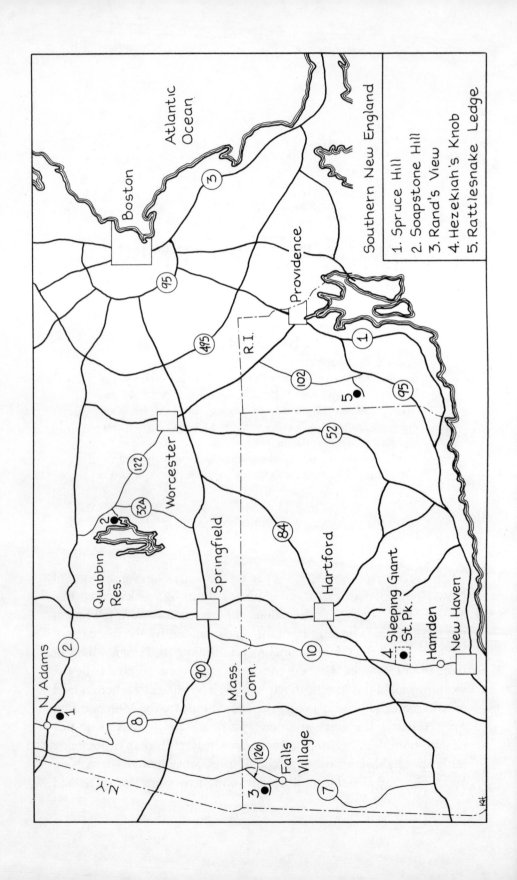

Southern New England

1. Spruce Hill
2. Soapstone Hill
3. Rand's View
4. Hezekiah's Knob
5. Rattlesnake Ledge

Paul Revere, who tramped westward along the Mohawk on his way to defend British fortifications during the French and Indian War.

Our walk begins in a beautiful patchwork of ferns and forest—red maple, birch, beech, hemlock, and oak, with hayscented and lady fern growing at their feet. Also next to the trail are mats of whorled wood aster, Japanese knotweed, and an occasional hobblebush. At 0.2 mile, a short distance after passing a power line thick with meadowsweet and hardhack, you'll reach a particularly fine fern garden. Tight clusters of lacy green leaflets are spread across the ground nearly as far as the eye can see, as if the gods had tried to ease their footsteps through the forest by wrapping the land in a soft, feathery carpet of fronds.

Ferns, along with the clubmosses and scouring rush that can be found along this trail, were in their prime 200 million years ago, when in the warm forests of the Mesozoic they attained tremendous size. Ferns release spore—perhaps as many as 50 million from a single plant—a few of which land on bare soil or on carpets of moss and germinate, growing into very small heart-shaped plants called prothallia. Prothallia contain both male and female reproductive organs. If a thin film of water is present, a swimming sperm outside the prothallium will join with an egg that was produced in a tiny vase-shaped female organ. This fertilized egg divides and grows into a plant that for a time obtains its nourishment from the parent prothallium, but eventually sends its own root into the earth and unfurls a small leaf to begin the manufacture of food. Upon maturity the plant will release its own millions of spores, and the whole cycle will begin again.

Our path continues past a mix of bluebead lilies, violets, jewelweed, false Solomon's seal, white wood aster, and an occasional Indian cucumber. If you're here in the fall, watch at about 0.5 mile for spiny balls of beechnuts littering the ground. While today beech is primarily known for its wood, which is commonly used to produce furniture and tool handles, there was a time when you could find beechnuts on the shelves of nearly any New England grocery. Besides being delicious to eat raw, the nuts were often roasted and used as a substitute for, or at least an additive to, coffee beans. The oil of the beechnut was frequently used in cooking, and herbalists long prescribed it as a remedy for worms. Indians and colonists alike

Meadowsweet

made decoctions of beechnut leaves to help relieve the pain of burns and rashes.

Continue climbing past a diverse mix of conifers and hardwoods, of sunlit openings and of cool, deep shade. Christmas ferns, which remain green throughout the winter, can be found at 0.8 mile, and later the trail will be peppered with baneberry, Canada mayflower, sensitive fern, bunchberries, and wild oats. In 1.5 miles you'll reach the rocky top of Spruce Hill, which is also known as Busby Mountain. From here the world is a sweep of hill and valley, capped by a blue sky that is often flushed with birds of prey. In the fall watch for migrating broad-winged, red-tailed, and sharp-shinned hawks, as well as American kestrels.

Directly below you to the west is the Hoosic River Valley, framed on the far side by Mount Greylock, which, at 3,491 feet, is the highest point in Massachusetts. Though from this vantage point you may not detect too much of a difference, Mount Greylock is actually part of an entirely different set of mountains than is Spruce Hill here in the northern Berkshires. Known as the Taconic Range, Greylock and its compadres are actually thought to have once been located on the east side of Vermont's Green Mountains. Five hundred million years ago there were grand collisions and uplifts occurring along a thick braid of geologic plates lying deep within the earth. The slow, dramatic rise of the Green Mountains actually lifted portions of what would become the Taconic Range and slid them west-

82

ward down their broad shoulders, where they finally came to rest roughly in the region where you now see them. Add millions of years of wind and water erosion, the patient downward slicing of rivers, and eventually the mighty grind of glacial ice, and you have nothing short of the mountain masterpiece spread before you.

Mount Greylock, by the way, takes its name from the crest of snow that cloaks it during the winter months. In 1946, scientists seeded clouds around this peak with dry ice, producing the first artificial snowstorm.

Red-tailed Hawk

SOAPSTONE HILL

Distance: 2.4 miles

Location: Quabbin Watershed. From the intersection of Massachusetts highways 32A and 122 near the village of Petersham,
head west on Highway 122 for 0.4 mile, and turn left onto West
Street. Proceed for 2.6 miles to a crossroad, and turn left. Follow
this road for 0.9 mile to a gate, marked by a number 37. Park here
and begin walking west along this gated road.

The Soapstone Hill walk is for anyone willing to drive a few miles of
twisted, potholed country roads in exchange for a long, remarkably
quiet view of the Quabbin Watershed—its 18-mile reach of blue
waters; its thick blankets of hardwoods tossed across a patchwork of
crumpled hills; the eagles, osprey, and red-tailed hawks that hang
from its skies on the warm winds of spring.

Our walk takes off from access gate number 37, winding
gently downward through a young forest of hemlock, birch, red and
black oaks, witch-hazel, white pine, and red maple, seasoned here
and there with mats of whorled and white wood asters, cinnamon,
bracken and interrupted ferns, twisted stalk, and sarsaparilla. The
route levels some as it continues to the west, and in 0.6 mile meets a
road taking off to the left (south) through a grove of red pines. As
beautiful as red pine can be, Quabbin managers are systematically
eliminating many of the old red pine groves that were planted here
shortly after the reservoir was built. In their place will be young
hardwoods, whose growth patterns and lack of acidic needles pro-
mote a better growth of understory plants, which offers both food and
protection for area wildlife.

Just past this road you'll cross a bridge over the west branch of
Fever Brook, a rather brackish flow that here is in its final, sluggish
drift before joining the waters of Quabbin Reservoir just to the south.
At the first road on the right just past this bridge, turn to the north
and follow this watercourse into a beautiful marshland. Beaver sign is
plentiful along here, as are the beating wings of great blue herons,
black ducks, red-winged blackbirds, blue-gray gnatcatchers, and
that herald of spring, the tree swallow. Tree swallows are especially
engaging to watch as they make dramatic swoops and dives above the
water in tight, fast pinwheels. Although there has never been a
shortage of researchers studying this bird, a few of its habits remain

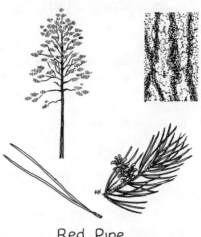

Red Pine

downright puzzling. For one thing, during some years on the breeding grounds, every member of an entire colony may suddenly disappear for several days at a time. Sometimes this mysterious, hasty departure even occurs during the females' incubation of the eggs, though with no apparent damage to the next generation. No one has been able to say for sure where, or why, the swallows go.

Other unusual behaviors include flying in small groups high above the breeding grounds and then diving down en masse back to the nests, as well as the old game of feather catch, where one or more birds drop a feather from high in the air, swoop down to catch it, and then release it again for yet another dramatic on-the-wing snag. (Think what baseball would be like with these guys in the outfield!)

At 0.85 mile, which is about halfway down the marsh, you'll see a faint footpath taking off into the woods to the left. This is our route to the top of Soapstone Hill, which rises 300 feet above where you now stand. This section of the walk definitely gets steep in places, so be sure to take your time with it. Less than 0.2 mile from the marsh you'll reach the rocky top of Soapstone Hill, with a beautiful, sweeping view to the south of Quabbin Reservoir (once the Swift River Valley) and its glittering braid of mountaintop islands. If you continue north along this faint pathway for an additional 0.1 mile you'll reach another promontory, this one perched on the edge of a rugged, tumbling plunge to the northeast, into the rolling woodlands of the Federated Women's Clubs State Forest.

RAND'S VIEW

Distance: 2.4 miles

Location: From U.S. Highway 7 in the northwest corner of Connecticut, turn east outside the town of Falls Village onto State Road 126 North. You'll come to a stop sign 0.6 mile from this turnoff. Turn left onto Point of Rocks Road, and continue 0.1 mile to Water Street, which takes off to the right, passing beneath a railroad bridge. In 0.4 mile Water Street makes a turn to the left across a bridge over the Housatonic River. Once across the bridge, stay right, and in 0.4 mile you'll turn left onto Sugar Hill Road. The trailhead and parking area are at the end of Sugar Hill Road, 0.9 mile from this last turn.

Despite a rather sharp climb toward the end of the walk, this 1.2 miles of Appalachian Trail is a pure delight—a mix of quiet deciduous forest, fern gardens, and cool, tumbling water, ending in a yawning mountain view that, on a clear day, reaches all the way to the soft green shoulders of Mount Greylock in northwestern Massachusetts. As some of the climbing sections toward the end of the walk can be slippery, be sure that your shoes are appropriate.

The first section of our path slips through a young forest on a small dirt road, framed on both sides by that classic signature of early New England agriculture, the stone fence. While you may wonder why in the world someone would be building stone fences through the woods, the truth is that when these stones were first piled here, this land was a tapestry not of forest but of fields. Early farmers cleared the land, and then immediately erected wooden fences around each and every pasture or field.

This penchant for fences consumed enormous amounts of wood (an oak fence might have to be rebuilt every seven years), and caused the English, who used no fences, to regularly question our sanity for erecting so many ugly enclosures around private property. At first, stones were used only infrequently as an enclosure. The farmer threw them along the edges of his fields during plowing. By the early 1800s, however, good fence wood had started to disappear at an alarming rate, and many farmers simply turned to piling their field stones against their wooden fences. The wooden portions of the fences, including a line of cap rails that probably topped the fence you're now walking along, slowly rotted away, leaving only the stones. As these fields were abandoned, various shrubs grew around the fence lines, which were followed by the kind of forest you see here today.

In 0.3 mile we'll take off to the right along a small footpath. Here you'll wind past hickory, birch, and an occasional white pine, growing from a forest floor carpeted with purple trillium, geranium, rue anemone, and miterwort. Miterwort, which in May is covered with a stalk of tiny, intricate white flowers, derives its name from the fact that its fruits resemble the peaked hat, or miter, commonly worn by bishops.

The real uphill portion of this trek begins at about 0.75 mile, alongside a series of stone and timber steps that trace the course of a small veil of falling water. Hemlocks and yellow birch can be seen here, and a close study of either is the perfect way to catch your breath during this vault toward the highlands. Yellow birch, with its shiny yellow- to silver-colored bark and rough, double-toothed leaves, is an extremely beautiful and commercially valuable hardwood, used in great quantities for quality lumber and furniture. Hemlock, an evergreen sporting needles that are dark green above and have two white bands beneath, does very well in cool, shaded areas such as this one. The bark of the hemlock contains significant quantities of tannin, which has long been used to produce finished leather goods. Hemlocks were once cut down in New England by the thousands simply for their bark, the rest of the coarse, durable wood left to rot in the forest.

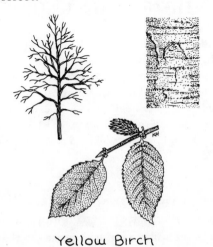

Yellow Birch

In 0.9 mile, very close to the crest of Wentauwanchu Mountain (almost as difficult to say as it is to climb), you'll see marker signs for a Nature Conservancy area, the 481-acre Patricia Winter Woodland–Hamlet Hill Preserve. This area is one of more than sixty sanctuaries owned by the Connecticut chapter of the Nature Conservancy, perhaps the finest, most capable preservation organization in the United States today. In Connecticut alone, the Conservancy has protected more than thirteen thousand precious acres.

Continue along a lovely stream lined with hemlocks and an occasional Jack-in-the-pulpit. The fleshy, peppery taproots of Jack-in-the-pulpit were once commonly gathered by Indians, a fact that led to yet another common name for the plant—"Indian turnip." At 1.1 miles is a fork in the path. The right branch leads in 0.5 mile to Prospect Mountain. We'll continue straight, though, to another split, and then follow the blue-blazed trail for 500 feet to Rand's View.

Rand's View is an absolutely delightful place, a collage of rolling pasture and thick, wild forest melting into the high, hazy lines of the Berkshires. Though strikingly beautiful in the fall, this perch feels like a summer kind of place to me—somewhere to be when the sun is walking, not running, across the sky, enough warmth pouring out of the blue to send body and soul into a fine and certain lethargy.

HEZEKIAH'S KNOB

Distance: 1.7 miles

Location: Sleeping Giant State Park. Heading north on Connecticut Highway 10 (Whitney Avenue) from Hamden, turn right onto Mt. Carmel Avenue. Go past the Mt. Carmel entrance to Sleeping Giant State Park to Chestnut Lane, which is located approximately 2.1 miles from Whitney Avenue, and turn left. Our trailhead is 0.8 mile up this road on the left side, in the bend of a sharp right turn. Begin walking on the trail blazed with white squares.

With all due respect to Hobbomock, the evil deity of local Indian lore who collapsed into a deep sleep here under the weight of a spell placed on him by good spirit Kietan, I must say that geologists have an equally engaging, if only slightly less fanciful, tale to tell of the origin of the sleeping giant. According to them, hot igneous rock streamed through fissures cut deep within a bed of 300-million-year-old sandstone, pushing the sedimentary rock upward until it formed a series of rounded ridge lines that rose and fell like ocean waves frozen against the ancient sky. Quick to yield to the forces of wind, water, and ice, this relatively soft sandstone eroded, leaving the hard igneous outcroppings that today make up the giant's legs, arms, body, and head.

Whatever creation story you prefer, there can be no argument that Sleeping Giant is one of south-central Connecticut's greatest treasures, a tumble of high, windswept knobs and ridges from which to really survey a bit more of the world, a way of putting into fresh perspective the hodgepodge of traffic and sirens and barking dogs that lies far below. Our walk begins on a trail marked by white square blazes, taking off through mats of white wood and large-leaved asters, wild oats, Canada mayflower, blue violets, round-lobed hepatica, and Solomon's seal.

Solomon's seal gets its name from the fact that the scar left on the rhizome when the old leaf stalk breaks resembles the seal of that wise old king Solomon. What's more, some early herbalists claimed that the good king (and respected magician) somehow managed to put that little seal on the roots by his own hand, in an effort to guide us to the plant's medicinal values. Well, who knows? Although the centuries-old claims that Solomon's seal can stop severe bleeding may be somewhat overly optimistic, the roots of the plant do contain allantoin, which is a substance used even today for treating cuts and abrasions. The somewhat similar false Solomon's seal, which also grows here, bears its flowers in white clusters at the tip of the stem, rather than having bell-shaped blooms that hang from the leaf axils.

We get down to the business of climbing fairly quickly on this walk, things taking an upward tilt at 0.1 mile. Take your time while moving up these steep rock stair treads, noting not only the beautiful redcedars beside you but the increasingly fine views that open behind you to the west. In a little more than 0.4 mile of ascent you'll cross a blue-blazed trail, and just beyond, the open, rocky perch of Hezekiah's Knob. From here you can look west and see the stone observation tower located on what is the left hip of the giant, and, at

Solomon's Seal

739 feet, the highest point in the park. The tower was a Works Progress Administration (WPA) project completed in 1939, and it immediately became a major tourist attraction. From this perch there are also sweeping views to the south and southeast, a gentle quilt of streets and factories and neighborhoods, which, in places, still seem surprisingly well wrapped in deciduous forest.

Less than 10 miles to the south and barely out of sight is the city of New Haven, home of the hallowed halls of Yale. The 1701 act of incorporation for Yale College was an unusually strong commitment to education—one that would soon grow to exempt any student not only from the military but from taxes, as well.

A particularly interesting way to date Yale is to look at a sampling of its old rules and customs. For a time, scholars were required to speak only Latin while "in their chambers." Instructors were to call an undergraduate by his Sir-name "unless he be the son of a noble man or Knight's eldest son." Newtonian science began filtering into the classrooms in the 1730s, yet it seems that there was a bit of a lag before the purchase of scientific equipment became any kind of a priority. Former student Lyman Beecher writes that in 1793 there was "a four-foot telescope, all rusty: nobody ever looked through it, and if they did, not to edification."

From Hezekiah's Knob we'll take a right (heading south) on the blue-blazed trail through a mix of chestnut, red and white oaks, witch-hazel, maple, and mountain laurel, the latter of which is especially profuse at 0.65 mile. Cross a green trail at 0.7 mile and, 0.1

mile later, take a right on the red trail. (If you'd like another view first, this time of the more rugged country to the northeast, go a short distance past the red trail intersection and up a small hill to a ridgetop overlook.) The red trail will hit a violet trail at 1.1 miles, where you'll take another right. Follow this trail 0.6 mile, staying left at the one fork that occurs not far from the parking area.

RATTLESNAKE LEDGE

Distance: 1.9 miles
Location: Wickaboxet State Forest. From Interstate 95 in Rhode Island, head northwest on State Highway 102. In 3.4 miles you'll come to Plain Meeting House Road; turn left. In 3 miles, on the right side of the road, is the small parking area and trailhead.

Wickaboxet (a Narragansett Indian word) was Rhode Island's first state forest, and it remains a quiet, untrammeled mix of rocky ledges and rolling hills cloaked in varying thicknesses of pine and deciduous forest. While you may see some weekend activity at Rattlesnake Ledge itself—a rock face popular with beginning climbers—the tree-lined roadways that meander beyond this point are washed with little more than the sounds of wind and birdsong, along with an occasional outburst of scolding from a nervous red squirrel.

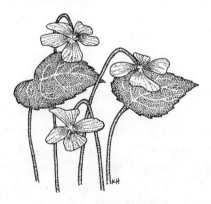

Blue Violet

Depending on what time of year you visit, the fringe of road-side vegetation just beyond the parking lot can in itself be a small feast for the eyes. Here are the ivory blooms of Canada mayflower, star-flower, and strawberry, lightly seasoned with a sprinkling of Rhode Island's state flower, the blue violet. The leaves of the common blue violet, incidentally, are extremely high in vitamins A and C, and in some parts of the East were once common table fare in salads or cooked greens. (A couple of old folk remedies actually recommend them for measles.) The root of a close relative, the garden violet, has a long history of use by herbalists in treating respiratory ailments.

Forty yards from the parking area, turn left onto a small, grassy roadway that climbs gently up a hill forested with white pine and red oak. Watch the roadside for clusters of ground cedar, a plant that looks very much like an elfdom version of a Christmas tree plantation. Also here are birdfoot violets, so named for the plant's leaves, which are clustered in the shape of a bird's foot. Unlike the blue violets you saw in the moist ground near the beginning of this walk, birdfoots like drier, sandier soils. Interestingly, the five petals of these blooms often come in two colors—an upper pair in a very deep purple, and then three lower petals in a light lavender. This striking combination has led the birdfoot to be called the most beautiful violet in the world.

Continue past clusters of blueberry, and, at 0.5 mile, a huddle of bigtooth aspen on the right. The leaves of aspen are known to shimmer in the slightest puff of air, a phenomenon once credited to a belief that an aspen was used for Christ's cross, an event so tragic that it caused all other aspens to tremble forever after. In truth, at the point where the aspen leaf stem joins the leaf, it is flat and extremely supple, a design that causes the leaves to quake in breezes that humans cannot even feel.

At about 0.6 mile, turn back on a road coming in from the right, and then, immediately afterward, turn left at a Y intersection. This stretch of the walk, much drier than the woodland where you began, passes by a loosely woven forest of pitch pine, which is an irregularly shaped tree with three needles and furrowed, dark gray bark. Pitch pine derives its name from the high concentrations of resin in its bark—so high, in fact, that colonists commonly fastened the knots from this tree to poles for use as torches. Pitch pine was

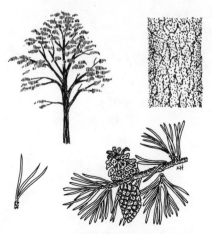

Pitch Pine

used in great quantities during the 1600s and 1700s as a source of turpentine and tar. Because these products were used regularly in the maintenance of sailing fleets, both pitch pine and white pine (which was used for masts) were protected under a set of "no cut" laws handed down to the colonists from the king, ever concerned that his Royal Navy stay well supplied. These regulations, rarely either adhered to or enforced, were on the books until the American Revolution.

Pass a smattering of sassafras trees at 0.9 mile, just before turning right and descending a small hill. Long before the arrival of the pilgrims, the discovery of sassafras in New England was touted by Old World politicians as a precious commodity that could help sustain colonial expansion in the Americas. At that time, the tree was valued not for flavoring or perfume but as a treatment for syphilis. When it was later found to have virtually no effect on this disease, sassafras merchants were quickly forced into handling new commodities.

The road soon makes another right, and, at approximately 1.25 miles, crosses a faint T intersection. Just past this point you'll be able to see Rattlesnake Ledge on the right. Make your way over to the base of the ledge past a mixed deciduous forest. This woodland is good for seeing several types of birds that you may recognize from your home bird feeder or neighborhood park, including northern orioles, black-capped chickadees, mourning doves, and white-

Northern Oriole

breasted nuthatches. On the far right side of the rock mass you'll find a fairly easy trail up Rattlesnake Ledge, the top of which will afford you a wonderful view to the south.

It was the timber rattlesnake that gave his name to this rocky perch. Connoisseur of small birds, squirrels, and mice, timber rattlers were once extremely common in this area. In fact, throughout most of the 1700s, groups of men would head for these ledges every spring and fall for "snake hunts," where they would kill the poor creatures by the hundreds. Today timber rattlers are quite rare (it is, in fact, illegal to kill them), and should pose no danger to you.

The rolling landscape spread before you was forested until the first half of the 1700s, when farms began spreading rapidly across the countryside. Besides cattle and sheep, turkeys were a very popular type of livestock during that era. Turned into pasture with the cattle, they got very, very plump simply by feasting on the chestnuts that at the time grew in nearly every nook and cranny of southern New England. (With the chestnut blight wiping out this source of food in the early part of the twentieth century, wild turkeys today satisfy their penchant for nuts by eating acorns and beechnuts.) With the combination of some very tired farm soil and a growing roster of better job opportunities in nearby industrial centers, many of these farms were abandoned in the 1800s, after which the forest quickly reclaimed them.

Vermont

MOUNT ABRAHAM

Distance: 5 miles
Location: Green Mountain National Forest. From the town of
Bristol, head north on Vermont Highway 17/116 for approximately 1.6 miles, and turn right onto a small road, following the
signs for Lincoln. Down this road 4.5 miles you'll see a route
taking off to the right toward South Lincoln. Stay left. Proceed
for 3.8 miles, to a parking area on the right. Our path (part of the
Long Trail) takes off from the other side of the road, a short
distance to the west of where you parked.

Most people who spend any time rambling along the lush stream
corridors and low ravines of the Green Mountains sooner or later have
an inkling to see what things look like from the top. Those who do
hear the summits calling should definitely consider a trek up the
southern flank of Mount Abraham. While this is not exactly a stroll in
the park—your outbound walk will require 1,600 feet of uphill
walking—by Green Mountain standards it rates as fairly easy. And,
once on top, you could hardly ask for a more spectacular view. From
this summit the world tumbles away in a cascade of rock and forest
and sky, ridge line after distant ridge line melting into the far horizons. Easily visible on the far side of Lake Champlain are the
beautiful Adirondacks, while to the southeast, Mount Ascutney casts

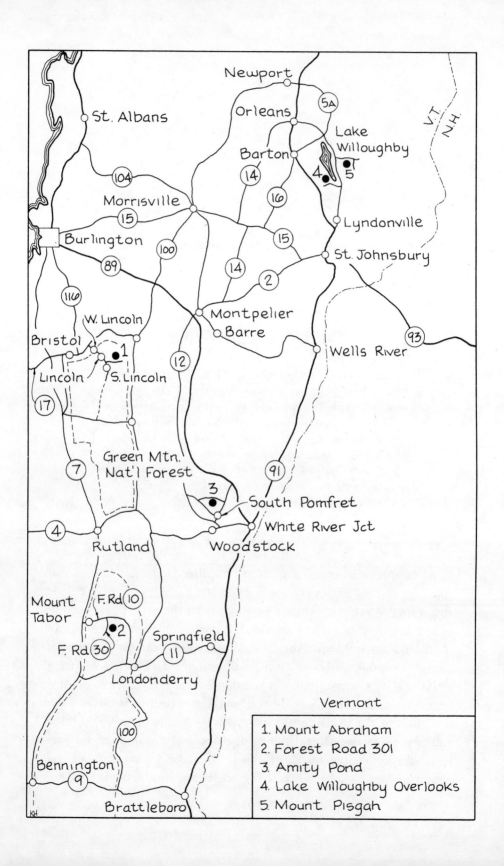

Newport

St. Albans

5A

Orleans

Lake
Willoughby

Barton

104

④
14

⑤

16

Morrisville

15

Lyndonville

15

Burlington

St. Johnsbury

100

89

14

116

2

W. Lincoln

Montpelier
Barre

Wells River

93

Bristol

①

12

Lincoln   S. Lincoln

17

Green Mtn.
Nat'l Forest

7

③

South Pomfret

91

4

Rutland

White River Jct

Woodstock

Mount
Tabor

F. Rd ⑩

②

Springfield

F. Rd ㉚

11

Londonderry

100

Vermont
1. Mount Abraham
2. Forest Road 301
3. Amity Pond
4. Lake Willoughby Overlooks
5. Mount Pisgah

Bennington

9

Brattleboro

a sharp outline far above the banks of the Connecticut River. If the day is especially clear, you'll also see a great swell of land rising to the north along the spine of the Green Mountains—beyond Mount Mansfield, beyond Jay Peak, all the way into southern Canada. Equally lovely in the east is New Hampshire's mighty Mount Washington, casting a soft, gray silhouette against the New England sky.

The first 0.5 mile of this walk is a gentle amble through a luscious weave of forest and ground covers, a scene that certainly supports Reverend Samuel Peters' decision in 1768 to call this region Verd Mont, or Green Mountain. To achieve this kind of plant density requires a fair amount of precipitation, and the Green Mountains receive 36 to 54 inches per year, the higher amounts falling in the upper elevations. Besides a host of mountain, striped, and sugar maples, the early sections of this path will take you through fine stands of birch, beech, and hobblebush. Especially common along the very beginning of the trail are thick carpets of whorled wood aster.

After 0.5 mile, when the going gets tough, take plenty of time to catch your breath and enjoy some of the bird life that abounds here. Blue jays can be seen catching food in various nooks and crannies of the forest for later dining. Black-capped chickadees, though common in many environments, seem to find these deep woods especially rich in the insects, seeds, and fruits that they need to survive. Here also are white-breasted nuthatches, scarlet tanagers,

Black-throated Blue Warbler

Yellow-rumped Warbler

black-throated blue warblers, and black and white warblers, as well as that maestro of birdsong, the wood thrush. As you make your way higher and higher up the mountain the bird roster will change. Other warblers will catch your ear, such as the yellow-rumped and Canada warbler, and once in the conifers, you may begin to see dark-eyed juncos and pine grosbeaks feeding on the ground.

Just as the bird life changes as you climb, so does the vegetation. Higher elevations typically mean wetter, colder conditions—perfect for both coniferous forests, as well as for moisture-loving ground plants like bunchberry, red-berried elder, and false hellebore. Two plants that will be with you during nearly all of your climb are tall meadow rue and bluebead lily, though each will become somewhat smaller in the face of the harsher upland conditions.

At 1.5 miles you'll reach a wall of red spruce and balsam fir. The close, compacted growth of these conifers, and the occasional dead snags standing stark against a much cooler, windier sky, leaves little doubt that you have reached the highlands. Indeed, at this point you'll be astride the backbone of the great Green Mountain anticline, a hard ridge of 500-million-year-old rock that stretches from the Hoosac Mountains of Massachusetts all the way to the Notre Dame Mountains of Quebec.

You'll reach the Battell Trail on your left at 1.6 miles, and a short distance later, the Battell Shelter. From this point you're ready for the final ascent—a steep trek up a long tumble of rugged rock stairways. One advantage of the intensity of this last bit of climbing is that you tend to be so focused on the task at hand that you many not realize just how far uphill you are going. Before you know it you'll be atop old Mount Abe himself, basking in wind and sun, and almost more scenery than a single pair of eyes can handle.

On a clear day in late fall this windswept, rocky perch is a wonderful place to watch migrating raptors. Indeed, if there is one thing that will push up the needle on your pleasure meter, it's catching sight of a red-tailed or rough-legged hawk hanging here on the edge of oblivion, bound in a whisper of wings for some rugged perch to the south.

FOREST ROAD 301

Distance: 2.2 miles
Location: Green Mountain National Forest. From Rutland, Vermont, head south on U.S. Highway 7 to the small village of Danby, and turn left onto Forest Road 10. Follow this route eastward for 6.75 miles, and turn right onto Forest Road 30. Follow this route for 1.4 miles, and turn left onto Forest Road 301. Park at the gate, and begin walking along this road.

Despite scars from a logging operation near the end of the path, this trek is much more engaging than the rather ho-hum name of Forest Road 301 might imply. The old roadway, in an area now completely closed to motor vehicles of any sort, carves a gentle line through a beautiful mature hardwood forest, ending on a high perch from which you can survey a great, green swell of mountains rising to the north.

Because the surrounding forest has yet to reclaim the swath of land that was originally cleared to make this road, you'll find thick fringes of the kinds of hardy plants that are famous for growing in disturbed, compacted soils. Some of these are so good at growing on poor ground, in fact, that they are considered to be measures for gauging the general health of the soil. Though these plants are seldom thought of as anything but weeds (and foreign weeds at that!) most have some interesting tales to tell.

99

Throughout much of this walk, for example, you'll find bladder campion, oxeye daisy, curly dock, scented bedstraw, and perhaps mullein. Use of mullein, with its tall, woolly stem and thick basal leaves, goes back two thousand years, to a time when Roman soldiers dipped the tips of the plant in grease and then lit them for torches. Tea from the leaves of mullein was not only taken by both Native Americans and Europeans for a variety of ailments but colonists routinely put the leaves in their socks to help stay the biting cold of a New England winter.

Curly dock (or yellow dock) has been eaten in America for as long as almost any wild plant you can think of. During the Great Depression, steaming bowls of young curly dock leaves made their way to many a dinner table. Curly dock tastes rather like spinach that has had a bit of lemon added to it, and in fact has half again as much vitamin A and twice the vitamin C as does that common garden vegetable. Indians routinely made flour from curly dock seeds, and some people continue to use the stems of the plant for what can best be described as a mock rhubarb pie.

Likewise, the young leaves of that ever-present biennial, oxeye daisy, have long been cooked, as well as used with other raw vegetables in salads. The bitter oil from older oxeye daisy leaves was at one time a primary medicine for gout, while European doctors used the substance to clear the sinus tract.

Down the road 0.2 mile you'll come to a grassy clearing on the right. These areas are sometimes known as deer parks, since whitetailed deer browse at their edges, bed down in them, or just plain loiter, chewing their cud before heading back into the woods. Come upon this clearing late in the evening and you may see several of these graceful creatures.

When I took this walk I happened to see several piles of coyote scat lying in the road. While some may view this clever creature as an indication of untouched wilderness, the coyote is actually extremely adaptable to the reckless, blustering ways of humans. It can run extremely fast—40 miles per hour in short bursts—swims remarkably well, and has amazing recuperative powers. Healthy coyotes have been caught that show severe bullet wounds completely healed; one male was still going strong after having his lower jaw shot off! In many parts of the country the coyote has thrived not only in the face of development but against millions of dollars that have been spent trying to eliminate it.

This drive by humans to eliminate the coyote, because it decimates both game species and domestic livestock, is hardly anchored in fact. Though these animals will occasionally take a young sheep or deer, the take is negligible. Indeed, one of the reasons the coyote can be so tenacious is because of its broad diet, which consists of everything from birds to berries. Coyotes make up one of the best mechanisms for cleaning the forest of carrion, and go a long way in keeping a lid on the rodent population. Nevertheless, it was only fifteen years ago that the Maine legislature was considering a $50 bounty on coyotes, despite the fact that there were less than five hundred animals in the entire state. Thankfully, the bill failed to pass.

In 0.8 mile is a lovely stream, after which you'll enter an area that has obviously been intensively logged. While most of this harvest was done on land that was moderately rolling, there were some cuts made on steep hillsides that are little more than open invitations to erosion. Eventually this land will be reclaimed by the forest

Eastern Coyote

through a process known as succession, whereby shrubs like rasp-berry are replaced by fast-growing but short-lived trees such as aspen, paper birch, gray birch, and pin cherry. These are then taken over by more shade-tolerant varieties including yellow birch and red maple, to which later may be added other trees of the climax forest, such as beech, sugar maple, and hemlock. Some trees, such as the birches, are able to grow again fairly quickly after logging, since they can sprout new saplings from stumps or roots. Most conifers, how-ever, do not have this ability.

Toward the back of the large, flat, cleared area at the end of the main road is a small track taking off to the right. Follow this track a few yards, and at a fork, take a left up a rather steep incline. Our turnaround point is 50 or 60 yards up this hill, at a line of trees that lies just a few miles north of the Peru Peak Wilderness. From this height you can look northward into the graceful rise and fall of the Green Mountain country, the forest lying on the distant hills like a thick, crumpled blanket of green velvet.

AMITY POND

Distance: 0.9 mile

Location: From the intersection of Vermont Highway 12 and U.S. Highway 4 in downtown Woodstock, head north on High-way 12 for approximately 1.1 miles, turning right at a sign for Suicide Six ski area. In 2 miles you'll reach a fork in the road at the village of South Pomfret, where you'll stay right. (Suicide Six ski area is to the left.) In just under 5 miles you'll see a road taking off to the left, marked by a sign reading To Interstate 89. Take this left, and veer left once again in approximately 1.7 miles. Amity Pond Natural Area is down this road 2.2 miles, on your left. The preserve is marked only by a very small sign reading Vermont State Natural Area. A small parking area is across from the entrance.

"It is our hope that this park may be a true refuge," wrote Dick and Elizabeth Brett, who twenty years ago generously donated this land to the state. "It is our hope that the sportsmanship of those who travel by machine will permit this small area to be a sanctuary for wildlife, native plants and the people who cherish these things in an atmosphere of quiet relaxation.''

And indeed Amity Pond does provide just that. The high spine of this preserve offers regal views of the Ascutney, Killington, and Pico mountains to the south. For the most part, though, this isn't so much a place where nature shouts down rocky escarpments and abrupt vistas, as it is one of warm, pleasant whispers over grassy highlands. Having been heavily grazed and doggedly timbered for centuries, Amity, it seems, has at last come to rest. You can almost feel the sigh of relief—in a summer breeze that lightly strokes the sedges, in a sleepy-looking green frog waiting at the edge of a pond for flies, in the rose-breasted grosbeaks that flit from forest to field looking for spiders and seeds.

Although there are several trails at Amity, some can be extremely hard to find, especially in the height of summer, when grasses cover them with thick cloaks of green. We'll be walking along a gentle, easy-to-negotiate blazed route that can be followed virtually any time of the year. Those who want more of Amity are encouraged to pursue trails to the many other nooks and crannies of the preserve, each as equally delightful as those presented here.

The first few feet of pathway will take you into a small grassy meadow, framed by a plantation of red pine, often planted both for shade and as an ornamental along highways throughout New England. The trail forks immediately, and you should take the right branch, which sinks quickly into the cool, green canopy of birch and sugar maples. The sugar maple, the famous signature tree of Vermont, has only had what can be considered a firm hold on the New England landscape for a relatively short amount of time. When a mile-thick sheet of ice finally began to retreat from the northeastern United States twelve thousand years ago, it left, of course, a landscape entirely bereft of trees. Nearly two millennia passed before spruce began to invade the region, followed by fir, and then, ever so slowly, by aspen and alder. It was much later that trees like the sugar maple migrated from the south. In fact, barely two thousand years have passed since this tree, along with yellow birch and American beech, became the dominant members of the northern New England hardwood forest.

The path climbs gently through the forest, soon coming out

on a high, sunny meadow peppered with milkweed and raspberry. Immediately to the right of a fence post with a blue diamond cross-country ski marker is tiny Amity Pond. According to local legend, many years ago two girls attending the East Barnard School made a solemn vow to each other that they would always remain the best of friends. As it turned out, one wed a man from the village of Pomfret, and the other a beau from Barnard. Remaining true to their promise, however, each year without fail they arranged by letter to rendezvous on a certain summer day for a picnic at the small pond that lay here at the height of land. And so this quiet pocket of water became known as Amity Pond.

Today Amity Pond, with its green fringe of red pine, maples, and aspen, is still every bit as delightful for a picnic as it was in the days of old. As water and shore plants continue to die and accumulate on the bottom of the pond, though, it grows ever smaller. There will come a day that best friends may share lunch not at the edge of a pond but beside a meadow.

Just past Amity Pond you'll reach a crest of land that offers beautiful views to the south and west. From here continue down the hillside, splashed with asters in mid- and late summer. Though the path may be faint here, use the blue diamond cross-country ski markers to guide you. At the bottom of the hill the Woodstock Trail comes from the left, but you continue straight into a beautiful wood-

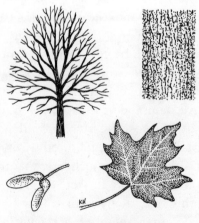

Sugar Maple

land. This path will continue to meander downward to a tiny rivulet at 0.5 mile—a mere trickle of water flowing through a hushed cathedral of maple, beech, birch, and an occasional mammoth white pine. This is our turnaround point.

On the way back, when you again reach the crest of the grassy hill you descended on the outbound walk (the "view spot," beside a large slab of rock), turn to the right (east) and head toward a blue diamond cross-country ski marker. You'll reach the starting point by first passing a camping shelter and then another small pond, this one fringed with clusters of aspen and willow, as well as by lovely mats of strawberry, red clover, milkweed, and sensitive fern.

LAKE WILLOUGHBY OVERLOOKS

Distance: 3.4 miles

Location: From intersection of Vermont highways 16 and 5A, head south on 5A to the beach at the south end of Lake Willoughby. From this point continue south on Highway 5A for 0.6 mile. Turn right onto a dirt road, and continue west for 1.8 miles to a small parking area on the right. (Stay right at the fork in the road at 0.5 mile.) The trail begins 10 yards up the road past the parking area, on the right. A small sign identifies this path as the Mount Hor Trail.

Lake Willoughby, a crescent-shaped basin of blue water set beneath massive glacial-scoured cliffs, is as enticing as any lake in New England. Great blankets of forested highlands lie folded around the perimeter of the lake, like tattered robes of green velvet tucked around the edges of a great sapphire. (Willoughby has long been called the "Lake Lucerne of America.") The scale of this land is really enormous, tending to amplify the general sense of wildness you'll feel here. The cliffs on the western and eastern flanks of both Mounts Hor and Pisgah rise to absolutely dizzying heights, their feet anchored in more than three hundred feet of cold, steely water. From the southernmost Willoughby Overlook you'll see an endless cascade of high ridges to the southwest, flowing all the way to the great White Mountains of New Hampshire.

The path for our walk to the Willoughby Overlooks begins a few yards west of the parking area, on the right (north) side of the road. Before you take to the trail, notice the beautiful purple-flowered raspberries along the road, a thornless member of the rose family that sports lovely pink or lavender flowers in summer. Your route through much of this slice of mountain country will wind through a young forest of sugar maple, birch, and beech. Even more engaging, however, are some of the ground plants that thrive in this moist, protected environment. During the first 0.25 mile of the walk, keep your eyes to the ground for Canada mayflower, lily of the valley, horsetail, and the long, whorled leaves of Indian cucumber. This latter plant is fairly uncommon today, although Indians of the area once harvested the root—which does indeed smell and taste somewhat like a cucumber—in significant quantities as a source of both food and medicine. Indian cucumber's genus name, *Medeola,* is a reference to the great sorceress and herbal healer Medea.

As you make your way through this forest, notice how the ground covers tend to grow in scattered pockets beneath the trees, some sparse, and some very thick and lush. While soil composition and moisture play a big part in how this tapestry is woven, another major factor is the amount of sunlight that reaches the forest floor. Profusions of plants growing along the trail are the result of the clearing of trees for the pathway. Such clearing leaves openings in the canopy that allow sunlight to pour onto the trailsides, thus giving rise to a greater variety and density of plants.

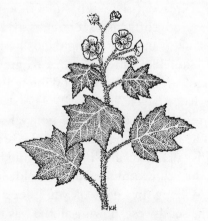

Purple-flowering Raspberry

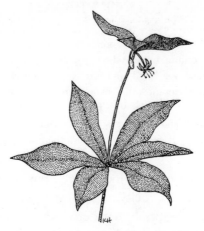

Indian Cucumber Root

At 0.75 mile you'll reach a T junction. Here we'll take a right, though those with a little extra climb left in them can take a left and, in 0.2 mile, be on top of Mount Hor. Near this intersection watch for the creamy white flowers of wild leeks, as well as the beautiful wood sorrel, a plant with cloverlike leaves and delicate white or pink blossoms, one to a stalk. Although common in New England, wood sorrel is actually a native of the British Isles, where many claim it to be the true shamrock. It was the three-lobed leaves of the wood sorrel, so the story goes, that Saint Patrick used to explain the concept of Christian Trinity to the pagan Celts.

Just under 1.4 miles the trail splits. Both forks go to very different overlooks of Lake Willoughby. Begin by taking the right branch, which offers tremendous views across the lake to the sheer walls of Mount Pisgah. The other overlook, 0.15 mile to the north, will allow you to see the rolling landscape that lies further to the north. Both overlooks certainly have their share of regal beauty, each a perfect testimony to the appropriateness of this lonely corner of Vermont having been nicknamed the Northeast Kingdom.

MOUNT PISGAH

Distance: 2.4 miles
Location: From the intersection of Vermont highways 16 and 5A at the north end of Lake Willoughby, head south on 5A for 1.5 miles to Mill Brook Road, and turn left. Follow this road for 1.7 miles, at which point you'll make a right turn onto a logging access road. In 1.3 miles you'll reach our walking trail, which takes off along another access road heading to the west. (You should see a small white sign marking the route.)

It would be hard to even imagine a more dramatic vista than the one to be had from the small, rocky roost located on the north edge of old man Pisgah. There is simply nowhere in Vermont where the world drops away in such sheer abandon, a long toss of wooded mountains and deep, green valleys upwelling from the steely blue waters of Lake Willoughby, shimmering in the sun more than fifteen hundred feet below. This perch is also excellent for watching migrating hawks beating southward during October and early November. This sheer summit actually caps the home turf of several nesting peregrine falcons, which were reintroduced into the Willoughby highlands several years ago. What's more, these inaccessible pockets are home to some very rare plants, including sweet broom and mountain saxifrage—arctic remnants of the cold, icy days that once prevailed here.

Although you'll have to endure 0.3 mile of steep uphill on this walk, it is by far the easiest of three possible routes to Pisgah. All in all, you'll save nearly nine hundred feet of vertical climbing. (One note of decorum here. If you happen to meet a line of exhausted people ascending the main north trail on a hot summer day, their chests heaving, their mouths sucking air, you may want to time very carefully your comments about this much shorter, far more gentle pathway.)

Fifty yards or so after leaving the parking area, the road will fork, at which point you should take the left branch. After this point 0.1 mile you'll see a small white sign and a series of white tree blazes on the left marking the trail to Pisgah. From here you'll be rounding the northern flank of the mountain, along a lightly forested slope that offers a few tantalizing views of Willoughby to the northwest. Look here for hobblebush, raspberries, wood aster, shinleaf, bracken, baneberry, false Solomon's seal, and sarsaparilla. Eventually the hardwood forest thickens, dominated by white and yellow birch, as well as red, sugar, and mountain maples.

When you intersect the main trail from the highway at 0.6 mile, take a left, beginning a short but steep trudge toward the sky. Notice how the forest changes as you rise to higher, more exposed slices of the mountain. The orientation of this upland toward the north means even cooler, moister conditions than those that would result from elevation alone—environmental factors that spruce, balsam fir, and northern white cedar handle very well. The cold-tolerant white birch has also established a firm hold here, as it continues to do all the way to the chilly reaches of Labrador.

By 0.75 mile the climb has lessened considerably, and, at about 1 mile, you'll intersect a path taking off to the right to the North Overlook. There is one fork near the very end of this 0.2-mile spur trail, where you'll want to keep to the left. Just a few yards past this junction the path will stop abruptly on a ledge overhanging the

Peregrine Falcon

very edge of oblivion—a sensational, breathtaking place. If you love soaring, tumbling views, you'll be delighted; Pisgah, namesake of the biblical mountain from which Moses first glimpsed the promised land, seems a most appropriate title. It's fun to watch the beautiful patterns of ripples that swell and melt away on the blue waters far below. These water dances, which even from shore can seem independent of any discernible wind, were once thought to be the handiwork of spirits.

The cobalt blue waters of Willoughby were once a rather modest river. It was the grind of ice sheets thousands of feet thick pouring out of Canada that changed these waters. Like a spoon pushing through ice cream, the glacier created a rounded, U-shaped valley where the earlier river had sculpted a V. Much of the bottom land gouged by the tip of this icy finger, along with plenty of other gravelly debris carried by the glacier, was deposited to form the height of land you see at the south end of the lake. By the time the various flowages finally stopped filling against this natural dam, they had reached a depth of more than three hundred feet, making Willoughby the deepest lake in Vermont.

New Hampshire

MIDDLE SUGARLOAF

Distance: 2.8 miles

Location: White Mountain National Forest. From the town of Twin Mountain, head east for approximately 3 miles on New Hampshire Highway 302 to Zealand Road. Proceed south on Zealand Road for 0.6 mile to a parking area on the right (west) side of the road. Both this trail and the Trestle Trail are located just south of this parking area, on the other side of a bridge crossing the Zealand River.

The three Sugarloaf mountains, so named for their resemblance to the cakes of sugar that were sold in colonial times, offer their wind-blown summits for far less effort than do most high perches in the White Mountains. From the top of Middle Sugarloaf you can gaze at a virtual symphony of peaks, from the awesome Presidentials exploding out of the forest to the east, to the softer, more distant highline of Vermont's Green Mountains in the west.

Our walk begins in a lovely forest canopy of balsam, maple, and yellow birch, with mats of Canada mayflower, bluebead lily, bracken fern, and bunchberry hugging the ground below. Singing a rocky song immediately to your right is the Zealand River, which twists northward toward the Ammonoosuc (literally, "fish place"), the combined waters then running across the neck of New Hamp-

111

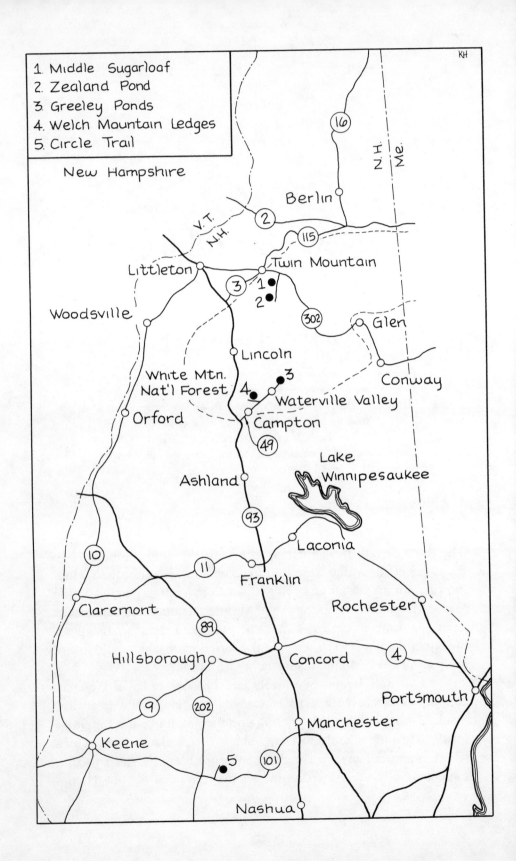

1. Middle Sugarloaf
2. Zealand Pond
3. Greeley Ponds
4. Welch Mountain Ledges
5. Circle Trail

New Hampshire

KH

shire bound for the Connecticut River. Take some time to enjoy this sprightly river, since at 0.2 mile we will leave all such valley things behind and begin our climb to the highlands.

The forest on this east side of the Sugarloafs, although young, is quite beautiful. Having not yet established the full, thick canopy of a mature mixed deciduous forest, the play of light is sufficient to afford you some lengthy views across the slopes, as well as into the twists and turns of a quiet braid of moist, quiet ravines. Sarsaparilla, clubmosses, sheep laurel, blueberry, Canada mayflower, and hobblebush weave textures into the forest floor, and, beginning in May and lasting well into autumn, set off tiny fireworks of colored blooms and berries.

Although this trail will not take you far enough to see a full-blown high-altitude forest (the summit of Middle Sugarloaf is about where such changes just begin in earnest), you may spot a few differences between this high ridge and walks you've taken at lower elevations. In the upper reaches of the walk, beech and hemlock will not be as prevalent as they were on lower ground, and you'll find more white birch growing among the yellow birch. At the very summit of Middle Sugarloaf spruce and fir are common, with a few mountain ash dotting the landscape where there were none before. Were this climb to continue its upward course another thousand feet, you'd see very little in the way of trees except the evergreens. It is at such higher altitudes, where cold temperatures create poorer soils and reduce a tree's ability to create new plant tissue, that conifers, which can conduct photosynthesis year-long, become the masters of the mountain.

Bunchberry

After a healthy huff-and-puff session of about 0.4 mile, at 0.9 mile you'll reach the saddle between North Sugarloaf and Middle Sugarloaf mountains. Turn left here, toward Middle Sugarloaf. Just before you reach the summit a trail will fork to the right, leading to the north face of the mountain. We'll stay left here, making the final quick assent to the summit. The top of Middle Sugarloaf is a rocky perch peppered with spruce, balsam fir, aspen, blueberry, tamarack, and shadbush.

Besides the long vistas—Mount Washington to the east, Mount Hale, North Twin Mountain, and Noble Peak to the south, and Vermont's Green Mountains to the west—note the lovely blanket of forest to the southeast covering the gentle twists and turns of the Zealand Valley. What makes this scene especially wonderful today is the fact that three-quarters of a century ago almost every inch of this valley lay rutted and barren of trees, robbed even of the river that again dances wet and wild between these mountain shoulders.

Timber baron J. E. Henry was born in 1831, into a New Hampshire household that offered little but poverty and hard work. Often the butt of bullying and jokes about his lower-class status, Henry swore that one day things would be very different. And different they were. Graduating from a job he began at fifteen driving freight wagons throughout northern New England, in the 1880s Henry began to acquire the first of the timber lands that would ultimately grow to more than ten thousand acres—the largest single tract of New Hampshire forest ever to be controlled by one person. For forty years Henry's lumberjacks laid their steel into the trees covering the landscape before you, wiping out what was arguably the most prime virgin forest to be found anywhere in the White Mountains.

Between Henry's timbering practices (he seldom disposed of his slash debris, and eventually descended into a kind of clear-cutting mania) and two devastating fires, perhaps both started by his locomotives, by 1903 Zealand Valley was a veritable wasteland. Ernest Russell wrote in a 1908 issue of *Collier's*, "It is as if the contents of some vast cemetery had been unearthed in that little valley." In the same feature Russell relates this comment from Henry, which hardly helped ease his reputation as master plunderer. "I never seen the tree yet," Henry told Russell, "that didn't mean a damned sight more to me goin' under the saw than it did standin' on a mountain."

The forests of the northern White Mountains were good to J. E. Henry. Upon his death in 1912, he left an estate worth more than ten million dollars. Fortunately, as C. Francis Belcher points out in his excellent book *Logging Railroads of the White Mountains*, he also left a groundswell of public outrage that ultimately led to the creation of the White Mountain National Forest.

It's hard not to wonder why today we still seem capable of learning such lessons only in the midst of ecological crises. When is the right time to react to acid rain? When will a critical wildlife habitat have shrunken past the point of no return? Unlike the remarkable return of the Zealand Valley forest, what will happen when our tinkering pushes nature beyond her ability to heal?

ZEALAND POND

Distance: 5.5 miles
Location: White Mountain National Forest. From the town of Twin Mountain, head east on U.S. Highway 302 for approximately 3 miles, to Zealand Road. Take Zealand Road south for 3.6 miles, where it will end beside our trailhead.

The trip to Zealand Pond is a heartening trek. Less than a lifetime ago this walk would have been through a scarred, barren wasteland—a shattered cathedral laid to waste by ruthless timber harvesting. The fact that this woods has come so far in healing itself, that in such a short a time it could again bloom so rich and full of promise, is staggering testimony to the potential of the earth to reweave intricate webs of life that have been shredded by human hands.

The walk begins in a wonderful forest of red maple, spruce, balsam fir, striped maple, and gray and white birch—a fairly young, well-spaced woodland that affords an endless variety of views through long, cool galleries of light and shadow. Black-and-white warblers and white-breasted nuthatches scour the branches of the trees looking for spiders and wood-boring insects; ovenbirds pick at the leaf litter for caterpillars, crickets, and worms. The friendly buzz of the black-capped chickadee can be heard ringing through the

115

trees, as well as, on occasion, the flutey, cascading melodies of the wood thrush.

This forest is also good for checking wet areas along the trail for wildlife tracks. Besides black bear, moose, beaver, deer, and woodchuck, you're walking through the heart of the region's lynx population. To actually see one of these lean cats, with their thick, luxurious fur coats and long, silky cheek ruffs, is considered one of New England's rarest and greatest wildlife experiences. Considering the long centuries of dogged trapping for lynx pelts, though, I consider it a thrill just to know that these magnificent creatures are still around. The lynx is an extremely shy creature that rarely enters large open areas, and prefers to den in secluded logs or rock crevices far from the foot of humans. Numbers of lynx fluctuate substantially with the population of its favorite prey, the snowshoe hare. When snowshoe hare are scarce, lynx tend to reproduce at a much slower rate.

At 0.55 mile is a footbridge. Immediately after crossing this bridge you'll see a trail taking off to the right, but you should stay

Woodchuck

Lynx

straight, on the blue-blazed path. Climb gently along a twisted mat of root systems jutting up from the trail, keeping your eyes open for spatters of whorled wood aster, wild oats, twisted stalk, and hobblebush. The braid of streams, rivulets, and ponds increases in density the further into the forest you go. In fact, by the time you reach the 1.5 mile mark, you'll never be more than a stone's throw from either the sight or sound of mountain water, as well as the lush mats of shrubs and wildflowers nurtured by such environments.

A particularly nice upland channel lies at 1.75 miles, where clear, cold water gushes from pool to pool, slip-sliding through earthen bottlenecks choked with speckled alder, mountain holly, and meadowsweet. Shortly past this spot you'll reach a chain of flooded lowlands fringed with tamarack, alder, tall meadow rue, and wild raisin. The local beavers' union has managed this section of the valley with various water projects for the past several decades. If you look carefully from here to our turnaround point, you'll spot several lodges built by these crafty engineers.

Beaver will often construct their lodge at the northern edge of a pond, thereby exposing it to the greatest possible amount of sunlight—a position that helps assure that the ice surrounding the structure will melt away as early as possible in the spring. These lodges are incredibly strong structures, usually built as mounds of sticks and mud from which chambers are then excavated from underneath. Typically there will be only one chamber in a lodge, the size varying according to the number of animals in the family. (Very large families, however, will have two chambers, each with its own entrance tunnel.) Most chambers adopt a sort of split-level design—a lower dining platform, and an upper shelf, covered with wood chips, where the beaver sleep. (Placing the sleeping area higher than the rest of the lodge helps keep it dry.) If the location of the lodge proves to be a good one, with plenty of food nearby, beaver may stay in the same one for many years, adding reinforcements to it each fall. After half a dozen years a lodge can look like a regular apartment building, measuring more than ten feet high and forty feet across!

At 2.4 miles, just before intersecting with the A–Z Trail, you'll meander through exquisite, leafy arches formed by white birch leaning out from either side of the path. Birch often lean like this into areas cut by trails, roadways, or streams, straining their necks for an extra splash of sunlight. These stretches, especially when set ablaze by fall colors, are among the most beautiful of any pathway on Earth. Robert Frost also loved the lean of birch trees, and in one of his poems is moved to remember days of climbing to the upper stories of the trees and then swinging down to the ground on their supple trunks. "One could do worse," he wrote, "than be a swinger of birches."

As you near the Zealand Pond you'll spot lovely gardens of sumac, wild sarsaparilla, bracken fern, shadbush, and silky dogwood. At 2.75 miles, about 0.25 mile past the intersection with the A–Z Trail, a small spur trail descends to the edge of Zealand Pond. Looking across the water, high against a sheer rock face, you'll see the white veil of Zealand Falls—a dramatic exclamation point for a stream that has made its way here via a dizzy 600-foot plunge from the high forests south of Mount Hale.

Birches, ponds, birds, waterfalls, wildlife. What an idyllic spot! Slow down. Take in as much of it as you possibly can.

GREELEY PONDS

Distance: 6.8 miles
Location: White Mountain National Forest. From Interstate 93, head east on New Hampshire Highway 49 for approximately 15 miles, to the town of Waterville Valley. Just before this highway dead-ends in the town, turn left next to the library onto West Branch Road. (You'll see a large tennis complex on the right just before this intersection.) This road crosses the Mad River over a one-lane bridge, then turns sharply to the right. Just before you reach a second bridge, 0.8 mile from the intersection with Highway 49, you'll see a road taking off to the right, with a large parking area beside it. (This parking area has a large trail information board beside it.) Park here, and begin your walk down this road. You'll find the Greeley Ponds Trail taking off to your left in 0.3 mile.

While this resort town was not officially recognized as Waterville Valley until 1967, the name probably dates back more than one hundred fifty years, to a time when it was used to denote both the valley as well as the surrounding peaks, which were then known as the Waterville Haystacks. It's hard to refute the appropriateness of the name *Waterville*, since, besides the Mad River, which we'll follow to its source, there is also an extensive braid of smaller mountain streams tumbling out of the high country from every direction.

Joining in this grand dance of water and mountain is the striking beauty of the forests themselves. Here are rich stands of spruce, fir, beech, and birch—a shimmering green tapestry stitched to the side of every swell, as far as the eye can see. In the mid-1920s this land, including all of the upper Mad River drainage from here to Greeley Ponds, was owned by the Parker-Young Company, which was making plans to clear-cut it. At the time the region included the largest remaining old-growth forest in the entire state.

While there was considerable objection to the plan, much of it fueled by the dogged efforts of the Society to Protect New Hampshire Forests, saving it would require some fancy footwork. In 1911, Massachusetts congressman (and New Hampshire native) John Weeks spearheaded the passage of a law that took Gifford Pinchot's notion of creating national forests out of publicly owned lands, and modified it to allow Congress to appropriate funds to purchase private

119

holdings, as well. It was this law that opened the door to establishing federal forest reserves in the East—no small feat. For years Weeks had met considerable opposition from conservative legislators, in particular Speaker of the House Joseph Cannon, who is credited with uttering the now-famous cry "not one cent for scenery!"

Despite the power that the Weeks bill afforded eastern conservationists, at the time Parker-Young planned to strip Waterville Valley, the only eastern lands that had ever been acquired for national forest designation had been properties that were already logged. An able group of New Hampshire citizens went to work, pulling every string possible, making very strong arguments to legislators about the importance of scenic lands. In an unprecedented move, Congress did in fact appropriate the funds to buy the Waterville Valley forests. (The fact that then-President Calvin Coolidge was from neighboring Vermont probably didn't hurt.) The battle of Waterville Valley did, in no small measure, help mark the beginning of a more enlightened American land ethic.

Although at 6.8 miles the walk to Greeley Ponds is fairly long, it is extremely gentle. What's more, you can turn around at virtually any point before reaching the ponds and still be very glad you came. From the parking lot 0.25 mile you'll see a large open area on the right. This place is good for looking at summer color, including the purple-tipped staffs of fireweed and the puckered yellow blossoms of the birdfoot trefoil—a plant, like so many here, introduced long ago from Europe. At 0.3 mile you'll see our path—the Greeley Ponds Trail—taking off to the left onto a smaller two-track road. Forming a roadside fringe beside a forest of birch and maple is a wide variety of common New Hampshire plants, including hayscented fern, partridgeberry, cutleaf and red-banded sedge, bunchberry, bluebead lily, purple trillium, flat-topped white aster, and selfheal. Selfheal is a member of the mint family that has been used medicinally for more than four hundred years. Perhaps much of its wide acceptance by herbalists occurred in the mid-1500s, when it was the primary treatment given to members of the German Imperial Army to treat a contagious illness called "the browns," which was marked by fever, sore throat, and a brown coating of the tongue. The Latin name of this illness later became the plant's genus name, *Prunella*.

By 1 mile into the walk you will have the delightful company of the Mad River close by your side. Other trails leave both right and left from our roadway at 1 and 1.2 miles, but we'll keep walking straight. At 1.45 miles, past tufts of strawberry and sweet-scented bedstraw, you'll come to a bridge that makes a beautiful crossing of the Mad River. This spot is good for a bit of simple tree identification. Looking upstream, next to the bridge is a fine white (or paper) birch. Many Indian tribes of the Northeast used this tree to make their canoes. The thin bark was stretched over frames made of Atlantic white cedar and sewn together with hemlock roots. The seams were then made waterproof by caulking them with resin taken from balsam fir. (Don't peel the bark of white birch, since doing so will damage the tree.)

A short distance upstream on the right is a beautiful white pine. This tree is the largest of the eastern pines, and to the colonists one of the most important trees of the forest, its combination of light weight and strength making it an ideal building material. If you turn around, on your left and slightly overhanging the bridge is a beautiful yellow birch.

The trail continues to wind pleasantly past wood and clearing, past orchids, trillium, and false violet, never far from the sound of the Mad River, which at this point is not mad at all. Fresh out of Greeley Ponds, it has so far gained only a whisper of spirit, one that will grow as water from countless other rivulets joins it on its run down the mountains. The Mad is angry only well down the valley, and even there only when prodded by heavy rains or melting snow. As far as

Bluebead Lily

121

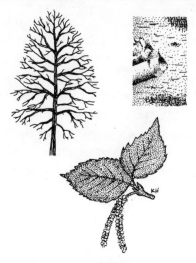

White Birch

Greeley Ponds themselves—the womb of the Mad River—there is only the quiet that comes with deeper waters, a shimmer of jewels set in high folds of timber and granite.

WELCH MOUNTAIN LEDGES

Distance: 2.8 miles
Location: White Mountain National Forest. From Interstate Highway 93, head east from exit 28 on New Hampshire Highway 49. About 5 miles east of the town of Campton the highway will cross the Mad River, after which you'll see a parking area on the right for the Smarts Brook Trail. Our turn is a short distance past this Smarts Brook parking area—the first bridge crossing the river on your left. Once across the river, follow the signs for the national forest access, which is located 1.35 miles from Highway 49, past a large condominium complex.

Though the majority of walkers on this trail actually make the steep, bare rock climb to the summit of Welch Mountain itself, our much easier trek to the high, blueberry-laden ledges lying to the south will offer you no shortage of opportunity to bask in a true New Hampshire mountainscape.

The long, wonderful swell of high country that stretches from here northward, which for centuries has been known as the White Mountains, has captured both the eye and the imagination of countless wanderers. Like magnets to the human spirit they drew the writers, poets, and adventurers of the nineteenth century—Nathaniel Hawthorne, Henry David Thoreau, Ralph Waldo Emerson, Henry Wadsworth Longfellow, William Cullen Bryant. They were equally magical to the Native Americans, who had come to know these peaks long before Samuel de Champlain first set eyes on them in 1605 from 10 miles out in the Atlantic. "Ask them whither they go when they die," wrote one visitor of the local Indians in 1672, "they will tell you, pointing with their finger, to heaven beyond the White Mountains."

After crossing a beautiful stream tumbling southward to a meeting with the Mad River, the trail winds through a fairly young forest of yellow birch, maple, beech, and hemlock. The hearty hobblebush strews branches covered with big, rounded leaves across much of the forest floor, with bracken fern, bluebead lily, wood sorrel, wild sarsaparilla, and an occasional purple trillium also close at hand. The path gets down to more serious climbing at about 0.4 mile, but this climbing lasts less than a mile before delivering you onto the face of an open, windswept table of granite.

Take your time along this bare brown shoulder, stopping for close-up looks at plants that you did not see, or at least not in such

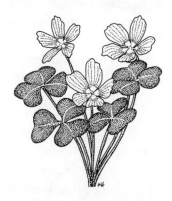

Common Wood Sorrel

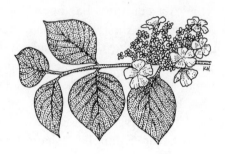

Hobblebush

profusion, in the forest below. Blueberries seem to appear from nearly every tiny pocket of soil, as do occasional smatterings of sheep laurel. You'll also find here the small, shrublike trees known as shadbush. The common name of this plant alludes to the fact that its clusters of beautiful white blossoms occur at the same time that the silvery fish known as shad make their way upriver in the spring to spawn. This particular combination of bloom and spawn never went unnoticed by the early Puritans, who were convinced that the simultaneous events were a special blessing to the faithful. (Shad were at one time pulled from New England's ocean rivers in incredible quantities, filling nets so full that teams of horses had to be employed to drag them out. Though English colonists usually snubbed the shad as a source of food, it did have its share of devotees. Perhaps most noteworthy of these was General George Washington and the troops at Valley Forge. It was an early run of shad in late February 1778 that literally saved the lives of Washington and his cold, hungry men.)

Follow the blaze marks along the rocks to a point where you can easily head south a short distance to the edge of the ledges. Here are clusters of red oak, bigtooth aspen, red spruce, and mountain maple, with patches of soft deer moss forming a shaggy carpet across the stone. At the end of the ledges is a long, lovely view of the forested fringe of the Sandwich Range Wilderness to the southeast, and the Mad River below, hurtling itself toward the Atlantic via the Pemigewasset and the Merrimack. Longfellow had a few words to say about the temperament of this river, which changes dramatically from its humble beginnings in the placid backwaters of Greeley Ponds:

> Men call me Mad, and well they may,
>   When, full of rage and trouble,
> I burst my banks of sand and clay,
> And sweep their towns away
>   Like withered reeds or stubble.

CIRCLE TRAIL

Distance: 0.4 mile

Location: Miller State Park. This park is located on the north side of New Hampshire State Highway 101, 3.8 miles east of the intersection of Highway 101 and U.S. 202 East. Turn into the park, and follow the entrance road 1.3 miles to the summit.

Note: The road to the summit is narrow and winding, not suitable for large vehicles or vehicles pulling trailers.

Miller State Park, crowned by 2,288-foot-high South Pack Monadnock Mountain, is the oldest park in the state of New Hampshire, donated in 1891 as a memorial to War of 1812 hero General James Miller. It provides a wonderful opportunity to experience a southern New Hampshire summit with no more effort than a series of rather hard twists on the steering wheel. (Those who would feel much too guilty about reaching a mountaintop without even breaking a sweat, however, can walk from the base on either the Blue or Wapack trails.) On clear days the views from this peak are remarkable, stretching southeastward all the way across Massachusetts into the concrete peaks of downtown Boston.

Once you've parked on top of the mountain, if you walk around the turnaround loop in a counterclockwise direction, the Circle Trail—marked by a series of red dots—will be found next to the last picnic table on your right. Though the route can be a bit of a challenge to follow at times, rest assured that the red paint marking dots are indeed there, either on the bark of a tree or on the face of a rock.

As you begin this walk, you'll be afforded a fine view of Monadnock Mountain, 12 miles to the west. This 3,165-foot mountain, whose name is actually a geological term for uplifts that have resisted the forces of erosion, is the highest point in southern New Hampshire. Like the mountain you are standing on, Monadnock is a residual of the Littleton Formation—a towering upswell of rock that remained unbroken by the great tongues of ice that scoured this landscape during the ice age. Much of the bare area visible along the upper 400–500 feet of Monadnock is not the result of harsh alpine conditions, which occur only at much higher elevations, but rather was created by early settlers who set countless fires on the mountain to drive wolves away from their sheep. (At one time Spanish Merino sheep were extremely common in this part of New England; in Vermont, they once outnumbered the people by 5 to 1!)

Monadnock is one of the most visited mountains in the world, once claiming regular audiences from the likes of Ralph Waldo Emerson, Henry David Thoreau, Rudyard Kipling, and even Mark Twain, all of whom probably stood looking east at the very place where you now stand. Twain, particularly poetic about the October vistas available near the base of Monadnock, said that "the sight affects the spectator physically, it stirs his blood like military music." Nor for that matter did the artistic attraction of this area die with the nineteenth century. Just to the west of here, near Peterborough, is McDowell Colony, a quiet retreat whose piney folds have attracted people like Thornton Wilder and Aaron Copland.

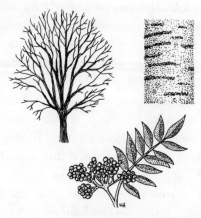

Mountain Ash

But enough of Monadnock. Let's take a closer look at her smaller sister. Our trail drops gently past tufts of meadowsweet, and then takes a right into the hush of a red spruce grove, the path peppered here and there with clusters of hayscented fern. As you exit this forest into a clearing, watch for nice mats of blueberry, which can be seen growing in abundance throughout much of this short trek. In 0.1 mile you'll cross an open area paved with flat rocks, and, shortly afterward, begin a short descent into a mixed forest of gray birch, spruce, mountain ash, maple, and sumac. (The hollow stems of this sumac, incidentally, were once used as sap taps for sugar maples.) At the bottom is a beautiful, cool hollow laced with ferns, bluebead lilies, Canada mayflower, and bunchberry.

Shortly after leaving the woods is an open, rocky area with a bench on the right—the perfect perch from which to survey views of the soft, tumbling swell of land to the north. When you've had your fill of scenery, continue around the summit toward the east, passing into a broken forest of yellow birch and maple, their feet wrapped in tight clusters of hobblebush. Besides the ever-present blueberries, there are also raspberries in here. In the spring you'll find splashes of purple trillium, or "birthroot," the latter name alluding to the fact that a tea from the plant was once given to women who had just given birth in order to help control bleeding. Certain Indian tribes also crushed the leaves of the purple trillium and applied the juice to burns and insect bites.

All too soon, at only 0.4 mile, you'll again reach the parking area. Perhaps you'll want to make this loop again, in the other direction. The views only get more enjoyable, the rush of wind through the rips in the tree canopy, more refreshing.

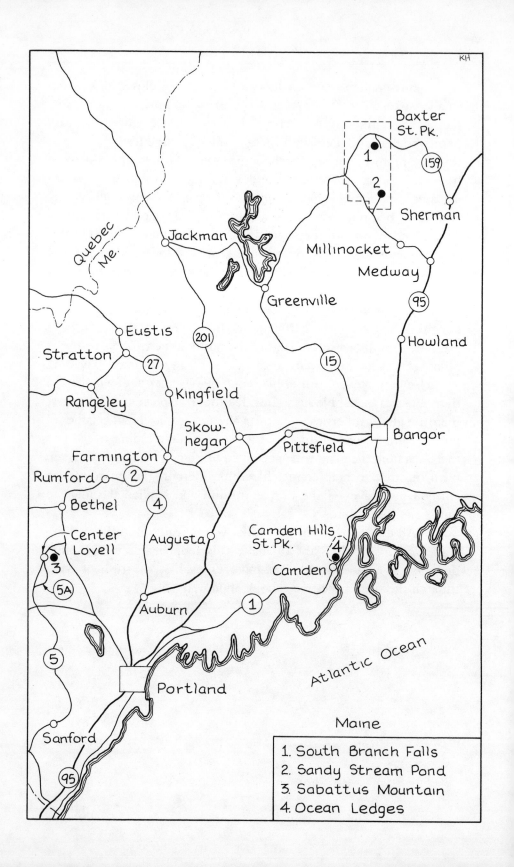

KH

Baxter St. Pk.

1

2

159

Sherman

Quebec Me.

Jackman

Millinocket

Medway

Greenville

95

Eustis

Howland

Stratton

201

27

15

Rangeley

Kingfield

Skow-
hegan

Pittsfield

Bangor

Farmington

Rumford

2

4

Bethel

Camden Hills
St. Pk.

Center
Lovell

Augusta

4

3

Camden

5A

Auburn

1

5

Atlantic Ocean

Portland

Maine

Sanford

1. South Branch Falls

2. Sandy Stream Pond

95

3. Sabattus Mountain

4. Ocean Ledges

Maine

SOUTH BRANCH FALLS

Distance: 1.2 miles

Location: Baxter State Park. From Interstate 95 north of Bangor, take the Sherman Exit, and then follow Maine routes 11 and 159 north for 8 miles to the town of Patten. From Patten continue west on Maine Route 159 for 27 miles to the north entrance of Baxter State Park, at Matagamon Gate. Continue west along the northern edge of the park on Perimeter Road, and turn left (south) on South Branch Road, toward South Branch Pond Campground. In 1.3 miles you'll come to a small parking area on the right (west) side of the road. Our walk begins here.

Standing in the quiet blanket of forest that warms the feet of Mount Katahdin, a glassy summer sky hanging overhead, it's difficult to believe that this landscape could be the child of violent, wrenching geologic changes. Yet millions of years ago, vast inland seas covering the region shuddered and sizzled in the face of thunderous earth-quakes and massive volcanic explosions. Countless millennia later, thick sheets of ice ground over the land with phenomenal force, gouging and polishing a vast braid of cirques and valleys like a hot metal scoop in a carton of ice cream. The easy walk to South Branch Falls will present a chapter of this history to you through a beautiful cascading stream, sliding northward across polished gray volcanic bedrock.

Our walk begins in a rather young forest containing white

129

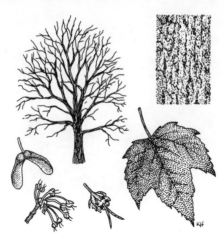

Red Maple

birch, beech, yellow birch, and red and striped maple. At 0.25 mile you'll also see a nice cluster of beaked hazelnut. The flowers of this small tree appear very early in the spring, well before any leaves are on the scene. It's a relative of the European hazel, which produces the filbert nut that many people find so tasty. At this early stage of its development the forest floor is still fairly well lit by shafts of sunlight, which pours like honey over clumps of bracken and interrupted ferns, bunchberry, Canada mayflower, ground cedar, and clubmoss.

At 0.5 mile you'll reach South Branch Ponds Brook. Head downstream here, crossing the large slabs of tilted gray rock that frame a beautiful series of sluice channels and cool, quiet plunge pools (pools much too inviting to pass on a hot summer day). This lovely sculpture, crafted over eons by the patient fingers of South Branch Ponds Brook, has been fashioned out of a rock known as Traveler rhyolite, a combination of lava and volcanic ash that has a chemical composition very similar to granite. Notice how these rocks were uplifted at some point, and now tilt decidedly toward the north.

Were you to continue downstream, you'd see this gray polished rhyolite yielding to a younger bed of sedimentary rock—a mix of pebbles, sandstone, and shales that were laid down in an ancient sea. It's in such sedimentary rock, especially around South Branch Pond Campground, that you'll find a wealth of fossils. Fossils, incidentally, are not just actual pieces of prehistoric life forms, but any trace that a life form did in fact exist. Thus the imprint of a shell or leaf or even a footprint is considered a fossil. In this particular region of Baxter Park some of the most common fossils are those of brachiopods, which are small, bottom-dwelling marine animals that look similar to clams. In some parts of the world they are known as lampshells, due to their resemblance to early Roman oil lamps. Brachiopods still exist today, but their heyday was 225–500 million years ago, during the Paleozoic. So far, scientists have described nearly thirty thousand different species!

It's humbling to stand beside the prints of organisms that were steadily going about their business more than 6 million human lifetimes ago. Likewise, the thought of the rise and fall of entire mountains, the filling and draining of vast inland seas, the inch-by-inch advances and retreats of enormous ice sheets, push the imagination into a dizzy spin of timelessness. Perhaps it is in such places as Katahdin, where the unstoppable inertia of the world seems showcased in every nook, on every horizon, that we stand the best chance of finding some kind of a window into the restless underpinnings of eternity.

SANDY STREAM POND

Distance: 3 miles

Location: Baxter State Park. From Interstate 95 north of Bangor, take the Medway Exit, and proceed west for 11 miles to the town of Millinocket. From Millinocket, follow the park signs northward for approximately 17 miles to the Togue Pond Gate entrance, located at the southeast corner of the park. From here follow the Roaring Brook Road to its end at Roaring Brook Campground. The trail leaves from the north side of a large parking area.

While this loop trail requires virtually no climbing, it nonetheless will offer you a generous helping of the pleasures of the high country. Plan to walk it very early some still summer morning, when Katahdin's headwalls are catching the first sunlight of the day, and moose are out in force just ahead of you, stamping king-sized footprints in the fresh patches of cool forest mud.

Although several trails take off near Roaring Brook Campground, the well-marked path to Sandy Stream Pond is easy to follow. After crossing Roaring Brook, the path will settle into a classic Maine forest of spruce, balsam fir, white and yellow birch, and striped and red maples. Watch the ground here for mats of bunchberry, hobblebush, snowberry, sarsaparilla, and whorled wood aster, as well as occasional starflowers, trilliums, and bluebead lilies. As you pass through wetter, more open areas along the loop, watch how the plants change. Suddenly there are colorful threads of meadow rue, meadowsweet, rhodora, blueberry, and cotton grass.

At 0.4 mile you'll reach an open area that offers beautiful views of 3,122-foot South Turner Mountain, a striking reminder that Katahdin is hardly Baxter's only member of the high country. In fact, from South Turner Mountain northward is a dramatic jumble of high peaks stretching for 15 miles, broken only once by the beautiful Wassataquoik Stream Valley. There are, in fact, 46 mountain peaks in Baxter State Park, 18 of which are more than three thousand feet high.

Moose

The open areas along this walk are wonderful places to spot moose. Those hopeful of seeing them, however, should be very quiet. While not endowed with particularly great eyesight, moose can hear footsteps and talking long before you get to them. A mere half century ago, poaching, disease, and loss of habitat through forest-fire suppression had reduced the Maine population of this great animal to perhaps no more than two thousand. Today, though, much to the delight of Maine residents and visitors alike, there are more than twenty thousand of them. As with all wildlife, never attempt to get too close to a moose, especially a female with calves. Far from being dumbstruck, a moose who merely stands and stares at your approach may well be deciding whether or not to charge. These giants, by the way, are perhaps the ultimate verification that your mother wasn't lying about the value of eating vegetables. A moose will eat forty to fifty pounds of greens every day—birch, aspen, willow, pond lilies, and so forth. Large bulls will tower more than six feet tall at the shoulder, and weigh nearly fifteen hundred pounds.

At 0.55 mile make a detour onto a view trail taking off to the left. This path will take you along the edge of Sandy Stream Pond for a short distance and then return you to the main trail not far from where you left it. The views of Katahdin from this view trail are truly magnificent. The two large cirques visible high on the mountain are North and Great basins, which were carved by the great sheets of ice that covered the landscape roughly ten thousand to eighteen thousand years ago. To the left of these cuts is 4,902-foot Pamola Peak, named for the fierce mountain god that is said to reside still in this craggy sky palace. There is a vast, rich weave of folklore about the Katahdin god Pamola—more, in fact, than exists about virtually any other mountain spirit in America. One tale says that Mount Katahdin was created by a council of the highest gods for use as their sacred meeting place. When Pamola, who was somewhat lower on the supreme-being social register, was refused a seat at the council, he retreated to the peak you now see, where he has lived ever since.

A surveyor who visited this area in 1804 relayed that the Indians around Katahdin believed Pamola lives on the peak during the winter, and then "flies off in the spring with tremendous rumbling noises." Later information revealed that Pamola stole a beautiful Indian maiden whom he protects from pursuers by hurtling thunderbolts at them. Anyone, in fact, who climbs Katahdin runs the risk of incurring the savage wrath of this big sourpuss.

Pamola is often portrayed as a strange mix of man and eagle. Roy Dudley, who for years lived at Chimney Pond near the foot of Great Basin, added further valuable information about what Pamola is really like by informing us that he smokes forest fires in his pipe, and is occasionally bothered by porcupines nesting in his ears.

Continue to work your way around the north side of Sandy Stream Pond. At 0.85 mile you'll reach the junction with South Turner Mountain Trail, surrounded by mats of interrupted and hay-scented ferns, Canada mayflower, cut-leaf sedge, bunchberry, sarsaparilla, and blueberry. Stay left here, and work your way southward past occasional dead snags of spruce and fir, the victims of spruce budworm.

At the junction with Russell Pond Trail, take a left. In another 0.6 mile you'll reach a fine bog area, peppered with pitcher plants, Labrador tea, elderberry, blueberry, and cotton grass. From here the trail continues through nice blankets of birch, balsam, and spruce, arriving at the intersection with the Sandy Stream Pond Trail at 2.9 miles, 0.1 mile from the parking area.

SABATTUS MOUNTAIN

Distance: 1.6 miles

Location: The village of Center Lovell is located approximately 22.5 miles south of the town of Bethel, on Maine Highway 5. From Center Lovell, 0.8 mile north of where Maine highways 5 and 5A intersect, turn right (east) onto Sabattus Road. Follow this road for 1.5 miles, and veer to the right on Sabattus Mountain Road. In 0.3 mile you'll reach a small parking area on the left side of the road. Our trail begins across from this parking lot.

In such places standing alone on the mountaintop it is easy to realize that whatever special nests we make—leaves and moss like the marmots and birds, or tents or piled stone—we all dwell in a house of one room—the world with the firmament for its roof—and are sailing the celestial spaces without leaving any track.

JOHN MUIR

Thanks in part to the way that glacial ice ground across the landscape eighteen thousand years ago, the twisted path up the north side of Sabattus Mountain gives no indication whatsoever of the magnificent views southward across the Oxford Hills awaiting you at the end of the trail. Viewed at sunset these vast drifts of upland, each blanketed with thick coverlets of deciduous and coniferous forest, tug especially hard on the imagination, sending it flying across some of the most untrammeled landscape in all of southern Maine.

Our walk begins in a logged field now in the early stages of forest succession. The stars of the show at this point are birch and aspen, but most of these will eventually yield the stage to more shade-tolerant species. You'll be passing through several stages of forest growth along this walk, ranging from very young saplings to small groves of mature white pines. This latter tree, identified by its shiny bundles of five needles, was a dominant resident in much of Maine for five thousand years, succumbing not to the forces of nature but to two hundred years of fast-flying axes.

As you enter a more mature woodland at just over 0.1 mile, keep your eyes open for nice gardens of bracken and woodfern, as well as clusters of Indian cucumber, wintergreen, white wood asters, whorled wood asters, blueberries, Canada mayflower, starflower, hobblebush, trailing arbutus, and pipsissewa. The rather lyrical name of this latter plant is a Cree Indian word meaning "breaks into pieces," which refers to the belief that prolonged consumption of a tea made from pipsissewa leaves would break down bladder and kidney stones. The plant was widely used as a diuretic throughout much of the American frontier, and some people also made compresses with it for the relief of pains in the joints. Even today the pipsissewa is not without its practical uses, an extract of the leaves being a common ingredient in the flavoring of root beer.

The trail continues to climb steadily on its 600-foot reach for the top of Sabattus, passing at 0.75 mile a nice clump of sheep laurel growing at the feet of several towering white pines. The journey comes to an end rather abruptly at a wide opening beside the remains of an old fire tower. Here you'll find several rocky outcroppings from which to drink in the view, most of which are cradled by beautiful red oaks, with a few tenacious gray birch hanging by their toes from the sheer south side of the mountain. (Like many of its relatives, the branches of the gray birch are so supple that heavy snows may pin them to the ground for several months without doing them serious damage.)

Looking across this great roll of timber, it's easy to believe that 87 percent of Maine (the Pine Tree State) is forested—a fact that accounts for it producing enormous quantities of lumber, pulp paper, and, not that anyone is counting, 25 million toothpicks every year. But even completely untouched and unharvested, the trees of Maine serve an invaluable role in the well-being of those who would simply pause long enough to take notice of them. "Keep a green tree in your heart," says an ancient Chinese proverb, "and perhaps the singing bird will come."

OCEAN LEDGES

Distance: 3 miles
Location: Camden Hills State Park. This park is located along U.S. Highway 1, 1.75 miles north of the town of Camden. Park at the lot located just to the left of the entrance station and just south of Mount Battie Road. Our path, which follows the Mount Battie Nature Trail, leaves from Mount Battie Road, just a few yards from the campground entrance road.

This lovely forested hill country, rising above the shimmer of Penobscot Bay, has long been considered the cradle of paradise by those looking for the ultimate seaside fantasy. Wealth and art have mingled with the natural beauty of this bayshore for nearly a hundred years. Paradise appeared before the turn of the century in the form of magnificent 250-foot yachts, their white sails billowed against the blue waters of Camden Harbor. Later it rose as beautiful music from white clapboard cottages on Rockport's Mechanic Street—from Josef Hofmann's piano, from Felix Salmond's cello, from the harp strings of Carlos Salzedo.

Today there are those who claim the delicate balance between humans and nature has been upset by a recent rush of people determined to have their share of the pleasures and profits that earthly paradises afford. And, when viewed from inside a car gridlocked in downtown Camden on a July afternoon, one would be hard-pressed not to agree. But all is hardly lost. Climb to either Mount Battie, or to our destination at Ocean Ledges, and you'll find that this slice of coastline still looks very fine indeed, a rich tapestry of steeples and seashore, spruce and sky.

Our walk begins in a rather young mixed deciduous forest of red oak, beech, white and gray birch, beaked hazelnut, and striped and red maple. Closer to the ground are splashes of Canada mayflower, interrupted, sensitive, and Christmas ferns, and clumps of arrowwood. (This latter plant takes its common name from the fact that Indians once used the young shoots in making arrow shafts.) Another plant you should see during the first mile of this walk is wild oats, a member of the lily family that produces beautiful creamy yellow, bell-shaped flowers from late April through June. Because these drooping blooms look rather like the soft lobe that hangs down

Round-lobed Hepatica

from the rear palate of a person's mouth, the plant was used by early doctors for treating disorders of the throat.

The practice of using plants for treating parts of the human anatomy because of their look, smell, or some other trait is known as the doctrine of signatures, which maintains that each plant offers a "signature" of the organ it is meant to treat. Thus, round-lobed hepatica, which resembled the liver, was used in treating liver disorders; Chinese lantern, with its bladder-shaped calyx, was used for disorders of the urinary tract. This view of medicinal plants is thought to have been pioneered during the Renaissance by Swiss physician Bombastus von Honenheim, or, as he was often called, Paracelsus. While today it may appear that Paracelsus was doing overtime in the wishful-thinking department, his contributions to medicine were in fact rather substantial. It was he, for example, who first realized the importance that chemistry had in the preparation of medicines.

In 1.1 miles, after passing nice patches of wintergreen, fern, and bluebead lily, you'll reach the Tablelands Trail. Turn right here, and proceed for approximately 0.8 mile on this pathway to Ocean Ledges. The last part of this section of trail is fairly steep, along a rocky path traversing a forest thick with young beech, as well as smatterings of northern red oak, birch, fir, and spruce. Those who trudge on, however, will most certainly have their reward at 1,300-foot-high Ocean Ledges. From this windswept, rocky summit the world falls away in a cascade of uplands fashioned by the advance and retreat of mighty glaciers. Far below are the shining beds of both

Lake Megunticook and Penobscot Bay. Up the ridge immediately to the northwest is Mount Megunticook, which, at 1,385 feet, is the second highest peak on the entire Atlantic coast. Directly to the west is the rugged knob of Mount Battie.

The peaks of both Battie and Megunticook are made of extremely hard rock, a metamorphose fired from the ancient sand and gravel beds that were once located at the edges of the continental shelves. It was the tremendous pressure and heat that occurred during the collision of the continents that transformed these gravelly beds into the rock you see today—a rock so hard that since the last thick fingers of glacial ice age retreated more than ten thousand years ago, very, very little erosion has occurred.

THE COAST

The great rhythms of nature, today so dully disregarded,
wounded even, have here their spacious and primeval liberty;
cloud and shadow of cloud, wind and tide, tremor of night and
day. Journeying birds alight here and fly away again all unseen,
schools of great fish move beneath the waves, the surf flings its
spray against the sun.

HENRY BESTON
The Outermost House

Set foot in almost any New England coastal preserve, from the windblown tip of Cananicut Island to the stark volcanic cliffs of West Quoddy Head, and you'll find yourself wrapped in a kind of timeless magic, a spin of mystery and deep, rolling rhythms found nowhere else but at the edge of the sea. Although beauty abounds up and down the Atlantic coast, the individual threads that weave the seaside tapestries of New England are especially rich and diverse. Here are soft, crescent beaches and mammoth rock promontories; wave-worn spits of glacial debris and marshes wrapped in thick blankets of cordgrass; places where the tide rises three or four feet with a whisper, and others where it comes in with a rush, burying headlands ten times that high. And nearly everywhere there are birds—sanderlings, knots, dowitchers, piping plovers, and sandpipers scurrying along the sand and mud flats; willets, great blue herons, snowy egrets, and clapper rails feeding in the salt marshes. And always beautiful eiders—sometimes great rafts of them—bobbing up and down in the ocean waves.

With the possible exception of the mountains, no slice of New England environment seems to engender such a sense for the restless

143

dynamics of nature as does this coast. How fantastic it would be to have a high-speed film of the past 200 million years, the earth's oceans and landmasses swirling and brewing like thunderclouds in a summer storm. The North American continent ripped loose from its moorings with two other continental landmasses 150 million years ago, taking with it small chunks of Europe and Africa that would eventually become a part of the upper New England coast. Ever so slowly the mass drifted westward, finally arriving at its present position 80 million years later. Great submergences, uplifts, and erosions followed. Long swells of mountains were created and then destroyed again, picked apart grain after grain after grain, by the patient, probing fingers of water and wind.

But it was in much more recent geologic times, over the past couple million years, that the coast would be sculpted and scoured by at least four periods of advancing glacial ice. The last of these, known as the Wisconsin Ice Age, peaked about fifteen thousand to twenty thousand years ago. In New England the Wisconsin glaciers reached about as far south as present-day Long Island and Martha's Vineyard, where they dumped their upland cargo of rocks and gravel into a sinewy ridge line known as a terminal moraine. So enormous were these ice flows, many of them reaching thicknesses of more than five thousand feet, that parts of the land actually sunk two hundred to three hundred feet under the sheer weight of them.

This sinking of the land didn't necessarily mean that the sea rushed in to fill the low areas. So much water was held by these gargantuan Pleistocene popsicles that the ocean line along much of New England may have been more than two hundred feet lower than it is today. This line of course changed when the climate finally warmed, and all that ice began to melt. Tremendous rivers of water poured over the land, spreading thick layers of glacial debris and sediment all across the land. (This process is precisely how the upper reaches of Cape Cod were formed.) As the melt continued, the ocean waters rose higher and higher, submerging much of the northern New England coast in the process. With the weight of all that ice off its back, however, the landmass rebounded, and then, like a rubber band stretched past its resting point, resettled downward once again.

The result of the great uplifts, the outpourings of molten rock, the drift of tectonic plates, and the grind of glaciers was only the setting of the stage for what would become one of the richest braids of life to be found anywhere along the Atlantic. Fine-tuned by the climate, currents, and tidal flows, the northern offshore islands became rich seabird rookeries and breeding grounds for seals; the submerged banks from Maine to Cape Cod gave rise to tremendous populations of fish; the salt marshes and mud flats of Massachusetts sustained flock after flock of wading birds. Not to mention the whales and the harbor seals, the oysters, crabs, clams, squid, shrimp, periwinkles, barnacles, mussels, scallops, sea stars, chitons, nudibranches, and so on.

Although we'll be taking a closer look at many of these creatures in the walks that follow, perhaps we should give a little center-stage attention here to New England's most famous, and probably its most representative, ocean inhabitant, the American lobster. So abundant were lobsters in colonial times that they were considered a trash food, fit for little else but fertilizer and feed for dogs. Even so, beginning with a small fishery at Cape Cod that was established around 1800, it took less than a century for lobster populations to become severely depleted throughout New England coastal waters.

Anyone trying to figure out how to eat a lobster for the first time might come to the conclusion that the creature was put together in the midst of havoc and happenstance. In truth, though, this is a remarkably efficient bit of engineering. The protective shell of a lobster is made up of chiton and lime, which is fashioned into plates of various sizes and shapes—from a large, single piece covering the lobster's back to a series of flexible sheets that protect the abdomen. This outer skeleton has to be shed ("molted") as the animal grows, a process that will occur about two dozen times over five years— generally speaking, the amount of time necessary for a lobster to reach one pound. During these molting stages, which typically last about two weeks, a lobster will lay low in its ocean burrow until the new shell hardens enough to protect it from predators.

The lobster has ten legs (its claws are considered modified legs), and moves through the water using small oarlike devices located on the underside of its body. If you look at a lobster's claws, you'll notice that they are not the same size. The smaller of the two has sharp teeth, and is used to cut and rip fish into pieces, while the larger one is a crushing claw, employed to smash the shells of mussels and clams. Though a large lobster has few enemies, occasionally it will lose a claw in a fight. No problem. Lost claws, as well as other legs, are replaced over a period of three to four molts.

While a one-pound lobster is typical dinner fare, it's hardly as big as these guys get. They are actually capable of living for a hundred years, and can reach the kind of proportions that B-grade monster movies portray. One specimen caught off the coast of Nova Scotia in 1977 weighed more than forty-four pounds, and measured 3½ feet from claw to tail! Large specimens are not often encountered, however, since, with more than 2 million traps off the coast of New England alone, very few have the chance to grow to any size. Today, in fact, a mature adult lobster has only little better than a 10 percent chance of escaping the dinner table, a statistic suggesting that the species has an absolutely unheard-of ability to maintain its numbers in the face of heavy predation.

Though most people prize lobster for its taste, James Joyce suggested that French poet and playwright Gerard de Nerval found this hearty crustacean to be, of all things, an ideal pet! As the story goes, Nerval was spotted one day leading a lobster through Paris' Palais-Royal gardens at the end of a blue silk ribbon. When quizzed about this by a baffled spectator, he matter-of-factly informed the fellow that a lobster is no more ridiculous a pet than is a dog. He went on to explain that they're actually very peaceful and serious companions, who never invade your privacy or nag you by barking. "What's more," he added, "they know the secrets of the sea."

Southern New England

BRIDE BROOK

Distance: 1.6 miles
Location: Rocky Neck State Park. From Interstate 95, take exit
72 to Connecticut Highway 156 and head east, following the
signs into Rocky Neck State Park. Once inside the park, follow
the day-use road for just over 1.5 miles. Just past a bridge crossing Bride Brook, you'll come to a large parking area on the right.
Our trail takes off from the far northwest corner of this parking
lot, near a group of picnic tables, and is marked by a wooden post
with a white blaze on it.

A walk in the deep woods of Rocky Neck, or a quiet moment spent
beside the thick carpets of marsh grass that cradle the weary wind-
ings of Bride Brook, are worlds away from the jumble of volleyballs
and bikinis and baking bodies typically strewn across this beautiful
pocket beach. (*Pocket beach* is the geological term used to describe
sandy, crescent-shaped beaches framed on either side by a prominent
headland. Rocky Neck is one of the finest examples in the state.)
When you've heard too many rock-and-roll countdowns, gotten one
too many whiffs of coconut oil, slip up this gentle trail and hang out
for a while with the bitterns, snowy egrets, cormorants, and king-
fishers.

   After only a few steps down the path you'll cross a rich tidal
flowage. Immediately to your right, on the top of a large elevated

147

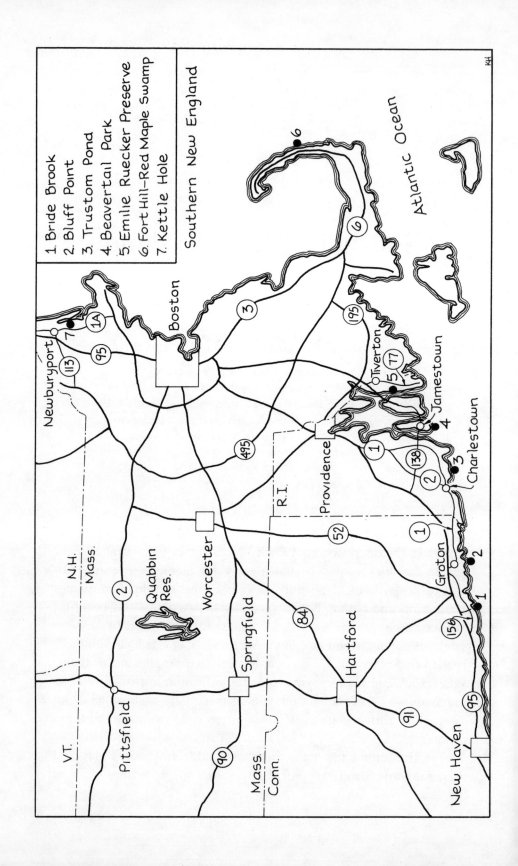

Southern New England

1. Bride Brook
2. Bluff Point
3. Trustom Pond
4. Beavertail Park
5. Emilie Ruecker Preserve
6. Fort Hill–Red Maple Swamp
7. Kettle Hole

Atlantic Ocean

Boston

Newburyport

Pittsfield

Worcester

Springfield

Hartford

New Haven

Providence

Quabbin Res.

Tiverton

Jamestown

Charlestown

Groton

VT.
N.H.
Mass.
Mass.
Conn.
R.I.

platform, is a big, beautiful osprey nest. Osprey are experts at building substantial nests, the male collecting most of the twigs and small branches that form the exterior of the structure, while the female gathers the mosses, grass, and bark used for the lining. Not long ago, high concentrations of DDT in the fish that osprey feed on nearly brought about the demise of this magnificent bird. The poison altered the shell structure of the egg, making it so fragile that it broke when the female tried to incubate it. Unlike some other species, osprey do not lay a new clutch of eggs if their first one is destroyed.

If the tide is out during your visit, take a look in the pockets of mud here for tracks of raccoon, whose forefoot prints are easily recognizable by their resemblance to the human hand.

On the far side of this marsh the path plunges back into a tangle of red maple, highbush blueberry, and black oak, as well as an abundance of Connecticut's state flower, the mountain laurel. Mountain laurel sometimes grows in extremely dense clusters (which some locals call "laurel hells"), and may reach heights of 12 to 15 feet. In winter these thickets are frequented by deer, who browse on the leaves. They also provide excellent protection for a variety of small mammals.

At 0.25 mile you'll come to a fork in the trail, where you should take the fainter, unblazed right branch toward the edge of Bride Brook. From here the path winds along the water's edge, past thick clusters of sweet pepperbush, bittersweet, and sassafras. Be sure to pause at breaks in the vegetation and make a careful scan of Bride Brook. Here you may see a marsh hawk, or even a belted kingfisher making loop cruises of its stream-bank territory, looking for a fish dinner. Just as common is the snowy egret, its spindly legs flashing as it sprints through the shallows in a mad dash for minnows.

One of the best views will be found at just under 0.5 mile, at a place where the trail seems to dwindle under the onslaught of shrub growth. Those here primarily for the Bride Brook show may want to turn around at this point. The more adventurous can pluck their way along the pathway for another 0.3 mile to a beautiful garden of cinnamon, hayscented, and Christmas ferns, framed on the east by dense thickets of witch-hazel, winterberry, dogwood, hickory, bittersweet, and rose.

Belted Kingfisher

If you do decide to follow this path to, or even beyond, the fern garden mentioned above, you'll be rewarded with a feeling of being really wrapped in wildness—that somehow you've penetrated a kind of inner sanctum of peace and quiet, where nature stands undiluted by the handiworks of humans.

Only for a tiny fraction of the long history of European settlement along this coast has there been any kind of ethic calling for the careful conservation of resources. The wolf began to disappear early, especially once the 1647 legislature approved a bounty of 10 shillings for every one taken. Bobcat and eastern mountain lion weren't far behind. The rich abundance of shellfish was also beginning to thin in some places along the coast by the middle of the seventeenth century. (At one point the town fathers of Fair Haven issued a complete ban on the harvest of oysters there, exceptions to be made for pregnant women who had sudden cravings for them.) Snowy egrets disappeared for a time in the late 1800s, overhunted for their feathers. The deer mouse is gone, as is the peregrine falcon and the long-eared owl. At last count there were three known barn owls left in the state, less than a dozen great blue herons, and one or two lonely short-nose sturgeons. Writing about the effects of war on the country-side in *The Red Badge of Courage*, author Stephen Crane said that it was

150

a surprise "that Nature had gone tranquilly on with her golden process in the midst of so much devilment." During most of the nineteenth century, the same could be said for times of peace.

It's good to know the calm of such places as this one, to feel your imagination opening again at the sight of soaring red-tailed hawks, or at the soft flash of a startled white-tailed deer. Yet isn't it remarkable how quickly we can forget the value of preserving such connections once they are out of reach of our everyday lives?

Absence, it would seem, can also make the heart grow harder.

Snowy Egret

BLUFF POINT

Distance: 4.2 miles
Location: Bluff Point State Park. From the town of Groton, Connecticut, head south on Depot Road, which takes off of U.S. Highway 1, 0.3 mile west of the Connecticut Highway 117 junction. In less than 0.5 mile you'll pass beneath a railroad bridge, at which point the road turns to dirt. About 0.2 mile further is a picnic area at the northern edge of Bluff Point State Park. Park here, and begin your walk by heading south past the closed gate.

Bluff Point is an especially beautiful slice of southern New England. Other than a little ear pollution from the airport across the Poquonock River, this nearly eight-hundred-acre parcel is one of only a couple remaining "unsaturated" pieces of real estate of any size on the entire Connecticut coast. Stitched across the length and breadth of the preserve is a delightful mix of vines, hardwoods, and conifers sprouting out of the bedrock, framed to the south by a shoreline peppered with great and little blue herons, mute swans, snowy egrets, buffleheads, mallards, and scaups. During winter, in fact, you can find scaups here by the thousands. It's great entertainment to watch them making dive after dive in search of a seafood dinner of crabs and barnacles, a feast they often combine with a cool, fresh salad of sea lettuce.

Into the walk 0.1 mile you'll reach a fork in the road. We'll be coming back on the left branch, but for now stay to the right, past fine mats of strawberry and Canada mayflower. A short distance later you'll reach a small meadow studded with oaks, cradled on three sides by an impenetrable weave of pepperbush, bittersweet, greenbrier, honeysuckle, grape, black raspberry, and rose. These tangles provide excellent food and cover for a host of birds; keep your eyes peeled for mockingbirds, catbirds, and bluebirds.

At 0.5 mile take the grassy path that branches to the right of the main road. This less-used walkway will take you along the quiet reaches of the Poquonock River, through a young forest of cherry, oak, and redcedar. Be very quiet and you may spot white-tailed deer nibbling on the bark, buds, or leaves of these young trees. This place is also good for finding sassafras, a tree that produces some of its leathery leaves in the shape of mittens. Sassafras root has a long

152

history of medicinal use for everything from purifying the blood to curing syphilis. For a brief time, in fact, it was second only to tobacco as a colonial export. But this little tree's links to humankind hardly ended with the advent of the industrial age. As late as the 1950s it was used as an antiseptic in dentistry, as well as for flavoring everything from toothpaste to root beer. Unfortunately, 25 years ago the USDA decided that the safrole contained in sassafras oil was a potential carcinogen, thus bringing to an end its use in commercial products.

A break in the vegetation occurs in 0.75 mile, revealing lovely views of the Poquonock River estuary. In just another 0.1 mile you'll see a small path to the right leading to a grassy glade on the river shore—a perfect place for watching swans, herons, and various other water birds that reside here during various times of the year. The nesting boxes you see on short posts are for wood ducks, while the much taller platforms are for osprey.

In another 0.1 mile you'll veer to the left, following a well-worn path back to the main road. Soon fine views of the coastline will open up, and in 1.6 miles, just past a boardwalk path that will take you to Bluff Point Beach, the trail splits. Stay right, and climb onto the headland of Bluff Point itself. From here you can see Fishers Island ahead and slightly to the right, and, further to the left, Rhode

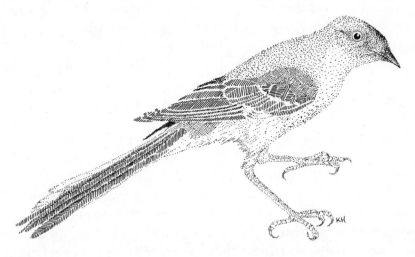

Mockingbird

153

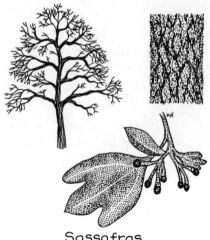

Sassafras

Island's Watch Hill, the latter used as an observation point by soldiers during the Civil War.

Continue to make your way eastward around this small peninsula of gneiss rock, past beach plum, salt spray rose, bayberry, and beach pea. At 1.7 miles take the right fork in the road, and proceed along the rocky beach. In 2.1 miles you'll join a well-used, grassy roadway. Continue up a gentle climb, past a small trail taking off to the right to an intersection at 2.8 miles. Turn right here, and then stay to the left. This path winds gently through a pleasant blend of forest and birdsong, finally arriving back at the main road, where you'll take one last right turn toward the parking lot.

Bluff Point is a frayed but beautiful thread of nature that can lead your imagination all the way back to the days when the first Englishmen stood here and marveled at the rich tapestry before them—a far cry not only from the lands they had left on the other side of the Atlantic but also from the Massachusetts colonies that they abandoned in order to take up a life of new opportunities in the verdant valley of the Connecticut River. With fearless Puritan Thomas Hooker in the lead, in 1636 his small "Newtown Contingent" of pioneers took their guns, cooking pots, and 160 head of cattle out of Cambridge on a 100-mile trek into the wilderness. Here, then, were pioneers, certainly as spirited and tenacious as any who would head to the Far West more than two hundred years later. In fact, besides general complaints about crowded conditions in the Massachusetts Colony, Hooker's petition to the Massachusetts court for new lands for his followers included the rather frank admission that they needed to leave because it was "the strong bent of their spirits to move thither."

And much of what those spirits found must have amazed them. Besides trees of tremendous stature there were birds and mammals beyond counting: wild turkeys, quail, partridge, otter, mink, deer, fox, and mountain lion. Even wolves were fairly abundant, and in 1647 a bounty of 10 shillings was offered for each.

Ambling through these woods very early on some quiet October morning, the chill of autumn nipping at your nose, those days, those adventures, may seem somehow closer than they ever have before.

TRUSTOM POND

Distance: 1.9 miles

Location: From the intersection of Rhode Island Highway 2 and U.S. Highway 1 near Charleston, head east on U.S. 1 for 3.7 miles, and turn right (south) onto the Moonstone Beach Road. Proceed down this road for 1.1 miles, and then make a right onto Matunuck School Road. The parking area and trailhead for the refuge is 0.7 mile down this road, on the left.

Despite the rush of growth that has overwhelmed, indeed nearly overcome, the natural areas of the southern New England coast, there are still a couple of jewels left in Rhode Island that are perfect for a slow, sweet saunter virtually any month of the year. It seems appropriate that in the state founded by Roger Williams, one of the very few New England leaders who displayed genuine respect for the rights of other humans ("Nature knows no difference between European and American [Indian]," he once said), that today there's a place like Trustom Pond, whose management reflects at least some measure of respect and admiration for the vast underpinnings of nature.

Our trail takes off from the far side of the parking area, leading quickly to an interpretive display that will tell you a bit about the history and nature of the area. We'll be following the trail marked

155

by a sign displaying the profile of a hiker. At a T intersection not far from the interpretive signs you'll take a right, and immediately afterward a left into an open field of alfalfa, flushed with the whistles of meadowlarks. The females of this species weave beautiful dome-shaped grass nests in the hollows of small depressions on the ground. This preference for ground-floor living, often in a farmer's field, leaves meadowlarks somewhat vulnerable both to trampling and to predators.

At the south end of these fields is a good example of how nature would manage things if left to its own devices. Shadbush, honeysuckle, viburnum, blueberry, and raspberry are all doing their best to lay rights to this sandy, acidic soil. The cloak of greenery grows steadily in intensity as you walk on, and by 0.3 mile you'll be totally immersed in beautiful thickets of cherry, scrub oak, red maple, grape, apple, and arrowwood. Like most of the habitats at Trustom Pond, this one has no shortage of bird life, including orioles, robins, towhees, catbirds, brown thrashers, and sparrows, which together weave a magical web of flashing wings and trilling birdsong.

At 0.65 mile you'll reach a T intersection. Take a left here, following a narrow peninsula of land to Osprey Point. At the tip of this peninsula, wrapped in a blanket of pepperbush and framed by spartina grass, is a small observation tower surrounded on three sides by the brackish waters of Trustom Pond. A long, narrow barrier beach completely separates this pond from Block Island Sound, although

Sweet Pepperbush

156

each spring during high water refuge managers cut a small channel through the sand to help replenish the nutrients of the pond.

The birds that will be available for your viewing depends, of course, on what time of year you visit. Safe bets are mute swans, Canada and snow geese, teals, pintails, mallards, wood ducks, terns, cormorants, egrets, and great blue herons. True to the name of Osprey Point, you'll also have a good chance of seeing one of these graceful raptors hovering over the pond looking for a fresh fish dinner, while a short distance away, red-tailed hawks will be scanning the meadows for mice.

On your return, stay to the left at the first intersection, which will take you along the western half of the loop trail back to the parking area. Here again is a marvelous, almost endless variety of plant communities, each nook and cranny brimming with everything from catbrier and scrub oak to fox grape and Austrian pine.

BEAVERTAIL PARK

Distance: 1.5 miles
Location: From Rhode Island State Highway 138 South (Wolcott Street) beside the Jamestown docks, go approximately 0.5 mile and turn right. This road leads to Beavertail Road, which will take you directly into Beavertail Park. Once inside the park, continue around the tip of the peninsula past the light-house, and park at parking lot 3. Begin walking south along the rocky shoreline toward the lighthouse.

If you relish a surging sea, the somber song of the foghorn, and the sight of terns spinning cartwheels in the salt air, then Beavertail is your kind of place. This particular walk is best suited to more intrepid walkers who are willing to work their way along the braid of sod cliffs and somewhat precarious bedrock ledges that rise and fall along the outer perimeter of the park. (There are easier footpaths located further inland.) If possible, plan to take a little extra time for exploring the shallow tidal pools and inlets you'll find along the way.

157

A short distance south of the parking area you'll pass the Beavertail Light, constructed in 1749 as the third lighthouse in New England, and the fourth to be erected anywhere in America. There's no question that this lighthouse, a celebrated sentinel of Conanicut Island, has seen its share of excitement. It was burned by the British in 1775, and then rebuilt 11 years later on funds approved by President George Washington. The lightkeeper's dwelling collapsed under strong winds in 1815, was swept out to sea by spring ice floes on the Providence River in 1875, and damaged once again during a hurricane in the fall of 1938. It was this 1938 hurricane, by the way, that exposed the foundation of the original 1749 tower, which you can see just to the south of where the current lighthouse now stands. (Though the Conanicut light is old, the idea of signaling ships by the use of lights is ancient. Most historians credit the Egyptians for coming up with the notion, which they accomplished by lighting fires on top of specially constructed towers. They were also responsible for the tallest lighthouse ever constructed. Built around 250 B.C., the Pharos of Alexandria stood more than four hundred feet high, and was used off and on to guide ships for nearly fifteen hundred years.)

Long before there were any guiding lights here, the seaman William Kidd, or, as you may know him, Captain Kidd, made a call here to his friend Thomas Paine. Aware that the captain had been angrily declared a pirate by the English government (somewhat unjustly, some still maintain), Paine tried to dissuade Kidd from making his planned landing in Boston the following day. Unfortunately, Kidd dismissed the warning. He was immediately nabbed in Bean Town and shipped back to England, where he was hanged. Hardly was the poor old pirate cold in his grave before people began writing all sorts of tales and songs about his supposed exploits. One of these ditties, titled "The Ballad of Captain Kidd," was for years sung by schoolchildren on both sides of the Atlantic.

Make your way round the tip of the island past tufts of English plantain and pasture rising toward the more protected eastern flank of the peninsula. In winter a remarkable variety of seabirds can be found on this more protected side of the island, including scoters, eiders, brants, and scaups. As you make your way northward, below you will be an abundance of two common intertidal plants. The first is bladder rockweed (sometimes called bladder wrack), which can be

Scaup

easily identified by the pairs of air bladders attached to its fronds. With these floats the plant can stay nearer to the surface of the water where the sunlight is stronger, thereby producing more food for itself. The only thing wrong with this ingenious adaptation is that these air pods tend to act as handles for the fingers of the surf to grab onto, sometimes with enough force to rip the plant from its moorings. To compensate, bladder rockweed grows fewer air chambers in exposed, rough water sites than it does in more protected locations.

The other common resident here is Irish moss, a beautiful, multibranched red to purple algae that sometimes forms thick, dense mats along the low tide line. This species is as tough as can be found on the Atlantic coast, able to withstand the assaults of the strongest waves. With the possible exception of the blue mussel, once established Irish moss will ward off invasion by virtually all competitors. This plant, by the way, is the source of carragheen, a substance used today for everything from a stabilizer for salad dressings and chocolate milk to a thickener for paints, pies, and toothpaste.

Into the walk 0.3 mile you'll find lovely spatters of yellow buttercups, as well as tufts of horsetail and redcedar. Ahead you'll spot a fine inlet carved into the rock, which at low tide is lined with long piles of blue mussel shells. To say that blue mussels are prolific is an understatement, considering that a single female may spawn more than 10 million eggs. This high reproductive rate is meant to overcome the fact that mussels in all stages of development are prey to a host of creatures, including starfish and crabs.

The larvae of these creatures settle onto the seafloor at the will of the waves, and, during the summer months, grow into immature mussels that then migrate up the tidal zone using a special "foot," eventually fastening themselves to the surface of a shoreline rock. Special protein threads produced in the mussel's foot—as tough and resilient as any synthetic fiber—are what allow this anchoring to take place. If the rock the mussel chooses proves to be in a bad location (not enough food, for instance), it can easily detach itself from its life lines and relocate to a better location.

At about 0.6 mile, near a small freshwater rivulet, you'll reach a tall wooden post on your right. Proceed up the shoreline as far as you wish, but on your return trip head east at this post along a small grassy pathway back to the entrance road. You'll find a wonderful array of bird life wrapped in these thickets, including flickers, sparrows, meadowlarks, and robins. What a delight to hear their morning and evening songfests, especially wrapped in the slow, soothing drum of ocean waves.

EMILIE RUECKER PRESERVE

Distance: 1.4 miles

Location: From the intersection of Rhode Island highways 77 and 177 in Tiverton, head south on Connecticut 77 for 1.7 miles, to Seapowet Avenue, which takes off from the right (west) side of the road. The parking area and trailhead are 0.25 mile down Seapowet Avenue, on the right.

Given the right location, it's amazing how much natural beauty can be folded into 50 acres. Emilie Ruecker's farm, which she donated to the Massachusetts Audubon Society in 1965, is definitely the right location. Besides being a haven at one time of the year or another for well over a hundred species of birds, there are beautiful wildflowers here, which lend soft splashes of color to the refuge from spring to fall.

The walk begins by heading north along the yellow trail, where you'll find lovely mats of cultivated lily of the valley. This hearty, very adaptable plant was brought from Europe to grace American gardens, but it wasted no time in breaking free from such confines to colonize the surrounding countryside. For centuries the white, heavily perfumed flowers of this plant have symbolized pureness, a notion that eventually led to their being used in bridal bouquets. This link to purity is also reflected in another common nickname for the plant, "our-lady's-tears," which is an Old World reference to the Virgin Mary. In fact, you will see lily of the valley in a great many European paintings of the Holy Mother. Although normally considered "poisonous," extracts of this plant were long used by folk healers to strengthen the heartbeat, as well as to ease the discomfort of gout.

The path will carry you on a gentle saunter past clusters of pine, honeysuckle, and spruce, many of which will be washed in birdsong. Keep an ear cocked for northern orioles, cardinals, hermit thrushes, Carolina wrens, and cedar waxwings. Cedar waxwings, with their wiry song of "seeee," are a very social lot, in late summer forming great berry brigades that scour the countryside for edible fruits. Adults have a special pouch in their throat that allows them to store a couple dozen small berries, carry them back to the nest, and then regurgitate them one at a time into the mouths of their ever-hungry youngsters. One of the more amazing behaviors of cedar waxwings is when half a dozen of the birds line up on a tree branch or

Carolina Wren

161

Cedar Waxwing

fence rail and pass berries down the row from one bird to the next, until one bird finally decides to end the game by eating the handoff.

Turn left at the blue trail, and then almost immediately, take another left past black cherry trees, Canada mayflower, and star-flower. This path will take you across a small bridge at 0.17 mile and then, if you stay to the right, you will travel counterclockwise around a small peninsula jutting into the salty waters of the Sakonnet River, much of it covered with thickets of ground juniper, bayberry, and shadbush. (The name *shadbush* refers to the fact that clusters of delicate white flowers bloom in the spring about the time that shad are swimming upstream to spawn.) As you make your way westward along this peninsula keep your eyes open for the glossy ibis, black-crowned night heron, great and little blue heron, and snowy egret. Like many beautiful water birds, snowy egrets almost became extinct during the last half of the nineteenth century when they were being killed by the thousands for their feathers, which at the time were a popular decoration for women's hats.

When you get back to the yellow trail, take a left, and loop clockwise around another small peninsula, this one rimmed by cord-grass, rushes, spike grass, seaside goldenrod, and saltwort. Besides

Black-crowned Night Heron

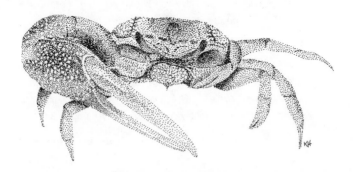

Fiddler Crab

clams and mussels, there's an abundance of fiddler crabs rushing back and forth across these mud flats, each with a single large claw held aloft, the scene looking rather like an annual convention of lunatic bass fiddlers.

Leave the shore and head south along the yellow trail. In the open, grassy areas near the southern rim of the loop keep your eyes out for the beautiful swamp buttercup. Soon after you complete the loop and begin heading south on the main stem of the yellow trail again, you'll see a red-blazed path taking off to the left. Passing by a beautiful cluster of mature sugar maples, the red trail sinks deeper and deeper into a hushed woodland of alder, arrowwood viburnum, oak, and hickory—a great stretch of path to see or hear woodcocks, olive-sided flycatchers, redstarts, and yellow-rumped warblers.

At 1.4 miles you'll reach an intersection. Continue straight along a rather faint trail back to the parking area. (The left branch will take you back to Seapowet Avenue, just a short distance east of the trailhead.)

FORT HILL–RED MAPLE SWAMP

Distance: 2 miles

Location: Cape Cod National Seashore, Massachusetts. From Exit 13 on U.S. Highway 6, continue north on U.S. 6 for approximately 2 miles to Governor Prince Road, and turn right. Park at the first parking lot on the left, just across the road from the Penniman House historic site. You'll find our trail behind the Penniman House, taking off on the right side of the barn.

With the landless gull, that at sunset folds her wings and is rocked to sleep between billows; so at nightfall, the Nantucketer, out of sight of land, furls his sails, and lays him to his rest, while under his very pillow rush herds of walruses and whales.

HERMAN MELVILLE
Moby Dick

Long before Edward Penniman, whose stately 1868 house marks the beginning of our walk, left Eastham at the tender age of 11 to seek a living on whaling ships, southeast New England had established itself as one of the premier deep-water whaling centers of the world.

Crews from this region would literally roam the world in search of whales, often making a spring-to-autumn run behind mass migrations that stretched all the way from Brazil to Greenland. Of special delight to New England whalers were the sperm whales, much coveted for the rich pools of spermaceti in their heads. Spermaceti was a kind of waxy oil that, besides being used in lamps, was added to tallow to make longer-burning, nearly smokeless candles. What's more, the ivory teeth found in the lower jaw of the sperm whale were highly valued for use in scrimshaw.

Once a whaling crew sighted a whale (which, yes, was often announced with a booming "Thar she blows!"), one of several small whale boats was quickly lowered off the mother ship. Into this craft climbed six hearty men, none of whom wasted any time laying his muscled arms into the rhythm of rowing, every mighty sweep of the oars pushing them closer and closer to a sounding whale. Once in position, one of the men would plunge a harpoon into the whale's side. Attached to the other end of that harpoon was a 1,300-foot coil of rope that the crew members tried to carefully measure out—as carefully as one could measure out a rope attached to a panicking 60-foot-long whale making a violent, life or death dash for freedom. It was this boisterous, hell-bent pull across the sea in a whaling boat that would one day come to be known around the world as a "Nantucket sleigh ride."

Just past the barn behind the Penniman House the trail will enter an old orchard, now a cool, almost impenetrable thicket of black locust, poison ivy, black cherry, multiflora rose, redcedar, and black oak. In just under 0.3 mile, however, you'll suddenly come out into a sunny, open area at the base of Fort Hill (one of three grassy hummocks so named on the Cape). On the short climb to the top you'll pass fine mats of milkweed, Queen Anne's lace, and chicory, whose beautiful blue flowers open at just about the same time each day. While you may be aware that the young leaves and roots of chicory have long been used for seasonings and coffee substitutes, the plant has also had a long history of use by herbal healers. The Romans used chicory to treat disorders of the liver, while people of the Middle Ages made poultices from the leaves to bring down the swelling of bruised muscles.

At the top of Fort Hill is a magnificent view, one of the finest in all the Cape. To the east is the edge of Nauset Marsh, a mix of

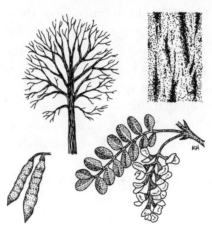

Black Locust

golden salt-meadow grass laced with long, twisted braids of tidal streams and mud flats, all bound by the blue arms of the Atlantic.

As lush as this land may look now, it was not always this way. The Plymouth colonists who founded Eastham in 1646—one of the first settlements on the Cape—had a fiery determination to subdue the land, just as the book of Genesis had commanded them. In remarkably little time their axes had cleared the forest to make room for crops, and hundreds of cattle had been turned out on the lush salt-grass meadows. Unfortunately, the layer of topsoil that overlay these sand plains, which had given rise to the illusion that this was an inexhaustible land of plenty, was a frightfully thin one. Despite laws handed down by the Massachusetts General Court prohibiting grazing and requiring the planting of beach grass in devastated areas, by the late 1700s, the plains of Eastham were worn out. "What was once a fertile spot," wrote one traveler to this area in 1794, "has become prey to the winds, and lies buried under a barren heap of sand."

Make your way down Fort Hill, past pokeweed, black cherry, black locust, redcedar, Japanese honeysuckle, and salt spray rose. At 0.5 mile you'll reach a fork in the trail, with a short spur taking off to the right to the edge of a tidal stream. Stay to the left here and continue 0.4 more mile to a shelter at Indian Rock. Be sure to pause here at least long enough to read the collection of interpretive signs, which will offer you some good natural and cultural history of the coast.

Straight ahead, about 0.2 mile past Indian Rock, you'll reach

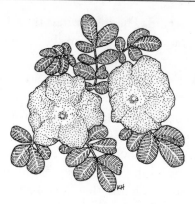

Salt Spray Rose

a pathway taking off to the left into Red Maple Swamp. The board-walk through this swamp of second-growth maple clusters is one of the most engaging sections of trail to be found anywhere on the Cape. While I found the forest especially lovely, sporting a kind of Garden of Eden lushness, those looking through a different set of glasses might find it an unsettling place, a backdrop for a chilling spook story. Many of the trees have great gnarled trunks with arthritic-looking branches, held to the sky like a huddle of old men begging the heavens to deliver them from the squeezing onslaught of fox grape and moonseed vines.

Also along this portion of our walk are wonderful clusters of sweet pepperbush, elder, catbrier, netted chain fern, bayberry, baked-apple bush, arrowwood, and swamp azalea. Everywhere you look, in fact, are mats of leaves of one sort or another. At 1.3 miles you'll reach a junction with a path going off to the right. Stay to the left, continuing to wind through the hush of the red maple forest. You'll meet this trail again 0.45 mile later, this time on the right, so be sure you stay left. Finally, at 1.9 miles you'll be at yet another junction where you'll stay to the right, almost immediately after which you'll take one more right back to the parking lot.

This latter section of trail through the Red Maple Swamp is an especially good walk to take on days when the Cape is wrapped in fog. Fog, incidentally, provides a significant amount of the moisture that many of these plants need to survive. According to Indian legend, the fogs of Cape Cod are no simple condensation. One day while returning from a successful raid against the Nausets, the great warrior Maushop heard the death wail of his wife wafting through the forest. Running to her side, he discovered that the Great Devil Bird from the South Sea had swooped out of the sky and made a meal out of his beautiful 16-year-old son.

Enraged, Maushop set across the waters toward what is now Martha's Vineyard, calling on the heavens to lend him the strength to slay the evil bird giant. Finding the monster asleep in a great oak tree, the bones of Indian children scattered around its trunk, Maushop crept into the branches, raised his tomahawk, and in one great swoop killed the bird. On the way home, Maushop paused on the island for a smoke, but found that his tobacco was so wet from his earlier ocean crossing that it would not burn. Covering the wet tobacco with pokeweed, Maushop was finally able to light his pipe, which burned with great, thick clouds of smoke. So dense did it become, in fact, that the morning breezes eventually carried it across the sound to Maushop's village, which his people immediately recognized as a sign that he had triumphed over the great monster bird.

And always after that, whenever a bank of summer fog drifted onto the Cape from across the sound, Indian children would hear of the great bravery of Maushop, and how once again, the smoke from his pipe was coming to them in the arms of the wind.

KETTLE HOLE

Distance: 0.6 mile

Location: Parker River National Wildlife Refuge. Traveling north on Interstate 95 north of Boston, take the exit for Massachusetts Highway 113, and then proceed eastward, following the signs for Massachusetts Highway 1A. In the town of Newburyport you'll see signs directing you to Plum Island and the Parker River Refuge. Once you pass the main entrance gate, proceed south and park at lot 3, located on the east (left) side of the road. Begin walking on the boardwalk that heads eastward toward the beach.

Note: Visitor hours at Parker River are one-half hour before sunrise to one-half hour after sunset. Because on summer days the refuge often fills to capacity by 9:00 A.M., you would do well to rouse yourself for a dawn visit.

This 5,000-acre reach of barrier beach, stitched with forest and marsh, capped by a long, brown tumble of sand dunes, is one of the most beautiful slices of natural coast left anywhere in southern New

England. Three hundred species of birds frequent this refuge during various times of the year. In the cool of November you may find more than twenty thousand ducks alone, as well as great clatters of snow and Canada geese, longspurs settling in from the Arctic, and mixed groups of pipets and snow buntings cartwheeling on the autumn winds.

The only way to traverse the trails and beaches of Parker River is very slowly and very deliberately. There is a whole other world hidden in these thickets of heather and salt spray rose, and in the long sweeps of salt-meadow grass and switchgrass.

About ten yards down the boardwalk that leaves eastward from parking lot 3, you'll see a small pathway taking off to the left into a tangle of barberry, rose, and bayberry. (It's the waxy coating on the fruits of this latter plant that is boiled off and then molded into bayberry candles.) Just beyond this fringe is the oldest forest on Plum Island—a lovely mix of aspen, maple, alder, black cherry, and oak, much of it bedecked in a lush cloak of grape and poison ivy. The reason this forest is so lush is because it lies in a very protected depression—sometimes referred to as a blowout—that was carved by the wind in the back side of a large dune field. Out of the stinging reach of sea and sand it has been able to enjoy the kind of steady growth not possible elsewhere on the island.

Hardly will you have entered this woodland when you'll leave it again, bearing to the right up the crest of a small dune. From here you'll have wonderful views across the entrance road into the marsh that cradles the Plum Island River. Descending from this hummock you'll hit an east-west trail, where you'll turn right. This route is simply a "back road" to the beach. Notice how the diversity of plant life has decreased dramatically from what grew in the protected pocket you passed through earlier. Only the most tenacious plants can play the game of life in this uncertain world of shifting sands. In the depressions on the back side of the large foredune that parallels the shore are clusters of beach plum, poison ivy, golden heather, and the leathery leaves of bearberry. Colonists, by the way, often stretched their tobacco supply by mixing bearberry leaves into it, while some coastal Indians used the plant as a treatment for bladder infections.

Once you top that tenuous wall of foredune and stand in full face of the sea, very little is left of the plant kingdom. Still hanging on

169

are clumps of beach pea and seaside goldenrod, but soon even these dwindle away. From here on the world belongs to American beach grass, a plant that not only doesn't mind sand but in fact requires a three- or four-inch layer of it even to survive. This blanket of sand stimulates the beach grass to send out horizontal root runners. Every ten inches or so these rhizomes sink another set of roots and then pop out another cluster of leaves—a kind of root race to grow just fast enough to stay one step ahead of the blowing sands. The great thing about beach grass is that once a sizable colony of it is established, it has a remarkable stabilizing effect on shifting dunes. When the colonists' cattle overgrazed the native beach grass at Truro on Cape Cod, the dunes immediately began to overtake the town's meadows. In 1739, the general court passed a law giving full protection to these areas. Yet even with this protection, along with vigorous grass-planting efforts each spring, the settlers were never able to fully recover all the acres they had lost.

Finally there is the beach itself, the final fringe of a peninsula that was fashioned by wind and waves, and great layers of rocky debris carried to the sea from the mainland first by tongues of glacial ice, and later by meltwater. Perhaps at no place more than a barrier beach–dune complex like this one do the dynamics of nature seem more obvious, or the exact borders of an ecosystem more uncertain.

Northern New England

ODIORNE POINT

Distance: 0.3 mile
Location: Odiorne Point State Park. Located southeast of the
city of Portsmouth, New Hampshire, near the village of Rye.
From the intersection of U.S. Highway 1 and New Hampshire
1A, follow Highway 1A south for approximately 4 miles to the
entrance of Odiorne Point State Park. Our footpath takes off to
the north from a paved road connecting the parking area to the
Russell B. Tobey Visitor Center. The trailhead is just west of the
visitor center.

Much has happened since Scotsman David Thompson dropped
anchor that spring of 1623 at the mouth of the Piscataqua River and
discharged his hopeful settlers—along with their miscellany of cooking kettles, tools, seeds, gunpowder, rope, and fishing nets—onto
this windswept neck of land, thereby beginning the first European
settlement (Pannaway Plantation) in what is now the state of New
Hampshire.

The name of this preserve, which is the last significant stretch
of undeveloped shore in the state, was taken from settler John
Odiorne. Odiorne began farming and fishing on this point in 1660.
Fully ten generations of his descendents, covering a period of more
than two hundred seventy-five years, continued to be a part of the
fabric of life on this rocky seacoast, their legacy broken only by the

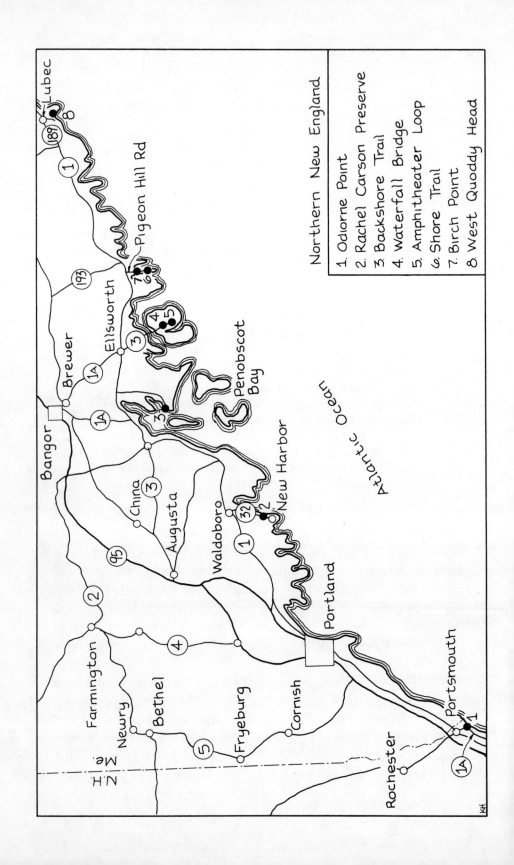

onset of World War II, when the U.S. government purchased the land and turned it into a coastal defense installation to protect the naval shipyard at Portsmouth Harbor. Almost overnight, a lazy mosaic of woodland and garden yielded to 16-inch guns and 155-millimeter antiaircraft cannon. The remains of concrete bunkers stand today alongside faint remnants of the pathways, gates, and fountains of the genteel—odd bedfellows indeed.

Either before you begin this walk or after you've finished, be sure to stop at the excellent nature facility and bookstore located inside the Russell B. Tobey Visitor Center. The staff is very good at answering the questions that a visit to such a magical slice of seacoast tends to engender. Our walk, which is really a free-form ramble up the coast, begins on a trail located just west of the Visitor Center. A short distance after leaving the paved road to head north you'll arrive at the edge of the coast. Stay right, passing rocky bluffs fringed by roses, sumac, alder, Scotch pine, tansy, and St. Johnswort, soon arriving at a fine collection of tidal pools. You can continue up the coast further, past a pebble beach to the tip of Frost Point. For this walk, though, let's concentrate on the remarkable mysteries held in these salty pools.

Besides the obvious need to watch where you walk in a tidal area, please remember that all creatures you handle should be returned to the exact place in which you found them. Living on the edge, so to speak, is a very precarious business. Just turning over a rock, for instance, exposes its residents to predators as well as to the drying effects of the sun—conditions that can lead to their early demise.

Many of the creatures at the edge of the sea are so good at camouflage that you can look them right in the oyster and not realize they're there. One of the best things about tidal pool watching, in fact, is that it forces you to really slow down, to focus on tiny things, slices of the world far smaller and more delicate than the broad brush strokes that paint our everyday lives. Let's begin by looking at a few of the more common, easy-to-see residents of Odiorne Point.

Of course there are barnacles here, those ivory-colored, volcano-shaped buttons you see glued fast to seaside rocks. This relative of the shrimp was in its larval stage a swimmer, though it soon traded in the life of a drifter for that of a homebody, constructing its

173

rigid house by secreting calcium carbonate plates and cementing them to a rock, ship, lobster trap, pier, and so on. (This "cement" the barnacle uses has as much holding power per square inch as any substance known to humans, a fact of which ship owners, who spend thousands of dollars scraping barnacles off their hulls each year, are painfully aware.) A barnacle essentially stands on its head in this bomb-proof home, and, when covered with seawater at high tide, sticks out a set of feathery appendages every few seconds to gather in plankton and various other food particles.

Two other common residents here are the chiton and the limpet. The chiton lives in an oval shell divided into plates, while the limpet resides in a symmetrical, cone-shaped shell that looks a great deal like a Chinese hat. Unlike barnacles, which are fixed in one place, limpets and chitons move slowly across rocks or the shells of other creatures, scraping off bits of edible organic material as they go.

You're also likely to see a particularly bold, active crab here— a mottled green color with ten scallops on the front of its dorsal shield. This is the green crab, and it has a particularly strong pincer, as many a barefoot beachcomber has found out. In fact, proportionally, a green crab can latch onto your big toe with twenty times the force that most humans can muster in their hands. The green crab is a carnivore, and is often spotted at high tide scurrying from side to side, in a tireless, fearless hunt for food.

Other creatures you're likely to see at Odiorne include dog whelks, rock crabs, spiral worms, periwinkles, mussels, sea urchins,

Limpet

174

starfish, and hermit crabs. There are really few things in nature more engaging than to peer into the nooks and crannies of the tidal zone. The activities of these creatures are performances from an ancient past, master links in a long, long chain of life. The story told in these pools never remains exactly the same. The actors, as well as the stage itself, can change dramatically with each new wash of seawater.

RACHEL CARSON PRESERVE

Distance: 0.2 mile
Location: From U.S. Highway 1 in the town of Waldoboro, head south on Maine Highway 32 for approximately 20 miles to the preserve, which is located approximately 1 mile north of the village of New Harbor. You'll find a small parking area here, immediately adjacent to the highway. Our destination is the salt pond, which is easily visible from the road.

This is not so much a walk as it is a very slow, deliberate ramble. The preserve, which is managed by the Maine Chapter of the Nature Conservancy, is a place particularly well suited to those who are willing to drop to their knees in front of a tidal pool or press their noses to a rock plastered with barnacles. The patient explorer will find here mysteries unfolding in a hundred nooks and crannies—tiny strands of the complex weave of life that wraps this bridge between land and sea.

In the short distance from your car to the gray granulite rocks scattered along the edge of the sea, you'll pass through a surprising range of habitats. Descending past a thin roadside fringe of gray birch, meadowsweet, strawberry, roses, and goldenrod you'll quickly reach the upper edge of the tidal zone. Here you'll find thick, slippery carpets of blue-green algae, the organism that many scientists consider to have been the first life form to ever leave its saltwater home and colonize the land.

This line is also marked by an abundance of rockweeds and knotted wrack, their air sacs tangled and tossed together like plates of pregnant pasta. The tiny air chambers you see on some of these plants, incidentally, allow them to float high in the water, maximizing their exposure to the sun. Here you'll also find an abundance of Irish moss, as well as rough periwinkles, blue mussels, and tortoiseshell limpets. Beneath this life line blue mussels continue to be abundant, as are common periwinkles, sea stars, and hermit and Jonah crabs.

Finally, this life line gives way to a submerged garden of rubbery kelp, some of which may weigh a whopping 25 pounds. Kelp is a plant that continually comes face to face with the force and fury of pounding breakers, yet it survives not by fighting but by "going with the flow," engaging in a loose, sinewy dance whose tempo is driven by the salty tongues of the waves. It also helps that kelp stalks are extremely well attached to their rock underpinnings, anchoring themselves with a strength that may require 800 to 1,000 pounds per square inch to break.

The Salt Pool, which sits center stage in the preserve, is a wonderful spot to see green crabs, smooth periwinkles, dogwinkles, and, if you're lucky, an occasional green sea urchin. True to its name, this subtidal resident is covered by a bright green pincushion of protective spines. Urchins feed both on kelp and by scraping algae off rocks by using a circle of five teeth that grind back and forth, powered by a strange weave of cartilage and muscle. Adjacent to this "mouth" is the digestive tract, and, in season, the gonads, which are considered to be delicacies by gourmet chefs around the world. Despite their spiny armor, sea urchins are preyed upon by sea gulls, cod, and lobster. It's thought that the overharvest of lobster, in fact, has allowed populations of sea urchins to grow to the point that they are a major threat to many important kelp beds along the Maine coast.

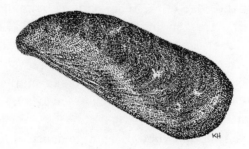

Blue Mussel

Framing either side of the preserve are folded gray layers of granulite, a rock created from sediments deposited on the ocean floor hundreds of millions of years ago, and then folded by violent collisions of the continental plates. The heat that accompanied this grinding in the earth was sufficient to turn some of the granulite into fiery-hot magma, which then flowed like warm honey through cracks in the more solid rock. These flows, called dikes, are easily visible along much of the shore north of the salt pool as colored braids running through the bedrock. What kind of rock comprises each dike depends to a large extent on the rate at which the magma cooled. These patterns, as well as a wonderful collage of boulder fields, sills, and warped strata, make this a geologic wonderland.

Such phenomena—drifting continents and rocks laid down one particle at a time on the bed of some strange, ancient sea—are enough to explode your concept of time to smithereens. And that was just the beginning! Yet to come was the grind of glaciers, as well as great erosions, submergences, and uplifts. It was very likely this scene spread before you now, the telltale signs of the long, slow dances of the earth, that also made Rachel Carson pause, and write in *The Edge of the Sea*:

Once this rocky coast beneath me was a plain of sand; then the sea rose and found a new shore line. And again in some shadowy future the surf will have ground these rocks to sand and will have returned the coast to its earlier state. And so in my mind's eye these coastal forms merge and blend in a shifting, kaleidoscopic pattern in which there is no finality, no ultimate and fixed reality—earth becoming fluid as the sea itself.

BACKSHORE TRAIL

Distance: 1.2 miles

Location: Holbrook Island Sanctuary. From the northern intersection of Maine highways 175 and 176, head south across the
Bagaduce River to a split in the two roads. Turn right here,
following Highway 176 in a counterclockwise direction around
the peninsula until you come to a small road taking off to the
right, leading to the village of Harborside. Follow this road for
1.7 miles to Indian Bar Road, and turn right. Make another right
at a fork in 0.85 mile. Our parking lot and trailhead are located
0.1 mile down this road on the left. (Continuing straight will take
you to the park office and picnic area.)

It would be hard to find a more idyllic blend of coastal natural beauty
than the mainland portion of Holbrook Island Sanctuary. Here the
old volcanic hills wear patchwork robes stitched with wildflowers and
mixed hardwood forest. There are freshwater marshes and ponds,
estuaries, mud flats, and beaches, each providing crucial habitat for a
surprising variety of bird and mammal life. You can sit atop any of a
dozen windswept grassy knolls and pull daydreams out of the blue
waters of Penobscot Bay, then set them adrift again on the out-
stretched wings of bald eagles and ospreys.

For all this beauty you can thank Anita Harris, the feisty
matron saint of nature on these 1,200 acres, as well as on her private
estate on Holbrook Island, both of which she gave to the state of
Maine (the island upon her death in 1985), primarily for the protection of the wild creatures that brought so much fulfillment to her
during most of her 92 years.

More than once did Miss Harris, as she was commonly
known, choose the good of nature over good relations with her
neighbors. Shortly after she and her sister acquired this mainland
sanctuary in the early sixties, they closed it to hunting and trapping.
In response, a gang of incensed, trigger-happy hunters proceeded to
slaughter an entire herd of deer. She was not particularly popular
when she fought the establishment of a copper mine on the edge of
the preserve. But perhaps at no point did she become more resented
than when she created a private nature preserve out of this property
and then claimed that, as such, the parcel should be given tax-
exempt status. When the courts disagreed with her, she promptly

donated the land to the state of Maine. "The villagers call me an old bitch," she informed Governor Ken Curtis before signing over the deed to this property in 1971. "Since the female of the canine species is loyal and intelligent," she added, "I take that as a compliment." In truth, were it not for the generosity and devotion to principle of this independent woman, the people of Maine—indeed, all of New England—would be far poorer.

Our walk begins in clusters of white pine, alder, cherry, and apple trees underlain by fallow meadows. The whole scene here presents a wonderful opportunity to see how nature can quickly and methodically reclaim what was culled from it by human hands. (At her own estate on Holbrook Island, Miss Harris helped things along considerably by requiring that, upon her death, all but one of the buildings there be demolished.) Here on the mainland the old fields are already well seasoned with clover, meadowsweet, curly dock, goldenrod, thistle, milkweed, and Queen Anne's lace, while each year the sun-loving members of the hardwood forest march a little further across the open ground.

Most of the above-mentioned meadow plants are considered weeds, a term Emerson once said we carelessly applied to any plant "whose virtues have not yet been discovered." In the case of several of the plants you see here, a use was indeed found, but ultimately forgotten. Consider, for example, Queen Anne's lace. The legend behind the naming of this plant says that Queen Anne pricked her finger while making lace, thus producing the single tiny red flower you see at the center of the bloom. (For centuries people believed that eating these red flowers would prevent epileptic seizures.) Queen Anne's lace is actually the daughter of our cultivated carrot, set free when the carrots that colonists grew in their gardens escaped cultivation and began roaming the countryside.

Likewise, the "spring greens" of curly dock were a common table vegetable during the Great Depression, while a tea made from the root of the plant has long been an effective treatment for constipation. The fluffy seeds of milkweed, on the other hand, came to our rescue during World War II. In 1942, the Japanese captured a group of East Indian islands that contained large groves of silk cotton trees, up to that point our major source of flotation material for Navy life jackets. Milkweed was found to be the perfect substitute.

We can go on and on about the links that modern life has to the plant world: quinine from Peruvian cinchona trees to treat malaria, heart medication from foxglove, emetine from the ipecac root to treat amebic dysentery, the secretions of barnacles in the development of superadhesives. If we need a pragmatic argument for slowing down today's high rate of plant extinction, the potential that unexplored species have as healing agents, or even as food sources, is a pretty convincing one.

At 0.2 mile you'll reach a T junction, where you'll make a right turn along the edge of a forest of sugar maple, red spruce, and white birch. At 0.4 mile, beside nice clusters of sweet fern, the path will enter the hush of the woodland—the domain of wood sorrels, Canada mayflower, and sarsaparilla, along with beautiful gardens of hay-scented, sensitive, and northern beech ferns.

The path will come out on the rocky shoreline of Penobscot Bay in 0.55 mile. (*Penobscot,* incidentally, is an Indian word meaning "rocky place" or "descending ledge place." The native people originally used the term in reference to a rough, rocky section of the Penobscot River between Treat's Falls and Old Town Great Falls.) This shore is an excellent place to see cormorants, gulls, great blue herons, bald eagles, and ospreys. During low tide, look for barnacles, blue mussels, and horseshoe crabs.

Horseshoe Crab

Bayberry

WATERFALL BRIDGE

Distance: 1.8 miles
Location: Acadia National Park. From the Bar Harbor–Hancock
County Airport, south of the town of Ellsworth on Maine Highway 3, head south, following signs for Maine highways 102 and
198. At a traffic light 6 miles south of the airport these latter two
routes will split. Continue to follow Highway 198 for 4 miles from
this traffic light, to a parking area located on the east side of the
road, just north of Upper Hadlock Pond. A small footpath takes
off through the forest from the north edge of the parking area,
meeting a carriage road in about 20 yards. Turn right here, and in
less than 0.1 mile you'll reach another carriage road, where you'll
turn left.

If you doubt that magic can happen when land meets sea, then
Acadia—a perfect expression of those two great Earth forces—will
open your eyes like no other slice of oceanscape in North America. If
ever there has been a place to, as the French poet Arthur Rimbaud
suggested, bathe "in the Poem of the Sea," Acadia is surely it. An
astonishing five hundred species of plants have been identified on
this largest of the Atlantic rock islands, as well as three hundred
species of birds, including nearly twenty species of nesting warblers.
Geological features abound: enormous boulders that were carried to

the tops of high granite peaks in the icy arms of glaciers; a beach where more than half of the sand grains are fragments from the broken shells of sea creatures; fanciful sea arches and caves cut into the volcanic tuff by the relentless battering of waves.

Once you've splashed your face here with the sea spray, once you've explored the headlands and the clear, rich tidal pools that cradle so much ancient life, then step back into the mountainous interior of this island for an entirely different perspective. This walk along one of John D. Rockefeller's famous carriage roads will carry you through fine spruce forests, past sweeping views of Upper Hadlock Pond and the coast beyond, and finally to a hanging veil of cool, tumbling water—the highest waterfall in the national park.

Turning left onto our carriage path at just under 0.1 mile (see directions above), you'll be in the thick of a beautiful spruce forest. Much of the eastern portion of Mount Desert Island was once covered with a thick forest of spruce and fir, but this was consumed in 1947 by a tremendous 17,000-acre fire. Today that area of the park is quilted with a mix of birch and aspen, trees quick to reclaim land suddenly opened to the sun. Eventually, however, the conifers will again reign supreme. As you continue to climb you'll pass several rocky areas where only a few plants have taken hold on the thick slabs of granite. Far from looking harsh, however, some of these rockscapes have the charm of a Japanese garden—a clean, spare patchwork of huckleberry, blueberry, white cedar, and spruce, each clinging tenaciously to the scattered pockets of soil.

Just before a T junction at about 0.4 mile, where you'll turn right, are nice bouquets of sweet fern and bayberry. It's the waxy, aromatic fruits of this latter plant, incidentally, that are used to make bayberry candles. After this last turn is a fine view straight ahead of the granite dome of 1,373-foot Sargent Mountain, sitting in a soft green frame of spruce, maple, and white cedar. Shortly after this view the road turns briefly to the southeast and rounds an open corner, affording glimpses of Upper Hadlock Pond and the ocean beyond.

Continue to climb steadily past long mats of sweet fern and sheep laurel, with maples, spruce, and white pines close behind. At 0.8 mile you'll reach Hemlock Bridge, which, true to its name, will afford you a glimpse of a spry mountain stream dancing through a lacy green curtain of hemlock branches. The next bridge, and our turnaround point, is another 0.1 mile up the road. Built in 1925 and appropriately named Waterfall Bridge, this beautiful span of stone lies before an airy veil of water, just passing through on its dizzy tumble from the rocky flanks of Sargent Mountain.

It is a sobering thought to consider the breadth of time necessary for these ribbons of water to work their erosional magic, for them, in their endless rush to the sea, to actually sculpt the land into shaded fissures hundreds of feet deep, as if this world were made of clay instead of granite. The slow peeling of mighty rocks, grain by tiny grain, is an image we have long held as an analogy to forever, a point beyond which it seems we cannot stretch our imaginations further. Shakespeare wrote in *Troilus and Cressida*, Act III, scene ii:

> When time is old and hath forgot itself,
> When waterdrops have worn the stones of Troy . . .

AMPHITHEATER LOOP

Distance: 5.5 miles
Location: Acadia National Park. From the Bar Harbor–Hancock County Airport, south of the town of Ellsworth on Maine Highway 3, head south, following signs for Maine highways 102 and 198. At a traffic light 6 miles south of the airport these latter two routes will split. Continue to follow Highway 198 for 5.3 miles from this traffic light, to a parking area located on the east side of the road, a short distance south of Upper Hadlock Pond. A small footpath takes off from the east side of the parking area. Follow this path for just under 0.1 mile to a carriage road, where you'll turn left.

Although like most ecosystems the delicate weave of life on Acadia is easily unraveled in careless hands, there nevertheless seems to be a certain strength, a tenacious permanence to this island paradise. It has already survived the missionary fervor that was launched upon it by French Jesuits in the early seventeenth century, as well as the aggressive advances of the land-hungry Virginia Company that, by the hand of King James I in 1601, was "given" not only the Maine seaside but the entire Atlantic coast. Frenchmen launched many a ship from these protected coves in attacks on English shipping vessels, while English soldiers raided Yankee settlers here from the time of the American Revolution to the War of 1812. By the 1880s, Mount Desert Island was on its way to becoming a playground for the rich— a place of spas and orchestras and full-dress balls; of polo matches, lawn parties, club houses, theater, and croquet; of Astors, Morgans, Carnegies, and Vanderbilts. Then, in late October 1947, a fierce fire began to rage across the island, fueled by wind gusts of up to 85 miles per hour. Before the flames finally came to rest on November 14, more than seventeen thousand acres had burned. Gone were timber, meadows, and more than two hundred twenty-five residences, including dozens of stately summer mansions of the rich.

An owner of one of these mansions, John D. Rockefeller, Jr., was responsible for the system of carriage roads—forever closed to automobiles—that you'll be walking along during our two Acadia treks. Although one can make a very good case that Rockefeller's uncontrollable penchant for road building was inappropriate on land set aside for preservation, a good portion of these carriage routes was constructed while the land was still in private hands. (Nearly one-third of this national park—more than ten thousand acres in all—was donated by Rockefeller.)

Follow the small footpath that leaves from the rear center of the parking lot to a T intersection with a dirt carriage road, and turn left. This route climbs gently through a lovely forest of spruce, striped maple, birch, white pine, bracken, and clubmoss. At the first intersection, reached at 0.1 mile and marked by an 18, stay to the right. Notice the long carpets of sweet fern along this section of road, a deciduous shrub that you'll see on drier sites from Nova Scotia to North Carolina. The leaves of sweet fern make a good tea, and some eastern Indian peoples made a wet compress out of them that they used for relief from the itch of poison ivy and poison oak. Also along the road are sheep laurel, wintergreen, blueberry, and meadowsweet, as well as thick mats of huckleberry.

Pause at a clearing at 1.1 miles for a magnificent view over your right shoulder of the Atlantic Ocean and the lovely Cranberry Isles. The assorted tales of intrigue and misadventures borne along these cold blue Atlantic waters would fill a bookcase. Perhaps none, however, has the sting of the ill-fated voyage of the *Grand Design*. The *Grand Design* was a large sailing ship that set sail in 1739 for Pennsylvania with more than two hundred wealthy Irish men and women, and a host of their bonded servants. Tremendous autumn storms pushed them far off course, and then dashed the ship into splinters against a remote granite peninsula that frames the entrance to Ship Harbor, at the southwestern corner of Mount Desert Island.

It would be hard to imagine a more remote, difficult location from which to be rescued. The very first settlers on Mount Desert— Mr. and Mrs. Abraham Somes and their four daughters—would not arrive for 23 years. With winter cold on their heels and no hope for help, the captain of the *Grand Design* and 100 single men made the decision in early December to cross the island and look for help. None of them were ever heard from again. By the time rescuers finally did arrive, brought in by a note the castaways had persuaded an Indian to deliver for them, there were only a handful of survivors left—all starving, wrapped against winter in the fine Irish linen they had carried with them across the Atlantic.

From this overview 0.2 mile a road will join you from the right. Keep to the left here, and in 0.5 mile you'll reach Amphitheater Bridge, the longest of Rockefeller's sixteen magnificent stone bridges. Not one to settle for second best, Rockefeller hired Frederick Law Olmsted, Jr., to design the carriage road system and its accompanying bridges. (Olmsted's father had gained fame as the designer of many of America's greatest city parklands, including New York's Central Park. His son was also an accomplished landscape designer.) Beneath the bridge runs lovely Little Harbor Brook, gingerly dancing out of the box canyon down a rock staircase framed by a forest of spruce, hemlock, maple, and birch.

From this point the road heads south, offering wonderful views into and across the forested canyon carved by the patient fingers of Little Harbor Brook. You'll pass fine huddles of white pine here, as well as gray birch, mountain ash, bigtooth aspen, and maple. Along the fringes look for hardhack and mountain holly.

At the forks in the road at 2.5 miles and 2.9 miles (posts 21 and 22), keep to the right. After crossing Little Harbor Brook Bridge at 3.3 miles you'll begin a slow, steady climb out of the valley through a forest thick with spruce groves laced with striped maple. In autumn

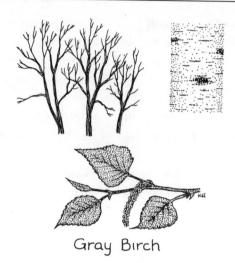

Gray Birch

the leaves of these striped maples splash wisps of mellow gold against the dark green conifers. The road will join the entrance road again at marker post 20, which is reached in 4.1 miles. Turn left. Tree lovers will want to take special note of this junction, as it contains several superb members of the Mount Desert Island forest community, including sugar maple, birch, white pine, spruce, and hemlock.

SHORE TRAIL

Distance: 2.2 miles
Location: Petit Manan National Wildlife Refuge. From the intersection of U.S. highways 1 and 1A in the town of Millbridge, head south on U.S. 1 for 2.7 miles to Pigeon Hill Road, and turn left. Follow this road south for 6 miles to the trailhead parking area, located on the right side of the road.
Note: The road past the parking area is private. Please do not drive vehicles beyond the designated trailhead parking site.

There is real magic on this granite isle, its interior a toss of spruce, alder, birch, and pine woven around fields flushed with bushels and bushels of blueberries. Deer, bear, porcupine, raccoon, and even fisher course through the forests. Dozens of bird species, from woodcocks to warblers, crisscross the spring and summer skies, while in autumn, the rocky shores erupt in great flurries of migration—eiders, laughing gulls, black ducks, cormorants, scoters, scaups, and Arctic terns. It would be difficult indeed to find a richer, more enticing place to walk.

From the trailhead parking area, follow the roadway southward for about 0.6 mile, where you'll see the Shore Trail taking off eastward through a field of blueberries. What stage of succession this field will be in when you visit is dependent on when it was last burned. Refuge managers fire these clearings every three years in order to provide "edge" for a wider variety of birds and mammals. You'll be able to tell roughly how long it's been since such a burning by the size and number of speckled alder growing here. Under the right conditions, alder is a tree that wastes absolutely no time in making a serious bid for control of any available clearing. In return, root nodules of the alder offer homes for the organisms that take nitrogen from the air and change it into a form that plants can use, thereby greatly enriching the soil. The leaves of speckled alder also provide good browse for both moose and deer.

The next 0.5 mile to the coast will be through a patchwork of woodland and clearing. Graceful spruce, birch, and red maples dominate the forest, with spatters of bunchberry and wintergreen building bright red berries at their feet. In open areas look for the lovely pink blossoms of sheep laurel, a plant once used by various Indian peoples for treating headaches and backaches. You'll also see jack pine here, a fire-dependent tree that specializes in settling areas that have been burned or logged. They do especially well in poor, sandy soils, and large groves of jack pines comprise what are often known as "pine barrens."

You'll come to an absolutely idyllic seashore cove 1.1 miles from the parking area, a gentle nook lined with cinnamon fern, cranberry, wintergreen, and baked-apple berry, the shoreline itself paved with a carpet of granite pebbles. From here you can make a fairly arduous hike south along the coast for another 2.5 miles, past a tangle of coves and bluffs, and, depending on the time of year, there are enough birds to satisfy the most feather-happy. The waters off Petit Manan provide an especially interesting mix of bird life because of a great overlapping of what is for many species their most northern breeding range, and for others, their most southern.

Of all the winged visitors here, the sea ducks are especially

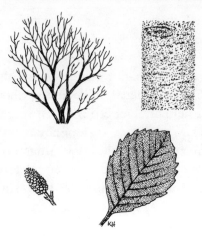

Speckled Alder

numerous. This place is excellent for watching common eiders, which at Petit Manan are along the southernmost fringe of a breeding range that extends all the way to Greenland. If you've ever come across the phrase "soft as a bed of eiderdown," this eider is the one they're talking about. The breast feathers of the female common eider are remarkably full and soft, and have been used in Europe for centuries to stuff blankets and pillows.

The female common eider lays her eggs in nests constructed on offshore islands, then faithfully sits with them almost without rest for nearly a month, during which time she will take no food. Soon after hatching the chicks are ready for travel, and loose groups of mothers and young head across the waters toward shallow, sheltered

Sheep Laurel

waters along the mainland. It's along such shorelines where they find the shellfish—mussels, clams, crabs, and so on—that make up the majority of their diet. Not ones for fancy dinner rituals, eiders simply gobble mussels and clams whole, the shells eventually crushed by a powerful set of stomach muscles. If you're here in the fall after the young have been reared you'll see males and females back together in great floating masses called rafts, the numbers sometimes reaching the hundreds or even thousands.

Also here are laughing gulls, at this point near the northernmost point of their breeding range, as well as beautiful wood and goldeneye ducks, scaups, sleek-looking black guillemots, surf scoters, black scoters, and Arctic terns, to name but a very, very few. It is the feisty Arctic tern, incidentally, that among all birds holds the record for the distance migrated each year. When an Arctic tern leaves here in the fall it will fly east along the Maine coast, cross the Atlantic, and continue down the coast of Europe and Africa, finally—perhaps ten thousand miles later—arriving at its wintering grounds along the coast of Antarctica.

The full exploration of the east side of the peninsula deserves an entire day. Don't feel bad, however, if you don't reach this point. Along the way is an almost endless number of wonderful distractions, each quite capable of undermining the need to end up anywhere else at all.

Arctic Tern

BIRCH POINT

Distance: 4 miles
Location: Petit Manan National Wildlife Refuge. From the intersection of U.S. highways 1 and 1A in the town of Millbridge, head south on U.S. 1 for 2.7 miles to Pigeon Hill Road, and turn left. Follow this road south for 6 miles to the trailhead parking area, located on the right side of the road. Our path heads west from the parking area through a large cleared field.
Note: The road past the parking area is private. Please do not drive vehicles beyond the designated trailhead parking site.

Your first steps along this delightful pathway are through a large open field, kept clear by regular burning in an effort to produce "edge habitat" for a variety of birds and mammals. In most summers this goal means one especially wonderful thing for human stomachs as well—blueberries! "As big as the end of your thumb, real sky blue and heavy," as Robert Frost would say. Although Maine's inland blueberry barons, who harvest nearly half the total North American crop of these juicy fruits, would not consider this field particularly productive, for about six weeks during most summers a casual stroller will think she's stumbled into a regular garden of eatin'.

On the far side of this clearing, just before entering a young woodland guarded by a feathery clump of tamaracks, you may also spot a few cranberries on the left side of the trail. Once inside this woodland, look for clusters of wild raisin backed by speckled alder, gray birch, and northern white cedar. The slow-growing northern white cedar has also been known as *arborvitae*—the tree of life— since the middle of the sixteenth century. And so it was for explorer Jacques Cartier and his crew, who in 1535 were saved from scurvy by drinking vitamin C–charged tea made from the tree's bark and foliage.

And, since we seem to be on a roll with food, you might also notice the patches of bracken fern on the right at just more than 0.1 mile. For centuries people from around the world have relished the young curled spring shoots of this fern, known as fiddleheads. There is some research to suggest that certain eastern Indian hunters feasted on fiddleheads during their spring deer hunt, in the belief that the plants helped hide their human scent from the noses of the deer. It's important to note, however, that while young curled shoots of these plants are edible, as the brackens age they become poisonous.

The path winds past additional clearings (with yet more blueberries), as well as past fine stands of balsam fir, white and black spruce, and aspen. By 1 mile, however, young white birch have absolutely stolen the show. Here they form a shimmering, delicate arch, their milky white trunks leaning over the roadway for a better look at the sky. Woven in between these light-skinned youngsters are the beautiful dark green branches of balsam fir. Together they form the loveliest of contrasts, the kind of striking patterns that make the forests of the Northeast among the most beautiful on Earth.

At 1.5 miles you'll pass a side trail to Lobster Point; stay left. Just 0.1 mile later the trail splits into a loop that circles Birch Point. On my visit, the left branch was impossible to follow. If this is still the case, work your way around the head of the peninsula counterclockwise, and then retrace your steps the way you came. When you reach the west side of the head you'll find fine views of Dyer Harbor, with Sheep and Sally islands clearly visible just offshore. Here the land above the high tide, defined by a crooked, matted line of bladder rockweed, becomes covered with blankets of grasses and wildflowers, including the beautiful lavender blooms of the beach pea. Visitors from the west coast will recognize this lovely trailing vine, since it is quite common on the Pacific coast from California all the way to Alaska.

Bracken Fern

WEST QUODDY HEAD

Distance: 4 miles

Location: Quoddy Head State Park. From Maine Highway 189 near the west edge of Lubec, head south on the South Lubec Road at the sign for Quoddy Head State Park. At a fork in 2.6 miles keep left, continuing for another 2 miles to the entrance road to the park, which takes off to the right in front of the West Quoddy Lighthouse. Our trail takes off along the edge of the bluffs, from the south side of the picnic area.

Note: As of this writing, the sign for Quoddy Head Park along 189 was visible only to those cars approaching from the west.

By the time you reach West Quoddy Head, the easternmost point in the United States, you will have without question left the hustle and bustle of the southern Maine coast far, far behind. There are no miniature golf courses here, no go-carts or petting zoos or T-shirt shops, no stores laden with "Maine" pen and pencil sets and piggy banks and lobster-pot table lamps. This is a place where, for the most part, the wild sea is still the only attraction. Waves batter against mammoth volcanic and gabbro cliffs, and southern breezes pull thick coverlets of fog across the bays. A bald eagle soars overhead. Rafts of eiders and surf scoters bob on the ocean swells, each making dive after dive to hunt for shellfish. In the distance, a lone minke whale rises to blow, and is gone.

Our walk begins on a trail that takes off along the shore from the far side of the picnic area. If you're a fan of tidal pools you may be interested to know that those below the picnic area contain rich populations of green and Jonah crabs, periwinkles, dog whelks, blue

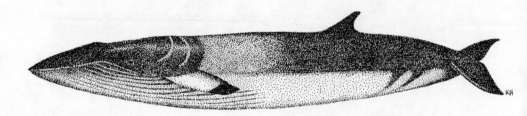

Minke Whale

192

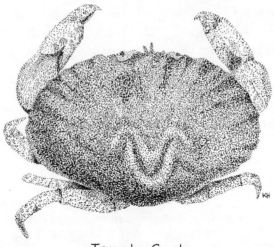

Jonah Crab

mussels, and nudibranchs. As you may have noticed on the interpretive sign located at the picnic area, this area has very high tides—nearly sixteen vertical feet. A major reason for these high tides is that the ocean waters flow from the south into inlets that become narrower and narrower as you move north, thus compressing the water into a smaller and smaller space, which causes a greater rise and fall than what occurs at the mouth. At the head of nearby Bay of Fundy, which lies between Nova Scotia and New Brunswick, spring and neap tides may rise and fall as much as fifty feet!

    Although most of us tend to take tides for granted, the phenomenon is really quite remarkable, a visible connection between our planet and that silent, glowing moon riding with us on our journey through space. The gravity of the Earth holds things in place on the planet, not the least of which are the oceans. Yet the moon (and to a lesser extent the sun) effects its own gravitational draw, actually pulling the waters up and then releasing them again each time it circles the Earth. We can predict the timing of this pulling (low tide) and releasing (high tide) based on the length of time it takes for the moon to make its journey around us. Generally speaking, there will be two low tides and two high tides every 24 hours, each advancing at a rate of approximately fifty minutes per day. If on the afternoon of your visit to Quoddy Head the low tide occurs at 2:00, for example, tomorrow that same tide will occur at 2:50, the following day at 3:40, and so on.

But if the moon orbits the Earth only once in a 24-hour period, why are there two high tides and two low tides each day? When the moon is tugging at the Earth, the ocean waters lying on the side farthest away from the moon are not pulled as much as the land in between. These waters actually bulge away from the Earth, causing a high tide to occur. Low tides simply mark the halfway point between the two simultaneously occurring high tides. (The sun is not without its own effects. Extreme high tides, known as spring tides, occur twice each month as the sun, moon, and Earth align with each other. Extreme low tides, on the other hand, known as neap tides, also occur twice a month, when the sun and moon are at right angles to each other. It's the moon's changing orientation to the sun that causes the heights of tides to fluctuate.) If this explanation seems much too colorless, you may prefer to stick with one ancient notion about the tides, which said that they were caused by the breath of a giant monster who lived at the bottom of the sea.

The walk along this coast is truly spectacular. Tattered blankets of spruce and fir drape the tops of high volcanic cliffs, rising 150 feet above the rush of the surf. Clusters of bluebead lilies, bunchberries, raspberries, and meadowsweet add splashes of color to the trailside, while mats of cinnamon fern lend a feathery touch to the bristle of the conifers. In just over 0.55 mile you'll see a small turnoff to the left leading to High Ledge. From this high perch, which is sprinkled with lovely patches of blue-flag iris, you'll have a com-

Harbor Seal

manding view of the ocean to the east. This place is excellent for watching some of the more intriguing mammals that spend time along this coast, including harbor seals, minke whales, and finback whales.

Harbor seals, shy but curious animals, can often be seen playfully leaping, rolling, and swimming in circles. These remarkable mammals are able to dive to depths of three hundred feet, stay under water for almost thirty minutes, and swim for short distances at speeds of more than twelve knots. You may not be able to see them during low tides, especially in warm weather, since they typically haul out for a bit of shut-eye. The staff at West Quoddy Biological Research Station, which you'll pass if you elect to return to the parking area by way of the road, has nursed many injured harbor seals back to health so that they could be returned to their ocean homes. Unfortunately, the most common ailment plaguing these seals is gunshot wounds. Fishermen, it seems, consider the harbor seal to be a major nuisance, and in nearby Canada, it's still legal to handle the problem with bullets.

In just under 2 miles you'll reach Carrying Place Cove, an inlet fringed with meadowsweet, clover, bluets, asters, and alders. This cove is a particularly good place to watch migrating seabirds in the fall. At 2.2 miles you'll come to a neck of land crossed by South Lubec Road; the trailhead parking area is approximately 1.8 miles down this road to the right. A portion of this neck is part of a 43-acre peat bog, the north side exposed to a height of ten to fifteen feet by both rain and the cutting action of waves. This kind of cross-sectional view of a bog is extremely uncommon, and the bog has been declared a National Natural Landmark. This bog is a beautiful place to explore, offering fine opportunities to see spatulate-leaved sundew, cranberries, Labrador tea, cotton grass, baked-apple berry, and pitcher plants. Those with an eye for birds should watch for sightings of both Lincoln sparrows and palm warblers in the brushy thickets. If you come here in early spring, the light trilly song of this latter bird will probably be the first warbler music of the season to fall on your ears.

FRESH WATER

By such a river it is impossible to believe that one will ever be tired or cold. Every sense applauds it. . . . Watch its racing current, its steady renewal of force: it is transient and eternal. And listen again to its sounds: get far enough away so that the noise of falling tons of water does not stun the ears, and hear how much is going on underneath—a whole symphony of smaller sounds, hiss and splash and gurgle, the small talk of side channels, the whisper of blown and scattered spray gathering itself and beginning to flow again, secret and invisible, among the wet rocks.

WALLACE STEGNER
Sound of Mountain Water

Coming to New England from the arid West, I was overwhelmed at the dazzling abundance of water here—water of all shapes and sizes: brackish and sweet, cloudy and clear, walking and running across the landscape at every turn of the trail. There are the mammoth lakes—Moosehead, Winnipesaukee, Sebago, and Menphremagog—their sprawling waters chopped each spring and fall by winds that will stir nutrients and oxygen back into their depths. There is the wide, meandering Connecticut River, and the fast, wild waters of the Allagash, not to mention ten thousand streams, brooks, and rivulets. There are rich, organic ponds and marshes, scattered across the countryside in such quantities that it seems as if some torrential rainstorm let loose and flooded all the lowland basins. And then there are the strange, hauntingly beautiful bogs, where mats of leatherleaf, sphagnum, laurel, and rosemary float on water as acidic as a puddle of vinegar.

This plethora of lakes, rivers, and streams suggests not only an abundance of precipitation in New England but also offers clear links to a landscape that has largely been sculpted by water in one form or another. It was water in the form of a two-thousand-mile-long ice floe inching out of Canada fifteen thousand to twenty thousand years ago that made sharp uplands smooth, carved great U-shaped valleys, and bulldozed the deep basins that would one day become lakes. Even today streams and rivers, always seeking the sea, shape the land by cutting ever downward into the earth. The future look of those twisted runs to the ocean depends a great deal on the speed of the flow, as well as the willingness of the underlying rock to yield to those flows. Sometimes the water walks slow and is sluggish, murky with the tiny particles of fields and mountainsides suspended in its depths. And sometimes it runs fast and furious, probing weak joints and cracks in the bedrock to form cascades, waterfalls, and plunge pools lined with ferns.

Within a single lifetime, however, such geological wizardry seems little more than a concept, a fantasy of what might have been or will be in the millennia yet to come. Much more apparent is the fantastic weave of life that springs within, upon, and beside the New England waters. Over there is a four-foot-tall great blue heron, poised on its thin black legs at the edge of a river, waiting for a fish to swim within reach. On this pond is a mated pair of Canada geese. Having been apart for a while, they are sharing a complicated ritual known as the greeting ceremony, bobbing their long black necks and singing a masterfully orchestrated honking song. Along that lakeshore a king-fisher is perched on a dead snag, about to plunge head first into the still waters to nab a fish with its long, sharp beak. The large, beautiful bird circling above it is an osprey. The osprey will accomplish the same feat on the wing, plucking a fish with its barbed talons from just below the surface of the lake.

No less noticeable in and around these waters are the plants and mammals. Watch that thick curtain of cattails; see the muskrat behind it, chowing down a meal of tubers? Hear the buzzing of the red-winged blackbirds? Look at the deep flush of violet in that clump of blue-flag iris, the bright, glowing yellow of the marsh marigolds, the soft ivory flower clusters of pepperbush.

As you explore the slices of freshwater environment that follow, watch how every seep of moisture completely alters the kinds of plant, animal, and insect life found. This profusion of life is one of the most remarkable consequences of beaver activity. Not only do their flooded areas sustain them but also other life, including swallows, loons, sandpipers, ducks, pond lilies, rushes, sedges, lotus, fish, frogs, newts, and muskrat. Water is most certainly the magic elixir, the spark that causes life on this planet to flame. And nowhere, perhaps, is that fact more beautifully stated than in the folds of New England.

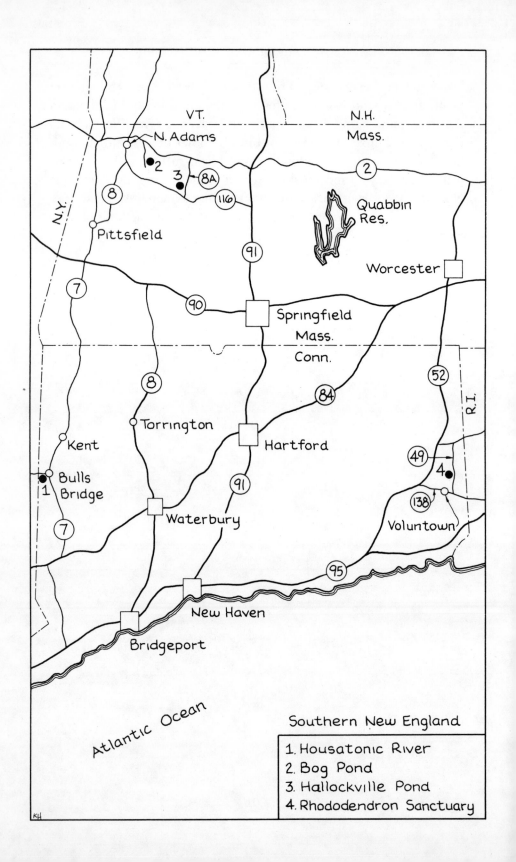

VT.   N.H.

Mass.

N. Adams

②

●2

3

8A

116

N.Y.

⑧

Pittsfield

Quabbin Res.

91

Worcester

⑦

90

Springfield

Mass.

Conn.

52

⑧

84

R.I.

Torrington

Hartford

Kent

49

4 ●

Bulls

Bridge

91

138

●1

Voluntown

⑦

Waterbury

95

New Haven

Bridgeport

Atlantic Ocean

Southern New England

1. Housatonic River
2. Bog Pond
3. Hallockville Pond
4. Rhododendron Sanctuary

KH

Southern New England

HOUSATONIC RIVER

Distance: 2 miles
Location: Head south out of the village of Kent, Connecticut, on U.S. Highway 7. At the town of Bulls Bridge, turn west on Bulls Bridge Road. You'll pass through a covered wooden bridge, and a few yards further, cross an open bridge over the Housatonic River. The trailhead and parking area will be on your left on the far side of this second bridge.

Nowhere is Connecticut walking more pleasant than along the beautiful Housatonic River. Along this single mile of waterscape—just a tiny slice of the Housatonic's 130-mile southbound run to Long Island Sound—there is a wonderful variety of sight and sound. One minute the river is roiling and splashing in great nosedives over sheer marble ledges and chutes, and the next, it becomes a sheet of clear, unbroken water, slipping past huddles of hemlock and red oak with barely a whisper.

Besides the Housatonic's fine company, the walk to Ten Mile River will also let you rub elbows and feet with a beautiful mix of hardwoods, conifers, and ground covers. In the latter category, along the first several hundred yards look for ferns, Solomon's seal, and round-lobed hepatica. This latter plant is easily recognized by its leaves, each containing three shamrock-shaped lobes that appear fused together at the base. As far as the botanist who named the plant was concerned, the shape of these leaves resembled the human liver. Hence, according to the doctrine of signatures—a theory that claimed each plant contained a sign of the treatment for which it was intended—he gave this plant the genus name of *Hepaticus*, which is derived from the Greek word for liver.

Likewise, the Solomon's seal, with its smooth, lance-shaped leaves and delicate green-to-ivory-colored flower bells, takes its name from another somewhat imaginative comparison. When the leaf stalk of this plant is broken from the root stalk, the resulting scar is supposed to look exactly like the official seal of King Solomon. This plant will form blue-black berries. These berries, I'm sorry to report, don't look like body organs or royal seals, but merely like small grapes.

Interspersed with hemlock, sugar maple, and red oak during the first 0.4 mile of trail are also several clumps of witch-hazel. Herbalists know this tree for the strong astringent that can be made from its leaves and smooth brown bark. But medicine is hardly the only story the witch-hazel has to tell. The young shoots of this tree have long been a favorite of dowsers in the making of divining rods. (Divining rods are the forked branches that dowsers claim can be used to locate underground water; more optimistic practitioners suggest that they can also be used to locate precious metals.) Over the centuries dowsing has had no shortage of skeptics. Sixteenth-century religious leaders such as Martin Luther were emphatically opposed to the idea of dowsing, a few going so far as to suggest that it was not water that pulled the rod toward the earth but the hands of Satan. Nevertheless, there are thousands of otherwise conservative farmers who wouldn't think of digging a well without the advice of a dowser.

If you're taking this walk in the fall, don't be surprised if a witch-hazel seed or two comes flying your way. When the hazel's fruit capsules open, they propel their cargo like bursts of gunfire, some seeds landing twenty-five feet or more from the parent tree.

In just under 0.5 mile the trail forks. Our walk follows the path on the left, along the white blazes of the Appalachian Trail. Watch the ground here for red columbine, ginger, violets, and that delicate orchid known as pink lady's slipper. The lady's slipper, incidentally, has a long history of being used to treat nervous condi-

Witch-hazel

tions ranging from insomnia to epilepsy. Like many of the more beautiful woodland flowers, however, keep in mind that this plant does not propagate well, and should not be picked.

At 0.6 mile you'll reach a fine view of the Housatonic River. The fact that the Housatonic has cut a beautiful gorge in this particular place is no accident. Underlying this corridor are thick layers of marble that yield easily to the erosive lick of water across their surface. The high hills and plateaus that lie immediately to the east and west are made up of granite, which is much more difficult for moving water to cut. The fingers of the Housatonic poked and probed, and, like all rivers, ended up working their magic along the paths of least resistance.

Pink Lady's Slipper

At 0.9 mile you'll descend through a cleared area with lovely spatters of dogwood and Japanese honeysuckle. Our turnaround point is a short distance past this plant life, on the far side of a footbridge crossing the Ten Mile River. To stand on this footbridge is to immerse yourself in an absolute symphony of rushing water—the Ten Mile fast-stepping out of the high, wild hills of eastern New York, and the Housatonic rolling strong and fast across the smooth gray bedrock of the northern Marble Valley.

BOG POND

Distance: 1.4 miles

Location: Savoy Mountain State Forest. From the intersection of Massachusetts highways 8 and 2 in the town of North Adams, head east on Massachusetts 2 for 4.5 miles. Turn right, and follow the signs for just over 3 miles to Savoy Mountain State Forest. Continue to follow this road toward the park campground. Our walk takes off on a small dirt track known as Haskins Road, located 0.2 mile past the campground on the left.

There are more than a few residents of northern New England who consider Boston and Massachusetts to be one and the same. Yet within the nearly eight thousand square miles of the Bay State are slices of nature rich almost beyond belief, not the least of which lie in the shadows of the ancient Berkshires. This land is the beat of bear and deer and even an occasional moose—a place steeped in blue sky, a land of drooping mountain shoulders cloaked in thick blankets of northern hardwood forest.

From the entrance to the campground walk south for just under 0.2 mile, and turn left (east) onto a small dirt two-track called Haskins Road. Immediately the world shifts from sun to shadow, as thick stands of birch, hemlock, maple, and beech crowd together in a race to snatch the light before it can fall to the forest floor. The first few yards of this road are a good place to find jewelweed, its spotted orange blossoms hanging like handmade lanterns from tufts of soft, gray-green foliage. When fully ripe, the elongated seedpods of the jewelweed will fire their batteries of seeds a considerable distance at even the slightest touch, hence another of its common names—spotted touch-me-not. The juice of this plant is well known for relieving the itching of poison ivy, and has also served well as a fungicide for treating athlete's foot.

At 0.4 mile you'll come to a small trail taking off to the right, marked with a blue blaze. Follow this path through clusters of conifers, birch, and beeches, with smatterings of hobblebush and ferns growing underneath. You'll be able to see Bog Pond shimmering through the trees at 0.6 mile, and, in another few yards, come to the shore itself.

Bogs are highly acidic places. Some of them in northern New England, in fact, may have one hundred times the acid levels of clean rainwater! As you might have expected, though, there are indeed some plants that have evolved to tolerate or even thrive in such environments. Among the ones that have mastered life in this particular bog are Labrador tea, leatherleaf, pitcher plants, and round-leaved sundew.

These latter two plants are insectivorous, which means that at least some of their diet consists of insects. Now since members of the vegetable kingdom can't flick a tongue or snap a beak to grab insects, they have to rely on more subtle means. The pitcher plant has a pool of water at the base of its leaves into which hapless visitors fall and drown. The sundew, on the other hand, has sticky glandular hairs that catch the insects' feet when they land for a meal. (There's some evidence to support the notion that a type of anesthetic is also released on the insect by short hairs on the inner leaves.) The movements of the creature to set itself free again stimulate a response in the plant to begin wrapping a network of hairs around its body. This procedure will typically begin less than two minutes after the bug has landed, and will be completed fifteen to twenty minutes later. Once the insect is digested, the tentacles open again, ready for the next unsuspecting victim.

HALLOCKVILLE POND

Distance: 1.5 miles

Location: Kenneth Dubuque Memorial State Forest. From the intersection of Massachusetts highways 2 and 8 in the town of North Adams, head east on Highway 2 for 18.1 miles, and turn right onto Massachusetts Highway 8A. Follow this road southward for 8.7 miles to the north end of Hallockville Pond, and park here. Our walk begins around the north end of the pond, circling it in a counterclockwise direction.

This 'round-the-lake loop trail is a nearly perfect mix of water and woodland. There are rocky coves blanketed with rubbery mats of pond lilies, and hushed, towering forests of hemlock and white pine. Here you'll find beautiful clumps of birch leaning over the water, straining their necks for a better view of the sun. In fall, the sky clears and drops deep shades of blue onto the surface of the lake; framed by loose splashes of gold, red, and evergreen, the place can seem to almost vibrate with color.

Park in the small turnout adjacent to the northeast corner of the lake and begin walking counterclockwise around the north shore, past a large cluster of state forest buildings. On the far side of the lake our path will head down the shore to the southwest, passing several marker posts, some of which have excellent interpretive information on them about the flora and fauna of the area. (A special interpretive brochure has also been prepared for this trail, and can be picked up at the offices on the north edge of the pond from mid-May to early October.) Pay close attention to the plant communities on this western side of the lake, since they will change fairly dramatically as you round the southwestern tip and begin walking back to the parking area again—testimony to the profound difference that orientation to the sun can make in the plants that grow in any given area. The more shaded back side of the lake, which faces the northwest, hosts a variety of plants that would not find enough moisture on the drier, southwest-facing side of the lake.

At 0.2 mile you'll pass through several beautiful gardens of New York fern, and shortly afterward, fine clusters of red and white pine, easily two of the most striking members of the pine family. (Red pine has two needles, incidentally, while white pine has five.)

208

Notice how few understory plants grow at the feet of these stately trees—in part because of the amount of shade they cast but also due to the strong acidity of the thick carpet of pine needles. This place is good for watching red-breasted nuthatches, golden-crowned kinglets, and, high in the canopy, Blackburnian warblers.

"Water," wrote Leonardo da Vinci, "is the driver of nature." That in mind, by all means pick one of the many sitting stones located along the south side of the lake and let this lovely liquid world show you a few of its mysteries. If you happen to be near a collection of lily pads, watch for sudden pops coming from underneath the leaves. The undersides of lily pads—well anchored and close to sunlight, food, and oxygen—make perfect homes for a variety of snails, worms, beetles, and caddis flies. The popping you may hear is the sound of fish nipping a meal from the underside of the leaves. Some types of floating pads are relished by beaver, who learn at a young age to roll them with their forefeet like a fine cigar, and then munch them as if they were hot dogs.

Look for mats of American yew as you round the tip of the lake, as well as increasingly dense stands of mountain laurel, which in June puts forth beautiful clusters of pink-white flowers. Also along the trail are occasional clusters of blue violets, Canada mayflower, sarsaparilla, and, near the very end of the walk, the tightly wrapped blooms of closed gentian.

Notice that several of the trees along this back side have been gnawed by beavers, who at various times have made this pond home. The only access tunnels for lodges built in the middle of a lake or pond are underwater. Therefore, once winter ice forms, a family of these nonhibernating creatures will see only the inside of their lodge, and their submerged cache of branches must sustain them until the spring thaw, along with an occasional tuber from the bottom of the pond. (Venturing beneath the ice cover for a leisurely snack from the family larder is no problem for these animals, since adults can easily hold their breath for fifteen to twenty minutes.)

Like many of us, beaver don't seem particularly eager for winter. As long as it's possible, beaver will maintain a hole in the ice sheet by bumping it open from below, and then enlarging it by breaking off pieces around the perimeter with their nimble front feet.

209

RHODODENDRON SANCTUARY

Distance: 2 miles
Location: Pachaug State Forest. The Mount Misery unit of the Pachaug State Forest. From Connecticut State Highway 138 east of Voluntown, head north on State Highway 49. In 0.6 mile, on the left, is our entrance to the state forest. Immediately after you make this turn is a fork; stay right. Follow signs for the public-use area until, at 0.9 mile, you arrive on the east side of a large playing field. Park here. The trail takes off from the north side of the field, beside a small sign marking the Rhododendron Sanctuary.

Of all the members of the heath family—a clan that includes blueberry, cranberry, and huckleberry—there is perhaps none more striking than the great "Rhododendron maximum." In this rich bog of the Pachaug State Forest the rhododendron reaches its greatest potential, a tangle of sprawling, free-form trunks corkscrewing twenty feet into the air, flying rosettes of thick, leathery leaves, and, in early July, delicate puffs of pink and white flowers.

Though beautiful, the tendency for rhododendrons in this area to grow in vast, almost impenetrable thickets has resulted in the plant occasionally being given "nuisance" status. What's more, the leaves and flowers of all rhododendrons and azaleas are poisonous. (Even honey made from the flowers is toxic.) Early settlers with an eye to the weather, however, did find one interesting use for rhodo-

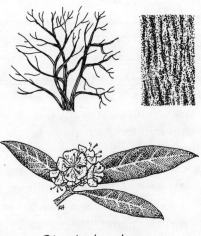

Rhododendron

210

dendron. As it turns out, the amount of curl in the plant's evergreen leaves can be used as a general guide to the temperature. Below about sixty degrees the leaves begin to droop in distinct increments that roughly correspond to ten-degree drops in the temperature. By the time the thermometer hits a point just above freezing, each will display a distinct backward curl.

Our walk begins in a pleasant open forest of hemlock, white pine, and an occasional red or white oak. In 0.1 mile you'll begin a short descent, marked at first by a loose weave of highbush blueberry, starflower, and Canada mayflower, giving way as the ground becomes wetter to cinnamon ferns, sweet pepperbush, rhododendron, Atlantic white cedar, and skunk cabbage. Atlantic white cedar was especially valued by early New England settlers, who used it for everything from floors to roof shingles to pipe organs. In fact, so prized is this durable wood that as standing timber became scarce, bogs were often dredged to extract dead cedars, many of which had been submerged for decades.

Continue to follow the blue blazes deeper and deeper into this great rhododendron-cedar jungle. The bird life is especially fine here, and you should have no problem seeing (or at least hearing) the Canada and Audubon's warblers, red-breasted nuthatch, brown creeper, and, in the very tops of trees, the olive-sided flycatcher.

Olive-sided Flycatcher

211

Brown Creeper

(One way to tell the brown creepers is that they tend to only work their way up tree trunks searching for insects, and not down, like some other birds.)

In less than 0.2 mile you'll come to a trail heading off to the left—this is a return path for the loop trail you're now on. Continue straight, and in a short distance you'll see the blue trail taking off through the bog. From here on there's no real path, just blue blazes that will guide you through a very wet, spongy bog. With appropriate footwear you'll find this a delightful amble through a dark, delicate world composed of cedar and rhododendron thickets, with occasional flushes of moss, arrowleaf, sweet gale, pepperbush, and pitcher plant.

Speaking of pitcher plants, the strange feeding mechanisms of this insectivorous plant are really fascinating. The leaves of the pitcher are joined in such a way that rainwater collects at the base into a small reservoir. An insect happens along, and is drawn to a better look by a series of brightly colored veins and nectar glands located along the upper edges of the leaves. Once inside, however, a fine mat of downward-curving hairs makes it nearly impossible for the insect to crawl out again. What's more, beneath these hairs is yet another trap, this one consisting of layers of sticky, loose cells that break away and adhere to the insect's feet as it tries to make its break for freedom. Eventually the tired, hapless victim falls into the pool of water and drowns. Using special digestive enzymes produced during certain months of the year, the pitcher plant then slowly breaks the insect's body down to release the bounty of nutrients stored there. Pieces of the insect that are indigestible are collected in a narrow stalk at the base of the plant.

Surprisingly, there is a small moth (*Exyria rolandiana*) that actually lays her eggs on the inside of pitcher plant leaves. The caterpillars that hatch in the spring distribute themselves one to a leaf. Here they set up house for the summer, feeding on plant material that grows along the inside of the fluted leaves. As it turns out, this home provides a level of home-maintenance freedom that would make an aluminum siding salesperson sit up and take notice. The only spinning the caterpillar has to do is to perhaps throw up a couple lines of webbing across the opening of the plant in order to keep from being eaten by hungry summer visitors.

After leaving the nature trail 0.1 mile, the pathway reaches a T intersection with a small road. Turn left, continuing to follow the blue-blazed trail (which soon leaves this road) until you reach a dirt road near the campground entrance. Turn left, and follow this road to the parking area.

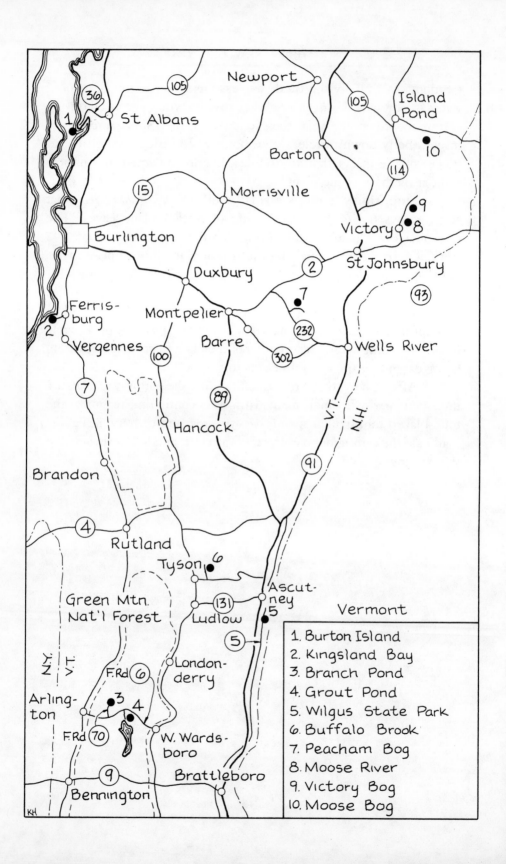

36
105 Newport
105 Island Pond
1 St Albans
Barton 10
114
15
Morrisville 9
Victory 8
Burlington
Duxbury St Johnsbury
2
7 93
Ferris-
burg Montpelier 232
2 Barre
Vergennes 302 Wells River
100
7
89 V.T.
Hancock N.H.

Brandon
91
4
Rutland
Tyson 6
Ascut-
ney
Green Mtn. 131 5
Nat'l Forest Ludlow
5 Vermont
N.Y. V.T. F.Rd 6 1. Burton Island
London- 2. Kingsland Bay
Arling- derry 3. Branch Pond
ton 3 4 4. Grout Pond
F.Rd 70 5. Wilgus State Park
W. Wards- 6. Buffalo Brook
boro 7. Peacham Bog
9 Brattleboro 8. Moose River
Bennington 9. Victory Bog
KH 10. Moose Bog

Vermont

BURTON ISLAND

Distance: 2 miles

Location: Burton Island State Park. From the town of St. Alban's, Vermont, head west on Vermont Highway 36 for approximately 5 miles, and turn left (south), following signs for Kill Kare State Park. A ferry will then take you from Kill Kare to Burton Island State Park. Once you arrive on Burton Island, you may want to stop at the park office just north of the dock slip for a map of the park. To reach our trailhead, walk through the camping area until you reach the westernmost camping shelter. (All of these shelters have been named after trees; the one beside our trailhead is called Juniper.) We'll be walking along the North Shore Trail, which heads west from beside this shelter.

Though only a couple of good stone skips from the mainland, Burton Island, where automobiles are not allowed, can seem like another world. How refreshing it is to find beautiful campgrounds bereft of a single sedan, to be able to peruse 250 acres of beaches and meadows and woodlands accompanied not by honking horns or racing engines but by bird song, by the scamper of raccoons in the middle of the night, by a whisper of waves lapping against the shoreline rocks. So appealing is the absence of cars here, so easily do campers transport their beer, bicycles, and bags of groceries from the ferry by simple

215

wheeled carts, that it begs the question why we haven't created more recreation areas through which General Motors is not allowed to march.

The trail we'll be walking begins 0.6 mile from the dock slip, beside the camping shelter tagged "Juniper." Things get interesting almost immediately, your first steps framed by a fringe of cow vetch, and behind that, a stately line of staghorn sumac. Both staghorn and smooth sumac were used by Indians for a refreshing drink (the hairy fruits were soaked in water), as well as for making a bark tea that was reportedly effective in treating sore throats. A decoction of smooth sumac root and branches was used by various Native American peoples as a treatment for gonorrhea. And the hollow stems of the plant were once employed as taps for sugar maples.

Roughly forty yards into the walk you'll pass between two large northern white cedars, and then a small huddle of aspen, their restless leaves dancing in the slightest puff of air. Also here is the common milkweed. Although often viewed as a lowly pest, milkweed (one of the few flowers along this stretch of trail that is actually native to America) actually has a rather impressive history of use. Reports were made of Virginia Indians using milkweed to treat skin disorders more than four hundred years ago. A couple centuries later, "modern" medicine got behind the plant, proclaiming that it was a particularly effective treatment for respiratory ailments. In the twentieth century, long after most American doctors had stopped using the plant for medicinal purposes, the harvest started once again. This time it was to collect the mature pods full of silky seed hairs, which became the primary stuffing material in Navy life jackets during the last years of World War II.

Beautiful Lake Champlain has been your constant companion along this walk, and a particularly nice view of it opens to the north at about 0.1 mile into the walk. Twenty thousand years ago, during the height of the Wisconsin Ice Age, this beautiful valley was covered in a mass of ice that stretched all the way to Long Island. After the end of glacial advance, when the long, icy blue fingers that had scoured and gouged the land finally began to recoil, meltwater began to accumulate here in tremendous quantities. By the time the large plug of ice north of here in the Saint Lawrence Valley finally melted, creating a passage to the Atlantic, the level of the lake was actually hundreds of feet higher than you see it today!

Northern White Cedar

The North Shore Trail continues to hug the waterline, past clusters of two more European introductions—white campion and purple loosestrife. Like the milkweed, loosestrife is far more than just a pest to gardeners. Greeks burned the plant to keep bugs at bay, and, in a more mysterious vein, hung large garlands of the plant around the necks of their oxen, believing that it encouraged the animals to work together as a team. Today herbalists still prescribe the plant as an effective treatment for diarrhea.

The walk changes abruptly as the path enters a forest of white pine, spruce, and speckled alder. Notice the thick carpet of pine needles here. Conifer needles are very slow to decompose, in part because they are covered by a waxy coating that helps the tree conserve moisture by allowing less water to escape through the pores.

Into the walk 0.2 mile you'll reach the quiet waters of Eagle Bay, a fine place to picnic, nap, or simply invest in a long, lazy Vermont daydream. What grand times there must have been in the 1850s for the children of Burton Island's sharecropping caretakers. Done for the season with daily boat rides back and forth to St. Alban's school, it's easy to imagine them hurrying through their farm chores in order to make fast tracks to the sun-drenched kingdom of Eagle Bay. Great men of the day may have at the time been wrapped in their own countryside adventures—Thoreau at Walden Pond, Whitman on the back roads of New York—yet none would have seemed of any more consequence than being a kid right here, smack in the middle of a slow, sweet Burton Island summer.

Leaving both the bay and flocks of ring-billed gulls behind, we'll begin our return trip along the Eagle Bay Trail, which heads into the woods beside a large birch snag. Unlike the bare floor of the coniferous forest we passed through earlier, the ground beneath this mixed deciduous forest is washed with shade-tolerant plants, including ferns, violets, twisted stalk, bunchberry, and Solomon's seal. At 0.5 mile the path again enters a more open area. Just after passing a stretch of wooden treadways, you'll see fine samples of red osier, pin cherry, and white ash, this latter tree being the preferred wood for making everything from snowshoes to baseball bats.

At 0.65 mile you'll spot a trail coming from the left, just this side of a dirt roadway. Turn back onto this pathway, and in about 0.1 mile, after passing a lovely cattail marsh on the left (complete with the buzz of red-winged blackbirds) and a magnificent swamp white oak on the right, you'll find yourself at your starting point.

Ring-billed Gull

KINGSLAND BAY

Distance: 0.85 mile

Location: Kingsland Bay State Park. Heading south on U.S. Highway 7, at the village of Ferrisburg turn right (west) onto Little Chicago Road (approximately 3 miles north of the town of Vergennes). Continue east on Little Chicago Road for approximately 0.95 mile, and turn right. Follow this road for 3.4 miles to the park entrance, and follow the entrance road to a large parking area just past the fee station. The loop trail begins along the edge of the bay near the tennis courts.

Kingsland Bay State Park is not only small but is reached only by leaving the beaten path and heading down a twisted braid of narrow country roads. What's more, as of this writing there wasn't a single sign to help you get there. All of this delightful inattention has helped to keep Kingsland Bay a relatively quiet, locals' kind of place, where close chums and their dogs get together on hot summer days for burgers and frisbee and sailboarding. The one trail here is along a small peninsula that juts out into the bay, offering an easy amble through a typical Vermont lowland forest, with some fine views of cool, blue Lake Champlain.

The amount of history that rose and fell along the shores of this 435-square-mile lake would fill many bookshelves. Unfortunately, we know very little about the slow turn of centuries that belonged to the various Indian peoples before the arrival of the Europeans. For the most part our tales must begin with the arrival of the French explorer, military man, and mapmaker who would ultimately lend his name to this long, blue reach of water—Samuel de Champlain.

It was in the fall of 1608, three years after he had first mapped the coasts of Maine and New Hampshire, that an Algonquin chief persuaded Champlain to lead an expedition into the waters of this great lake to strike down the Algonquin's archenemies, the Iroquois. After a couple of rather uneventful days, on the night of July 29, 1609 across the water from where you now stand, Champlain and the Algonquin did indeed meet the enemy they were seeking. Messengers were sent from the Iroquois, and, since the darkness of night made it nearly impossible to know who was friend and who was foe, both sides agreed to begin the battle at first light.

219

As the darkness lifted, Champlain saw that he was easily outnumbered three to one. Undaunted, he led the Algonquin on a slow, confident march toward the advancing front line of the Iroquois. When the fearless Frenchman got within thirty yards, he reports that he saw the Iroquois leaders make a move to draw their bows. "I took aim with my arquebus and shot straight at one of the three chiefs," he writes in his journal, "and with this shot two fell to the ground and one of their companions was wounded who died thereof a little later." Champlain's Algonquin friends could have hardly been more encouraged. They instantly erupted into a boisterous attack that sent the alarmed Iroquois running like rabbits into the shadows of the forest.

It has been suggested that with that one shot from his arquebus, Champlain set in motion a long history of intense division between the Algonquin and the Iroquois—a feud that France and Britain would use in their battle against each other for control of the New World. But while this notion probably gives the July 30 melee much more impact than it deserves, there can be no doubt that it did help to fuel the anger of the Iroquois, who, 32 years later, embarked on a series of some of the most bloody raids in history against the French and their Algonquin friends.

Our walk, through much more peaceful environs, begins in the cool shade of a forest thick with sugar maple, white cedar, hemlock, black cherry, and shadbush, the ground peppered with white trillium and an occasional false Solomon's seal. About 0.1 mile into the walk are nice huddles of white oak, shagbark hickory, hemlock, and hophornbeam, or, as it is also known, ironwood. A very short spur trail leads to the left at 0.2 mile to a fine view spot. From here you can see a long sweep of the Adirondacks, rising into the New York skyline from the far shores of Lake Champlain.

As you leave this rather pleasant perch and continue down the trail, you'll pass through a stately stand of red pine, the name derived from the tree's beautiful thick, red-brown bark. Although for over two hundred years people have been calling this tree Norway pine, this is a complete misnomer, since the mighty red is most certainly a native of the New World. Red pine grows very well even on poor soils, sometimes able to push out eighteen to twenty-four inches of growth in a single year! As such, it's a favorite tree for replanting forests that have been cut or burned.

Our path rounds the small headland at 0.45 mile, and then, after a short climb, doubles back toward the main park area. Just after this climb another spur trail takes off to the left, this one leading to a view spot looking toward the northeast, surrounded by some lovely clusters of honeysuckle. Continue to make your way back through the forest, accompanied by white oak and hobblebush, as well as a few basswood poking their branches out into the footpath. In 0.85 mile you'll emerge near the tennis courts, just a few yards from where you started your trek.

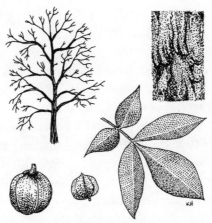

Shagbark Hickory

BRANCH POND

Distance: 1.6 miles

Location: Green Mountain National Forest. Coming from the north, follow Vermont Highway 100 to the single bridge in the town of West Wardsboro. From this point head south for 0.2 mile and turn right (west) onto Forest Road 6. Proceed for 11.3 miles to Forest Road 70, and turn right. Follow this road for just under 2.5 miles to the end of the road. Our trail takes off on the right.

And the pond's stillness rippled as if by rain instead is pocked with life.

MAXINE KUMIN

Though the hidden southern finger of Branch Pond is quite close to the parking area for this walk, following this easy pathway through a cool mixed forest to the pond's east side is a much nicer way to get acquainted. The woods are lush with ferns and patches of wood sorrel. Bluebead lily and purple trillium line the trail, and mats of hobblebush can be seen hugging the great, shining trunks of the yellow birch. What's more, you're very likely to hear the beautiful song of the hermit thrush here. Each outpouring of this camouflaged ground nester is slightly different than the last—a different pitch, and a slightly rearranged crescendo of clear, fluid notes. These lovely tremolos, dripping off the leaves of the forest like drops of fresh rain, are as sweet as any birdsong in America.

At just under 0.3 mile you'll intersect the Branch Pond Trail, where you'll take a left. This path, laced with a thick braid of roots, winds briefly out of the forest at 0.45 mile to the fringe of a quiet marsh. Watch here for green heron gliding silently past huddles of twisted tree skeletons, looking like the last survivors of some ancient spirit world. Soon the path ducks into the forest again, and, in a beautiful stand of yellow birch at 0.7 mile, intersects the trail to Branch Pond. Take a left here, and walk 0.1 mile to the edge of the pond. The last few yards of the pathway will take you past a beautiful collection of sheep laurel, their pink, spotted, saucer-shaped flowers looking like miniaturized versions of that showiest of eastern upland plants, the mountain laurel. In June, you may also be treated to the lovely blossoms of blue-flag iris.

Perhaps more than any other inland environment, ponds are absolutely flushed with life, although much goes unnoticed by human visitors. It is a very complex, very interwoven web of life, thousands of events unfolding in any given hour, on any given summer day. Surely as you stand here, somewhere a fish is eyeing a group of whirligig beetles floating on the surface of the pond. The beetles, on the other hand, are scanning the depths for danger with one set of "underwater eyes," while watching for their own dinner of insects to fall onto the surface of the pond with another set. Water striders strike at young mosquitos emerging from their larval stage. A dragonfly nymph zips quietly through the water, propelling itself by first drawing water into the digestive tract, and then using special muscles to squeeze it out again. A diving beetle grabs a bubble of air with its wing covers—an instant scuba tank, of sorts—and dives beneath the water, perhaps not to surface again for many hours. And of course there are frogs and newts and turtles and crayfish, toads and birds and worms and spiders and snakes.

Beneath all this semivisible activity are the one-celled phytoplanktons. These algaes and desmids and diatoms maintain structures and methods for locomotion that are 2 billion years old. Yet under the microscope, some are as uncannily futuristic looking as anything dreamed up in the studios of Hollywood. These "invisible" organisms, by the way, form the very foundation for all the life of the pond—the underpinning that holds on its back virtually every ascending level of the food chain.

Red-spotted Newt

GROUT POND

Distance: 2.9 miles

Location: Green Mountain National Forest. Coming from the north, follow Vermont Highway 100 to the single bridge in the town of West Wardsboro. From this point head south for 0.2 mile and turn right (west) onto Forest Road 6. Proceed for 6.4 miles to the Grout Pond entrance road, and turn left. Follow this road for 1.2 miles to a parking lot and picnic area at the bottom of a hill on the northwest corner of Grout Pond. (A boat ramp is nearby.) Our walk continues east along this road, running along the north shore of the pond.

This easy 2.9-mile stroll winds in and out of forest and clearing, the rippling blue waters of Grout Pond never more than a stone's throw away. But for a few scratchy patches of wood nettle growing on the back side of the pond, this path traverses what is essentially a very friendly environment—in the warm months a gentle mix of shade and sunlit shore that can slow the most harried walker. Henry James is supposed to have said that "summer afternoon" were "the two most beautiful words in the English language." Head down, feet up along the shore of Grout Pond, it's hard to disagree.

From the parking area at the end of the road we'll be heading clockwise around the lake, beginning on a roadway that will eventually narrow to a footpath. Besides the commonly celebrated trees of the Vermont forest, such as sugar and striped maples, beech, and balsam fir, you'll also be passing a couple species that you may have overlooked, such as mountain maple and hophornbeam. The bark of the mountain maple is an important food to deer. Ruffed grouse of the area, which in summer can be found nesting along the grassy fringes of the forest, relish the young buds. (Ruffed grouse, though, relish a lot of things. Studies in various parts of the country have identified more than six hundred types of plants in their diets!)

It should come as no surprise, then, that ruffed grouse also feed on the buds of the hophornbeam you'll see along the first 0.5 mile of the walk. The "hop" in this name refers to the resemblance that the fruits have to the hops used in making beer and malt liquor. Hophornbeam is also sometimes called ironwood, a reference to the extremely hard wood that has been used for centuries to fashion tool handles.

The walkway inches closer and closer to the lakeshore, with several nice side trails going to small shoreline picnic areas. At 0.5 mile you'll be able to look across the pond to the southeast and see the forested flank of 3,556-foot Mount Snow. In this area, just about the time that the road yields to a footpath, look for fine stands of both mountain holly and witherod. This latter plant is a viburnum, and like most members of this genus, it has very slender, supple branches. In fact, the first part of the plant's common name, *withe*, is a term referring to any flexible branch used in basket making. The fruit of the witherod, which appear in August and September, tastes a great deal like raisin. As you continue along the lakeshore, scan the lake once in a while for loons.

In 1 mile you'll intersect the Kelly Strand Road Trail. Turn right to keep following the loop path around the pond. The next part of the walk is through a cool, moist forest, the shady trailsides lined with ferns, bunchberry, wood sorrel, and bluebead lily. Listen here for both the lilt of warblers and the soft rattle of downy woodpeckers. As you round the southeast corner of Grout Pond, to your right will be a wonderful wetland area. The bird houses in this corner pocket of the lake are for wood ducks, which land managers maintain year-round by adding fresh wood shavings to the floors of the nests. Wood ducks aren't the only ones who appreciate this housing subsidy. Mice, bees, and wasps have been found inside the boxes, as have flying squirrels. (These marvelous little creatures don't actually fly, but rather use a special membrane located between their front and rear feet to glide out of trees—sometimes for distances up to one hundred fifty feet. Because they're nocturnal, they are rarely seen by humans.)

At 1.8 miles is a T intersection, where you'll take another right. Watch out for wood nettle on this stretch of trail, whose stinging hairs can irritate the skin. (Appropriately, along the wetland area you just passed are clusters of jewelweed, the leaves and stems of which can be ground to produce a juice that substantially reduces the irritating effects of both nettles and poison ivy.) Also here are selfheal, tall meadow rue, whorled wood aster, and red-berried elder.

Across the lake to the north of where you now walk lies Stratton Mountain, where, in 1840, Daniel Webster delivered a stirring oratory in support of William Henry Harrison's bid for the presidency—part of the famous Log Cabin and Hard Cider Campaign. (Webster would later lend his masterful editing touch to President Harrison's inaugural speech.) It's interesting to note that New Hampshire–born Webster was once so petrified at the thought of public speaking that he couldn't even get out of his seat when called to do so at Exeter Academy. Yet he went on to become perhaps the greatest orator in American history. Enormous gatherings of people, occasionally topping a hundred thousand, would come to hear just about anything that Daniel Webster had to say. Across the water at sleepy little Stratton Mountain, he drew a crowd of more than fifteen thousand.

Champion of New Englanders, praised at one time or another by everyone from Lincoln to Emerson, Webster, who died in office as secretary of state, was an extremely influential statesman. It was under the direction of this staunch Federalist that American currency eventually gained a solid position within the United States Bank. The Monroe Doctrine, which announced to the world that the American continents "are henceforth not to be considered as subjects for future colonization by any European power," had a great deal of Daniel Webster in its brief but powerful message. Famous patriotic

Downy Woodpecker

Flying Squirrel

statements such as "One country, one constitution, one destiny" and "The people's government, made for the people, made by the people, and answerable to the people" were Webster's. It is reported that lying on the cusp of death in 1852, the last words this statesman ever uttered were "I still live." For a long time, in the hearts of many, many Americans, he still did.

At 2.5 miles you'll reach a dirt road. Other routes lead from this one, but if you continue circling to the right you'll reach the entrance road at 2.7 miles. Turn right once again, and in 0.2 mile you'll arrive back at the trailhead parking area.

WILGUS STATE PARK

Distance: 0.6 mile

Location: Take the Ascutney exit off Interstate 91, and follow U.S. Highway 5 south for approximately 1.5 miles. The park entrance will be on your left. Immediately after turning into the park, turn right into the picnic area parking lot. We'll be walking along a riverside nature trail, located on the far side of the picnic area.

Just a stone's throw from U.S. Highway 5, this short, shady amble along the Connecticut River offers a wonderful respite to the road-weary traveler. There seem to be few prescriptions as effective for relieving stress as fifteen minutes spent on a wooded riverbank, casting idle thoughts into the quick of the current. Not that such mental drifting is anything new. Virgil was waxing poetic about such things more than two thousand years ago. "May the countryside and the gliding valley streams content me," he wrote. "Lost to fame, let me love river and woodland." Virgil would have liked the Connecticut River.

The Connecticut, a name derived from an Indian phrase meaning "long tidal river," is New England's longest watercourse, winding its way 410 miles from the crumpled, forested uplands along the Canadian border to the waters of Long Island Sound. Thanks to a massive cleanup effort, today the Connecticut is once again a beautiful river, having gained back at least a few shreds of the splendor it seemed to hold for former Yale president Timothy Dwight in the early 1800s. He wrote in *Travels in New England and New York*, "This stream may, with more propriety than any other in the world, be named THE BEAUTIFUL RIVER. The purity, salubrity and sweetness of its waters; . . . the uncommon and universal beauty of its banks . . . the rude bluff and the shaggy mountain, are objects which no traveler can thoroughly describe and no reader can adequately imagine."

Beyond beauty, however, this river valley has seen more than its share of human history. Great villages of Pennacook and Abnaki Indians once lived here, raising crops, tapping sugar maples, and spearing shad along the riverbanks. Although the river was discovered in 1614 by a Dutch sea captain named Adriaen Block, the first settlement along these upper reaches (in what would one day become Vermont) was a square fort of pine built south of here by the British in 1724. As was so often the case, after the arrival of the Europeans there seemed to be no end to the skirmishes in this valley—battles with the Indians, fights with the French, onslaughts from the British, and a tirade of verbal firepower between Ethan Allen and Eleazer Wheelock (cofounder of Dartmouth) over who would ultimately control this verdant land.

In the interim, however, there came a time when hardy settlers began trodding up the banks of the Connecticut to this region, bound to the north country to clear themselves a fresh start from an unsettled, uncivilized land. Most such beginnings were remarkably humble, typically centered in a crude, dirt-floored cabin of hand-hewn logs, which was often constructed around a large tree stump that served perfectly as the family dinner table.

Besides the pleasure of having the Connecticut River for company, one of the more enjoyable aspects of this walk is the fact that several trees along the trail have been identified, which makes the trek perfect for budding naturalists anxious to get a close-up look at a handful of New England's more common trees. Since names are only a beginning, however, let's spend some time talking about some of the lore surrounding a few of these long-time Connecticut Valley residents.

White Pine (at the beginning of the walk, on the left): White pine has as illustrious a history as any tree in New England. White pines were absolutely perfect for making strong, one-piece masts for sailing ships. In colonial times, in fact, it was strictly against the law for colonists to cut down any white pine measuring over three feet thick at the stump (one of many laws that the colonists chose to ignore). So big were these trees that it was not uncommon to need seventy pair of oxen to skid one out of the forest!

White Oak (0.1 mile in, on the left): While there has perhaps been no group of trees more important to American Indians than the oaks, most Native Americans had a special place in their hearts for certain white oaks. This favoritism is because some white oak trees

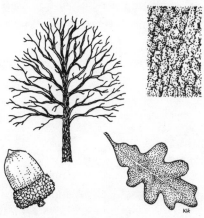

White Oak

produce acorns that have fairly low levels of tannic acid—that bitter, very disagreeable taste that puckers your mouth (and, if you ate enough, would eventually harm your digestive tract). Removing tannic acid from acorns required long periods of leaching in water, which the Indians accomplished either by burying them in the ground or hanging them in streams, sometimes for several months. Only then would they be fit to grind into flour, mix into mush or pemmican. Obviously, locating a white oak with fairly sweet nuts on it, whose tannins could be leached quickly and easily, was something worth celebrating.

Yellow Birch (1.8 miles in, on the left): Of all the birches, yellow birch has the longest, most varied history of commercial use. Leading carriage makers chose yellow birch from which to craft their hubs, since the wood of this tree is very resistant to cracks, and tended to hold wheel spokes tightly for years after they were anchored. Likewise, many New England ship builders preferred yellow birch for making any part of a vessel that was to remain underwater. Tool handles are also constructed of this birch.

Much of the lore about birch trees in general has nothing to do at all with commercial possibilities. For instance, slender birch branches were used not only for spanking children but for flogging prisoners at least as far back as Roman times. (One legend, in fact, claims that Christ was beaten with birch sticks.) In addition, witches supposedly rode the midnight skies on brooms made the birch. Light, pleasant teas continue to be made from the leaves of the birches, and Europeans long favored a wine made from the twigs and sap.

BUFFALO BROOK

Distance: 3 miles

Location: Head north out of the town of Ludlow on Vermont
Highway 100. At the village of Tyson, turn right onto Kingdom
Road, following the signs for Camp Plymouth State Park. In 0.7
mile, turn left onto a road that will take you to the park entrance
station. Instead of turning into the park, however, continue
straight for about 40 yards, to a small dirt road taking off to the
right. Take this dirt road for 0.1 mile, and park at a small, grassy
clearing on the right. Our walk follows this dirt road.

This walk, which follows the gentle turns and tumbles of Buffalo
Brook, is particularly pleasant early in the morning or in late evening.
It's then that the buzz of the chickadee and the shout of the ovenbird
can be heard ringing through the woods, adding a bit of punctuation
to the sizzle of stream water falling over the folded braids of rock.
Certain sights along this walk—massive white pines, or ribbons of
stone made smooth by countless centuries of ice and water—hint at
the almost overwhelming patience with which the wheel of nature
tends to turn. Yet within the last few ticks of that clock, there have
been some rather interesting human dramas in this area.

Half a dozen miles to the east, for example, between Caven-
dish and South Woodstock, was the eastern main line of Vermont's
highly developed underground railroad, where for three-quarters of a
century countless slaves moved north toward the promise of freedom

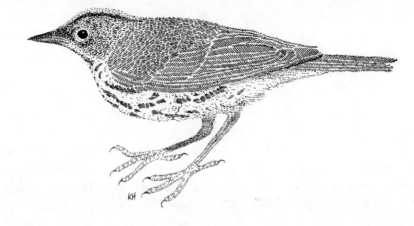

Ovenbird

231

on Canadian soil, carried much of the way in wooden crates or in wagons with false bottoms. Indeed, Vermont had a long history of antislavery attitudes. In 1777, while still a republic, it drafted the first constitution in which slavery was prohibited. Open defiance of the Fugitive Slave Law of 1793 became fairly common in the courts, a position that perhaps began in 1815 when a Middlebury judge stated that the only proof of ownership he would honor in extraditing a man into slavery was a "bill of sale from God Almighty." Based on population, more Vermonters fought the Union cause in the Civil War—one out of every four men—than residents of any other state. Only one in ten was actually drafted.

Seven years after Lee surrendered to Grant at Appomattox, Calvin Coolidge was born a few miles north of our walking path, near the town of Plymouth. In 1924, after making it through a hotbed of scandals he inherited as vice-president from Warren Harding, who died in office, Coolidge was elected the thirtieth president of the United States. He was an extremely serious man, often referred to as "Silent Cal." One story tells that during a formal dinner an attractive woman seated next to Coolidge informed him that she had just made a bet that she could get more than two words out of him. "You lose," was all Coolidge said.

As you make your way along the roadway, look at 0.1 mile for nice clusters of shinleaf, a ground cover with elliptical leaves and stalks of fragrant, waxy white flowers. The leaves of this rather common member of the wintergreen family contain a chemical similar to aspirin. They were once used to make a plaster, known as a shin plaster, that was placed on cuts and wounds to reduce pain. Also on the ground in this area is the beautiful bluebead lily, as well as Canada mayflower and wood sorrel.

The walk continues to follow the stream at a very gentle grade, passing through a lovely forest of hemlock, birch, beech, and maple, with fringes of tall meadow rue, clearstem, and selfheal, the latter plant famous as a remedy for sore throats. Also common in the dry, gravelly sites along this walk is coltsfoot. The early-blooming coltsfoot was known by the Romans as cough dispeller, while the English called it coughwort, both names hinting at the plant's long use as a remedy for persistent coughs, asthma, and bronchial congestion. Asthmatics in this country for years found relief for their condition by smoking coltsfoot leaves, at least until more effective anti-histamines arrived on the scene.

You'll cross Buffalo Brook several times during this walk, giving you a perfect chance to explore some of the easily overlooked wonders of a stream environment. Here is the net-winged midge larva that hangs on to rocks in the middle of a rushing current by means of special suction cups. What's more, it can create or release suction at will by retracting or extending a pistonlike device located in each cup. By letting some of its suction cups loose, and then anchoring them in a new place, it can move over rocks without being swept away by the current.

The adaptations of stream dwellers to flowing water are truly fantastic. Even the shape of a fish is no small accident, its sleek, supple body allowing it to swim upstream with a minimum of energy. One species of caddis fly actually weaves a net in the fork of a tiny twig, which it uses to snare food drifting in the current. Blackfly larvae, which grow up into one of the most detested insects of the northern New England woodlands, anchor themselves to webs of silk spun against a rock, snatching food from the slow current with a pair of hairy appendages. If a blackfly larva is accidentally dislodged from its rock, it can return by reeling itself back upstream with a safety line anchored to the home web.

At 1.3 miles you'll reach a fork in the stream. Stay right. You'll come to our turnaround place in another 0.2 mile, at a point where Buffalo Brook comes from the left, along a faint roadway, and Reading Pond Brook continues straight up the main forested ravine. You may want to sit for a while on the point of land lying between these two watercourses, surrounded by, as John Milton once described it, the "liquid lapse of murmuring streams."

PEACHAM BOG

Distance: 4.8 miles

Location: From Interstate 91, head west on U.S. 2 for 18.2 miles
to Vermont Highway 232, and turn left (south). Follow this road
south for 8.4 miles to the main entrance into Groton State Forest.
Down this road 1.7 miles, on the left, just past the Big Deer
Campground, is the nature center and parking area. Our walk
takes off from the far side of this lot.

*I have frequently found that I was attracted solely by a few
square rods of impermeable and unfathomable bog—a natural
sink in one corner of it. That was the jewel that dazzled me. I
derive more of my subsistence from the swamps which surround
my native town than from the cultivated gardens in the village.*

HENRY DAVID THOREAU

Groton State Forest lies along a particularly lovely swell of mountains. Much of the reserve's 25,000 acres, once blanketed with great
quilts of conifers, is today covered with fine forests of yellow birch,
red maple, and white birch, a change caused in large part by intense
fires that seared these uplands early in the century. The sheer size of
the reserve (the state's second largest landholding) sustains a rich
variety of wildlife, including black bear, fisher, mink, moose, and
deer.

The charm of this place doesn't stop at the boundaries of the
state forest. Surrounding Groton is a delightful braid of twisted
country roads, leading to some of the most idyllic Vermont villages
imaginable. A couple of these, including nearby Peacham (sometimes called the most photographed town in Vermont), are perched
atop hills that afford fine views of the surrounding countryside. Such
elevated sites were chosen not for the scenery but rather as an
attempt to eke a few more frost-free days out of the growing season by
planting crops well above the colder air of the valley bottoms. (In the
mountains, of course, there soon comes a point where elevation
means colder, not warmer, weather.)

Before you head down the trail, notice the fringe of tamaracks
growing here, rimming the parking area with their lacy branches like
a plantation of pale green feather dusters. Tamaracks have needles

234

that actually turn gold and drop each autumn, leaving a huddle of ragged gray skeletons that look very much like dead conifers. (Occasionally, though, what you're seeing *is* a dead stand of trees, killed by infestations of the larch sawfly.) For early northern New England Indian tribes, tamaracks had a special tie to the white birch trees that also surround much of the path to Peacham Bog. The bark of the white birch provided shell material for constructing canoes; the sinewy roots of the tamarack, on the other hand, provided the thread with which that bark was sewn together.

Once you top the small hill beside the parking area and enter the forest, watch the ground for extensive mats of both bunchberry and wintergreen. The damp, cold New England winters did much to aggravate rheumatism in early Indian peoples, and one of their favorite remedies for the discomfort was wintergreen tea. Colonists discovered the benefits of the beverage rather by accident, as they searched for substitutes to the brew supplied to them by the East India Company, which was no longer available during the boycott of the 1773 Tea Act. Scientists later discovered that the oil of the wintergreen plant is composed primarily of methyl salicylate, which is indeed a very close relative to aspirin. What's more, wintergreen oil (now synthetically produced) is still in use today as an ingredient in externally applied muscle ointments.

At 0.4 mile is a trail intersection, the path to Peacham Bog continuing straight through a strikingly beautiful weave of balsam

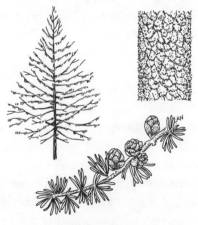

Tamarack

and birch. You'll cross one of two strip cuts you'll be following for much of the walk 0.2 mile later. This area, which was cut during summer 1984 and is now filled with raspberry, pin cherry, and blackberry, is well along the way to becoming an honest-to-goodness birch forest.

We mentioned earlier that the birch woods replaced large stands of conifers—more than eight hundred fifty continuous acres in this particular section of forest—when fires swept through the woods around the turn of the century. Whether or not a conifer forest ever returns to a severely burned or heavily logged area depends a great deal on the soil that lies underneath. Places with thick layers of well-drained soil may see a long-term shift to a beech-maple forest. In much of this area, however, where glacial deposits have created thin, poorly drained soils, the more adaptive conifers could probably once again have their day in the sun. In this sense, a significant portion of the deciduous color shows we enjoy each autumn in northern New England are not natural per se but the result of our having driven out the conifer forest through centuries of relentless logging.

At 1.25 miles you'll pass through beautiful gardens of hay-scented fern and woodfern, with patches of bunchberries never far away. A pocket of brackish water opens at 1.75 miles—the southwest leg of Peacham Bog. Our path then plunges into the spruce-fir forest, finally reaching a spongy slice of true peat bog 0.5 mile later, near a nice mat of snowberry. Here indeed is a world very different from any other, a hauntingly beautiful carpet of sphagnum, sedges, leather-leaf, laurel, rhodora, and rosemary—all spiked with green huddles of tamarack and black spruce. Not many plants can withstand the high levels of acidity found in such a bog, which registers just slightly higher on the pH scale than vinegar. Please keep in mind that the vegetative mat of a bog is extremely fragile. Do not wander off the main trail.

These 200 acres are especially unique in that they form what is known as a raised bog. A raised bog, which occurs only when sufficient moisture is present, is a phenomenon whereby thicker and thicker layers of saturated peat accumulate, ultimately building a dome-shaped mass that actually rises above the level of the original cavity. This action may not seem so amazing until you realize that the water level is also higher in the middle of the bog than it is at the edges—a defiance of gravity, if you will. Very little is understood, however, about the long-term mechanics of this bit of natural engineering.

MOOSE RIVER

Distance: 1 mile
Location: From Interstate 91, exit at U.S. Highway 2 and head east. Approximately 3 miles east of St. Johnsbury, you'll come to the intersection of U.S. 2 and Vermont Highway 18. Continue east on U.S. 2 for 8.8 miles, and turn left on a road with a sign pointing to the community of Victory (now just a small scatter of buildings). Our parking area, called Mitchell's Landing, is located on the left, 4.6 miles down this road. From the parking area, walk 0.2 mile south along the entrance road until you see a wooden snowmobile bridge on the left crossing the Moose River. This is our walking path.

This short stroll along the beautiful Moose River, ideal for a quick stretch of the legs or a streamside lunch, can be easily combined with our other stroll at Victory Bog (see page 239), which also leaves from the same parking area. Together they will give you a short but very sweet introduction to one of the richest, quietest wildlife preserves in the state of Vermont.

The view from the snowmobile bridge crossed at 0.2 mile is one worth savoring. Upstream to the northeast is an especially wild patchwork of mountains and wetlands, the liquid fruits of this watershed running beneath you on a fast dance to the Connecticut River via the Passumpsic. (The Connecticut River drains more than a third of the land in the state of Vermont.) One hundred fifty years ago the Moose River was used to float pine and spruce cut along these banks to downstream sawmills. The lumbering business got a real shot in the arm when the Victory Branch railroad was punched up the valley in the 1880s. (During some of this walk you'll be traversing the old track bed.) To say that logging had a profound impact on the New England landscape is a tremendous understatement. The old Bog Pond Mill alone, which from 1892 to 1900 was the commercial center of the village of Victory, ran more than 5 million board feet a year through its steam- and water-driven saws. Scarcely twenty-five years after those blades first started turning, the old-growth virgin spruce forest of the Moose River drainage was gone.

From the bridge our path takes a sharp right turn, following the Moose River downstream for the remainder of the walk. Look along the path for club mosses, whorled wood asters, foamflower, strawberry, meadow rue, and meadowsweet. The hillside on the left is thick with spruce, but nearer the path a more deciduous mix of maples, birch, and alder take the stage. At 0.3 mile you'll see the remains of an old railroad trestle on the far side of the river, a remnant of the lumbering days discussed earlier. From this point the pathway is a bit more overgrown, but if you follow it another 0.1 mile you'll come to a still, peaceful pool of water—a last pause for the Moose before it begins a rocky tumble southward to the sleepy village of Concord.

This river is well named. A quiet walk down the paths of Victory Bog during early morning or late evening will give you a better-than-average chance of spotting moose. The same long, gangly legs that allow moose to maneuver so efficiently when dining in the muck of a swamp also help them traverse deep snows. Unlike deer, who in winter will travel together in lines to trample paths through the snow, the towering moose has no need to engage in such community projects.

VICTORY BOG

Distance: 0.8 mile

Location: From Interstate 91, exit at U.S. Highway 2 and head east. Approximately 3 miles east of St. Johnsbury, you'll come to the intersection of U.S. 2 and Vermont Highway 18. Continue east on U.S. 2 for 8.8 miles, and turn left on a road with a sign pointing to the community of Victory (now just a small scatter of buildings). Our parking area, called Mitchell's Landing, is located on the left, 4.6 miles down this road. The trail takes off across the road from, and slightly to the right of, the parking area, and is marked by a 2.

The trails at Victory Bog Wildlife Management Area have almost no markings on them, tend to end quickly in the middle of nowhere, and, in more than a few places, are half overgrown with a shaggy tangle of grasses, weeds, and shrubs. The place, in other words, is about as perfect a wild getaway as you'll find anywhere in Vermont.

The Moose River traces a silent, twisted path here through an incredibly rich freshwater marsh and bog. A great sweep of mountains fills the eastern horizon, each autumn set afire by the fluttering reds, oranges, and golds of millions of maple and birch leaves. Moose tracks can be found in almost every lowland patch of mud, as can those of mink, weasel, otter, beaver, and muskrat. Under the cover of the surrounding hardwoods are marten, bear, and even Canadian lynx. Birds absolutely abound, with more than a dozen species of warblers and sparrows alone. Bitterns, green herons, and great blue herons stalk the lowland marshes; osprey, marsh hawks, and rough-legged hawks hug the skies overhead.

It is this primitiveness of Victory Bog that gives it such appeal. You'll certainly enjoy this place if you're the kind of nature enthusiast who doesn't mind donning long pants and picking your way through a tumble of untrammeled nature. A visit to Victory is less a walk than it is an exploration. Literary historian Walter Bagehot once made a statement that applies well to the enjoyment of places like Victory Bog: "To a great experience one thing is essential—an experiencing nature."

Across the road and slightly to the south you'll find a grassy pathway descending through the woodland to the edge of the Moose River. From the edge of the water turn left, and wind your way

239

northward along what is really an old railroad bed. By 0.1 mile you'll
be framed by fine, sprawling mountain vistas on the right, and a
wonderful cattail marsh on the left, the latter a favorite hangout of
red-winged blackbirds, marsh wrens, and muskrats. If you've read
many nature books you may already be well aware of the extensive
list of uses humans have come up with for cattails, but a few of them
are worth repeating. For starters, practically all of the plant is edible
(not to mention highly nutritious), from its starchy rootstalks to its

Great Blue Heron

fuzzy brown flower head. The roots taste like potatoes, the young stalks like celery or cucumber, and the developing flowers a bit like corn. The pollen is a wonderful addition to breads and pancakes. Indian peoples used cattail leaves extensively in weaving, soaked the flower heads in animal fat to make torches, and employed the downy seeds as both diapers and padding for cradle boards.

Continue through clumps of spruce, alder, tamarack, honeysuckle, blueberry, currants, meadowsweet, and shadbush, taking plenty of time to explore the wild edges of Moose River. Watch carefully for sudden eruptions of wings along the water, which usually belong to the robin-size spotted sandpiper. This bird is typically very reclusive, one that you would likely never see if you were walking in a more heavily visited area. In a fascinating reversal of typical mating habits, it is the female spotted sandpiper that attracts the male with a strutting courtship display. Once the eggs are laid the male may get left behind to incubate and raise the young while she goes in search of another mate. In fall the sandpipers will not cluster but slip quietly away a few at a time in the dark of night, many bound for wintering grounds in South America and the Caribbean.

MOOSE BOG

Distance: 1.2 miles

Location: From the junction of Vermont highways 114 North and 105 East in downtown Island Pond, head east on Highway 105 for 8.8 miles, and park at a large turnout on the left (north) side of the road. (This turnout is 0.8 mile east of a railroad crossing.) From the parking area, walk east along Highway 105 for 0.2 mile to our walking road, which is a small, two-track road taking off to the right (south).

Moose Bog, in the heart of the Wenlock Wildlife Management Area, is as wild and untrammeled a natural tapestry as you could hope to find in all of Vermont. Indeed, its blanket of spruce-fir forest, its sandy, two-track roads riddled with moose tracks, its forests and clearings alive with nearly a dozen bird species on Vermont's rare and endangered list, are more what you would expect to find in the far reaches of Maine or southern Canada. For an investment of barely a mile of walking, this trek will take you further into the thick of nature than you may have thought possible.

As noted above, leave your car at the large parking area on the north side of Highway 105 and walk east for 0.2 mile to our walking road, an old logging route on the right. A few yards up this road is a fork. Stay left, on the branch blocked from vehicle traffic by a large boulder. Around this junction you'll find a nice garden of Canada mayflower, as well as beautiful clusters of bunchberry—a member of the dogwood family that in June sends creamy white flower bracts above its whorl of smooth green leaves. Just past this junction the road becomes wrapped in a thick curtain of conifers, the delicious scent of balsam dripping off the summer breeze.

It's here that the especially fortunate walker might get a glimpse of the elusive spruce grouse. (You may have seen a notice posted near the highway, requesting that you report spruce grouse sightings to the Department of Fish and Wildlife, which is trying to track their dwindling populations.) Though approachable to the point of being downright tame—they have long been referred to as "fool hens"—spruce grouse, with their white-spotted sides and rust-tipped tail feathers, are so few in numbers and so good at hiding beneath conifer branches that to see one in this area is a rare treat. During summer spruce grouse will eat a wide variety of nuts, berries, and the shoots of young plants, reducing their diet in winter to one long helping of evergreen needles and buds. Like many birds who have adapted to the long, frigid winters of the north country, the spruce grouse dons a fine cloak of feathers to hold back the cold, including fine, thick leggings that extend all the way to its feet. If in the end you are empty in your effort to spot spruce grouse, you may wish to try your luck at locating other fairly elusive residents of this spruce-fir forest, including black-backed woodpeckers and boreal chickadees.

In approximately 0.2 mile we'll turn right onto a footpath that takes off opposite a small, crescent-shaped clearing. This trail begins on a bench blanketed with spruce, and then drops gently through tufts of orange hawkweed and bristly dewberry, as well as thick mats of bog laurel, which in summer you'll find flying beautiful clusters of pink, saucer-shaped flowers. Also here is Labrador tea, the name of the plant derived from the fact that seventeenth-century

Bog Laurel

frontiersmen of the Northeast prepared a fragrant, rose-colored beverage from the leaves.

Soon our path exits the weave of spruce and laurel to arrive on the spongy peat shores of Moose Bog. The lovely reach of open water here, surrounded first by a fringe of leatherleaf, sphagnum, and pitcher plants, and then by somber huddles of black spruce, creates a truly wild scene. Here the pulse of nature seems to beat particularly strong and unfettered, a swell of life that is dancing not to the whims of humans but only to the slow, deliberate turn of the seasons.

As you make your way toward the edge of the pond (please stay on the existing path) you'll notice that the ground is springy, each step squeezing water as though you were walking on a saturated sponge. The surface of this bog, known as the mat, rests on top of a layer of partially decomposed dead plants (and, to a much lesser extent, animals), which is commonly referred to as peat.

Despite their very special beauty, their special blend of life, bogs are one of the least understood and fastest disappearing ecosystems in the world. Thus far, humans have tended to view bogs only by what can be taken from them. They vacuum them with giant suction machines to produce bags of peat moss for gardeners, treat raw sewage in them, farm fruits and vegetables on them, and are currently looking to mine them on a grand scale both for home heating fuel as well as for producing electricity. One would hope that, while there are still a few unspoiled places left in the Northeast, we would come to view bogs as worthy ecosystems just as they are.

Vermont State Naturalist Charles Johnson makes the point elo-
quently: "Reasons there are enough for us to watch over the Northeast's peatlands, from Cape May to the Allagash, from Lake Erie to
the Gulf of Maine—to cherish them as gifts and fellow travelers on
earth's odyssey—to allow some to exist on their own, to go where
they will."

Retrace your steps to the logging road. Before heading to your
car, you may want to explore a bit further down this two-track road.
From the trail junction 0.1 mile are some fine stands of cedar, speckled alder, and tamarack. This is also a good place to look for moose.
These remarkable creatures were once common as far south as Massachusetts, and here in Vermont, were plentiful enough (and easy
enough to shoot) that they provided early settlers with a great deal of
their daily meat. With records of individual settlers killing seventy-
five or eighty moose in a single season, it's no wonder that populations
declined rather quickly. Despite a rather ungainly appearance, the
typical 900- to 1,400-pound moose is well suited to move easily
through marshes and bogs. What's more, they show remarkable get-
up-and-go when threatened, having been clocked at speeds of 35
miles per hour for short distances. Cow moose have one or two young
in June; the bouncing babies typically weigh a whopping 25 to 35
pounds.

New Hampshire

FULLAM POND

Distance: 2 miles
Location: Pisgah State Forest. Head south on New Hampshire
Highway 10 to the town of Winchester. Once downtown, across
from the town hall, turn right onto Elm Street, which will immediately cross the Ashuelot River. Elm Street soon veers to the
right, becoming Chesterfield Road; 4.4 miles from where you
first turned onto Elm Street is a gate at the edge of the Pisgah
State Forest. (John Hill Road comes from the right near here.)
From this gate, proceed 1.45 miles to a road taking off to the
right marked by a 12. Turn right here, and drive for 0.5 mile to a
gated road on the right. Our walk takes off along this gated road.

Encompassing 13,000 acres, Pisgah State Forest is the largest tract of
undeveloped land in all of southern New Hampshire, and it offers
perceptions of nature that one would expect to find only in the long
sweeps of national forest lying far to the north. Each step along this
road will carry you deeper and deeper into the wilds, until, at the
north edge of Fullam Pond itself, you'll find yourself in the center of a
marvelous mix of beaver, deer, heron, and hawk, all wrapped in an
enticing blanket of trackless woods. Quiet days spent in such places
can offer a new appreciation for the wisdom of land preservation. The
writings of people like wilderness advocate Bob Marshall take on new
meaning. "One looks from outside at works of art and architecture,

245

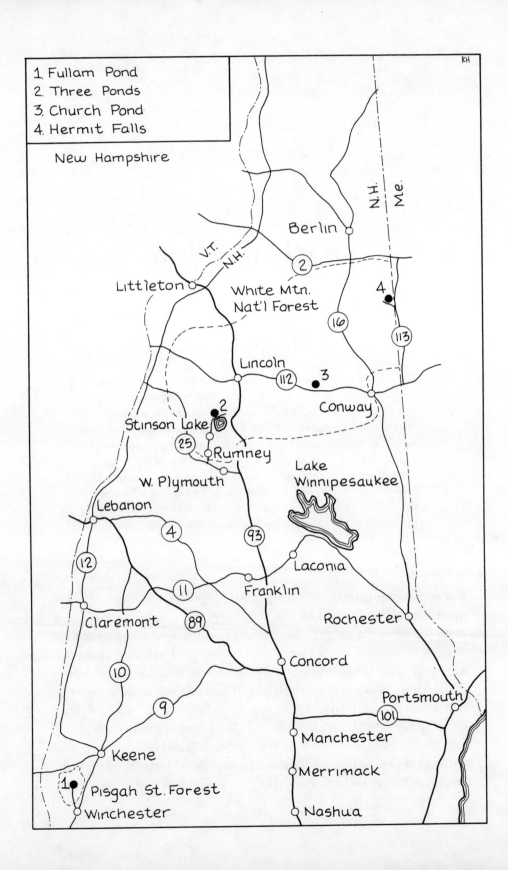

listens from outside to music or poetry," he wrote in *Scientific American* more than a half century ago. "But when one looks at and listens to the wilderness he is encompassed by his experiences of beauty, lives in the midst of his esthetic universe."

The forest here is a fine mix of soft- and hardwoods. Yellow and gray birch add slivers of light to the more somber huddles of hemlock. Clusters of witch-hazel dot the route, while striped maples, also known as moosewood, nod their supple trunks over the dwindling brim of the road. On the ground are shinleaf, Canada mayflower, bunchberry, bracken fern, and interrupted fern, as well as purple trillium and false Solomon's seal.

Take special notice of the hemlocks mentioned above. This conifer is particularly beautiful and one of the most easily recognized. Its branches are long and slender, and often droop to give the tree a rather shaggy appearance. (Pioneer women often used these branches as brooms.) The needles are spread in two rows, and have two white lines on the underneath side. If you have a good hand lens, take time for a close-up inspection of the many small pores—stomata—that dot the underside of each hemlock needle. These tiny holes, which are more easily seen on the hemlock than on most other trees, are what regulate the flow of air and water in and out of the "leaf."

Hemlock bark contains high levels of tannin. In the early part of the nineteenth century the bark was stripped from hemlock trees throughout New England at a rapid rate to be used in tanning shoe leather. You'll likely see, or at least hear, the incessant chatter of red squirrels gathering seeds in these trees. During winter months the porcupine also makes regular rounds of the hemlock groves, chewing away on both branches and bark.

Large hemlock groves produce such dense blankets of shade that none other than hemlock seedlings, which are very tolerant of low sunlight, can manage to get a foothold. Until fire, disease, or logging operations disturb these groves, there will be no contenders to threaten their position.

The road continues on a gentle meander through the woods, picking up small patches of ground cedar and wood nettle along the way. At 0.5 mile notice the white pine needles and cones visible on the road. At times these are the only clues that this stately tree is even present, so high do its bristly canopies lie above the rest of the forest. (Indeed, many times you'll find that looking for leaves lying on the ground is the best way to identify what species are really present in a forest, since in maturity many trees tend to self-prune lower branches that no longer have access to the sun.) The inner bark of white pine was used first by Indians and then by settlers as a remedy for coughs and sore throats, while some herbalists used the gum of the tree to produce a medicine for rheumatism. So strong and useful in building was the white pine that colonists chose it as their emblem on the first flag of the Revolutionary War.

Another plant to watch for here is the Indian pipe, a short, ghostly white plant that, through a partnership with root fungus, takes its nourishment from decayed organic material. At just under 0.7 mile, on either side of a small stream running through a culvert beneath the road, take a left off the main road. (Because of the thickness of the vegetation, you may hear the stream rather than actually see it.) This path is very faint at first, but becomes quite clear once you've made your way a few yards along it.

A short distance down this road you'll begin to see quiet pools on the right side of the trail, where beaver have backed up the stream flow. Look closely, and you'll find tree stumps with the beavers' teeth marks still plainly visible. The chewing teeth of the beaver, like those of many rodents, are remarkable in that they become sharper with use. The back of the incisor is made of a soft dentine, while the front is composed of a hard enamel. When a beaver chews on trees,

Indian Pipe

those rear layers wear down at a much faster rate, giving the teeth an angled shape. What's more, because the lower pair of incisors rubs against the upper pair, they tend to sharpen themselves with use.

Nudged against clumps of blueberry and clubmoss is the north channel of Fullam Pond, 0.3 mile from where you turned off the main road. Although the view is hardly the most encompassing one of Fullam, it is certainly one of the wildest. The thick braid of trees pushing their way to the very edges of the pond, the dead trunks rising from the water with arms frozen gray against the sky, give this place a delicious feeling of seclusion. Breathe it in deeply, and then take it with you wherever you go.

THREE PONDS

Distance: 4.4 miles
Location: White Mountain National Forest. From New Hampshire State Highway 25, approximately 3 miles east of West Plymouth, head north on the road to Rumney and Stinson Lake. The trailhead for our walk is on the left (west) side of this road, about 0.6 mile past the north end of Stinson Lake.

The rich blanket of forest and ponds lying northwest of Stinson Lake is a particularly peaceful place to ramble on foot, the kind of gentle setting that pulls you into a dozen little nooks and crannies for a closer look into the remarkable doings of nature. The sense of calm here is a far cry from what awaited southern New Hampshire resident John Stinson, the man who lent his name to both this lake and to the mountain southeast of here. Surprised by a band of St. Francis Indians during a trapping expedition in the spring of 1752, Stinson and one of his companions lost their scalps on these peaceful shores, while a third man, 24-year-old John Stark, was spirited off to Canada. (Despite this apparently brutal affront, Stark, who remained with his Indian captors for five weeks before being exchanged for a pony, would later say that he was treated far better than were prisoners of war in any civilized country. Stark went on to become a respected soldier in both the French and Indian and Revolutionary wars.)

You'll probably be struck by the lush pockets woven into the fabric of this forest—stream banks, beaver ponds, marshes, and cool, shaded ravines. This walk is wonderful for getting a better feel for how not only soil type but moisture levels influence what plants will be found in any given area. Some plants, such as hobblebush, can exist across a fairly wide range of conditions, while others, like marsh fern, are quite particular about where they set up shop. Using moisture as a beginning guide, you'll be able to predict where a surprising number of plants will be found long before you actually arrive there.

When beaver come in and flood the land—a phenomenon you'll see on this walk—they change the entire plant community in the process. As the water level increases, so do many of the plants that beaver relish most, including iris, water lilies, rushes, and spatterdock.

At 0.1 mile you'll reach a trail junction. Stay left, following the path marked with yellow blazes. This forest is pleasant—a flutter of maple leaves, the golden shreds of yellow birch bark, the shiny, aromatic boughs of balsam fir. On the ground you'll spot horsetail, whorled wood aster, sensitive fern, selfheal, and bluebead lilies. At about 0.3 mile into the walk the path will pass through large mats of wild sarsaparilla. The root of this plant, which you'll almost never see growing by itself, was once used as a flavoring for root beer, as well as for a once popular drink known simply as sarsaparilla. Herbalists continue to prescribe a tea made from this plant as both a stimulant

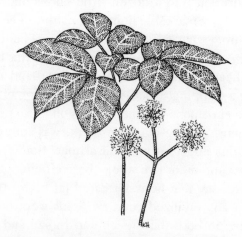

Wild Sarsaparilla

250

Beaver

and general tonic. (The berries, which usually ripen in July, are not edible.)

The trail continues through more open areas, past a small marsh, and at 0.9 mile, after passing by a thick garden of hobblebush, arrives at Sucker Brook. After crossing the bridge over this stream, take a right. Water in some engaging form, either stream or pond, will be with you for the rest of the walk. As you make your way along Sucker Brook, keep your eyes on the ground for violets, Indian cucumber, shinleaf, and partridgeberry. This latter plant was used often by New England colonial women, who made a tea from the leaves as a remedy for menstrual cramps. The berries, which have a faint taste of apple in them, are sometimes added to jellies and jams.

Just before you reach the first of several stream crossings at 1.5 miles, you should see a large flooded area on your right. If you comb the fringes of this pond you'll find the stumps of several trees that have been cut down by beaver, their incisor marks still very visible in the wood. Though occasionally a beaver is killed by one of the trees it is cutting, far more often it perceives the fall of timber in time to dash away—if possible, into the safety of a nearby pond. There the beaver will remain for a while, watching for predators, finally emerging (this time with other members of the family) to cut the branches. Armed with ever-sharp incisors, it takes a beaver only about ten minutes to

251

drop a six-inch birch. Perhaps motivated by some Rodent Hall of Fame that we humans know nothing about, there have been records of beaver cutting down absolutely mammoth trees. One of these in British Columbia measured more than three feet in diameter and was one hundred ten feet tall!

The trail continues crisscrossing watercourses, at times passing by several beautiful round-leaved orchids. Still more beaver sign will be found in the pond area on the left at 2.1 miles. This place is also good for looking for both blueberry and huckleberry. Besides being good to eat, herbalists have long prescribed a tea made of either young blueberry or huckleberry leaves to prevent kidney stones. Also along the trail here in summer are the delicate ivory blooms of false violet.

By 2.1 miles you'll be beside a relatively large pond, actually the middle of the "Three Ponds." At 2.2 miles the trail will fork. The right branch heads uphill, and eventually makes its way north to another pond a short distance from here. We'll stay on the left branch, which goes down to a pleasant shoreline opening. There's a fairly nice high, remote look and feel to this land—one that may leave you feeling it should have required a lot more huffing and puffing to get here. Then again, what did that guy who said "good things never come easy" really know? Maybe he was the same one who thought up those workaholic tags about beaver, like "eager beaver" and "busy as a beaver," when, in fact, this little engineer usually labors very little during the warm months. Sitting on some sunny shore at Three Ponds, I much prefer Gershwin's thinking:

> Summertime
> And the livin' is easy.

CHURCH POND

Distance: 2.2 miles
Location: White Mountain National Forest. This walk takes off from between sites 18 and 19 in Passaconaway Campground, which is located on the north side of New Hampshire Highway 112, 22 miles east of Interstate 93.

If you happen to be among those rare souls who are able to enjoy (or at least tolerate) sloshing through roughly 0.3 mile of wet bog trail, you'll find this walk to be among the most engaging of any in the White Mountains. Besides getting a close-up look at a true peat bog, sprouting rich mats of laurel, black spruce, small cranberry, leatherleaf, and Labrador tea, Church Pond itself is a true beauty— a wild-looking pool of water fringed by a regal stand of red pines.

Our walk begins in Passaconaway Campground, which takes its name from the great Pennacook Indian chief Papisse-conwa ("bear cub") who, in the early 1600s, ruled a powerful federation of tribes that were spread throughout northern New Hampshire. This chief led his people bravely through thick and thin, including a long, bitter period of disease and death that descended on the tribes after the arrival of the colonists. When Papisse-conwa died, legend says that he rose into heaven from the summit of Mount Washington, ascending in a great sled drawn by a pack of wolves.

You'll find the Church Pond Loop Trail taking off between campsites 18 and 19. The first order of business on this walk is to ford the Swift River, which the Pennacooks called Chataguay, or "the main stream." When you reach the far side you'll find a thicket of speckled alders waiting for you, a tree that provides valuable browse for both deer and moose. The water-loving alder is remarkably resistant to rot. In fact, it was a cousin of this tree—the European alder—that Hollanders used to create the piles on which they raised the city of Amsterdam. From the north shore of the Swift, the path follows a gravelly channel for a few yards, and then takes a right into a forest of maple, birch, and conifers. Soon you'll come to yet another water channel, although this one, at least in mid- to late summer, can be crossed merely with a bit of light-footed rock hopping.

In 0.3 mile you'll come to a place where the loop trail splits; stay left. For the next 0.3 mile you'll be in a tranquil forest of spruce, balsam, and white pine, the path in places covered with a carpet of needles so thick that your footsteps will not make a whisper. Look here for clumps of blueberry, Canada mayflower, shinleaf, trillium, bunchberry, and bluebead lily. At 0.5 mile there are also nice clusters of bracken, interrupted, and hayscented ferns, and, a short distance later, small mats of wintergreen and snowberry.

By the time you reach the 0.8 mile mark, you'll be in an honest-to-goodness bog, the open, spongy vegetation mats peppered with clusters of tamarack and black spruce, huddled like ragged old men against the wet and cold. As you make your way along this very soggy path (as peat bogs are very fragile, try your best to stay on the existing trail), you'll be surrounded by lovely bunches of bog laurel, which in June are bedecked with striking pink and white flowers, as well as leatherleaf and Labrador tea. Keep eyes and ears open for both boreal chickadees and white-winged crossbills, the latter using its hooked, crossed beak to retrieve seeds from the cones of black spruce.

There is a wild, very remote feeling here—the quiet of the bog, the crumpled quilt of conifers rising westward toward Sugar Hill and Greens Cliff. Standing here, toe-deep in brackish brown water, it's interesting to consider the slow rate at which such ecosystems are formed. It may take more than a century to create a single inch of peat; in the lower reaches of the bog, cut off from oxygen, the process is even slower. A foot and a half of peat bog may represent more than two thousand years of effort.

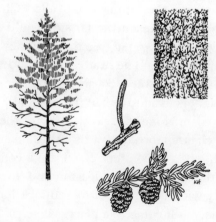

Black Spruce

Nearly half of this peat consists of humic acids, which are substances that tend to act as preservatives for organic materials. Pull a 200-year-old cedar log from the depths of a peat bog, for example, and it's likely to have an amazing amount of its original structural integrity. Particularly common in this brew is a waxy, resinous substance known as bitumen, a word you may recognize from the type of soft coal we call bituminous. The bog on which you're now walking may one day be a coal deposit, in the same way that today we mine coal from what were, millions of years ago, vast peatlands.

Interestingly, core samples taken from such peat bogs provide remarkable windows for looking into events of the past. The eruption of an ancient volcano, for instance, will show in the bog as a thin layer of ash. We can trace the sudden influx of Europeans on the continent by noticing the increase of ragweed pollen. But there are also more recent, much more troubling developments to be found in the upper layers of bogs—the sudden surges of lead that have accompanied the spread of automobiles, and higher and higher levels of poisons such as DDT and PCBs. Some future visitor from space landing by a peat bog would hardly need much more information to understand what have been the environmental costs of rampant industrial growth.

In 1 mile you'll come to the end of the bog, and at 1.1 miles you will find yourself in a beautiful grove of tall red pines. Here you'll have your first view of beautiful Church Pond. Linger for a while to explore the quiet inlets of the pond, to soak yourself in the sun and piney air. Rather than follow the loop, which will take you through longer, even more severe, sections of bog, it's best to return to the campground the same way you came.

HERMIT FALLS

Distance: 3 miles
Location: White Mountain National Forest. From U.S. Highway 2 in extreme southwestern Maine, head south on Maine Highway 113. In a couple of miles you'll see a signed turnoff on the right leading to Wild River Campground. From this point continue straight on Forest Road 113 for 7.9 miles to another road taking off to the right, which you'll follow for 0.6 mile to a parking lot at the south end of Basin Pond. You'll find our trail on the west edge of this parking lot.

It would be hard to think of a more beautiful beginning to a walk than a slow saunter beside the still waters of Basin Pond. This magnificent 1,500-foot-high amphitheater was carved roughly fifteen thousand years ago by the head of a massive glacier that flowed from here into the Cold River Valley to the east. Today's visitor will find the basin cradled by a striking mosaic of timbered slopes and ridges, and sheer, vertical walls of granite that make dizzy plunges into the valley below. On a very calm day, Basin Pond turns into a glassy reflecting pool, providing a double dose of not only bold mountainscape but of lovely clumps of shoreline birches, their slender ivory frames looking like ballet dancers frozen in the middle of a pirouette.

The path first enters a woodland community consisting primarily of birch and maple, with a few dark green dashes of balsam fir and hemlock. On the ground you'll find hobblebush, blueberry, bracken, ground cedar, meadow rue, and partridgeberry, as well as

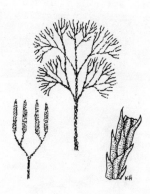

Ground Cedar

some nice mats of wintergreen and bunchberry, the latter especially beautiful when bedecked with lovely red fruits.

As was so true throughout New England, the plants of the northern forests have a long history of serving people as both grocery store and pharmacy. From the hobblebush, blueberry, and even bunchberry came edible fruits. Wintergreen contained an aspirinlike substance that proved effective in treating the discomforts of colds, flu, and muscle aches. Some Indians wiped their bodies with bracken fern fronds in order to mask their scent during hunting expeditions. Tea from hemlock bark was a popular treatment for bladder infections, and Native Americans and frontier doctors alike applied balsam resin as a healing salve for cuts and burns of the skin, and steeped the twigs of the tree in water for use as a laxative.

In 0.4 mile you'll reach the far end of Basin Pond—a beautiful wetland of tall grasses, sedges, and water-loving plants fringed with maples, birch, and alder. This spot is fine for seeing an occasional moose, as well as marsh wrens, tree swallows, and snipes. It's the snipe, incidentally, that gives off that strange whistling you may have heard while hiking around wet areas. The birds announce their territory by making a series of steep, dramatic dives from high above the earth, during which air rushes through the tail feathers and creates this eerie sound. A snipe's diet consists of roughly two-thirds animal matter, most of which is the larvae of aquatic insects, earthworms, and snails.

Common Snipe

257

As the road continues to meander westward you'll be given some beautiful glimpses through the weave of birch, beech, and maple of the high rocky rim of this glacial cirque. Science did not generally realize until about a hundred fifty years ago that glaciers covered not only the mountains but much of the North American land surface. This "ice age" (referred to as the Pleistocene) saw not just one but many advances and retreats of glaciers across the land. Some landscapes felt sheets of ice thousands of feet thick grind across them, each carrying the rocks and debris that would scour and polish their faces like an enormous belt of sandpaper.

At 1.3 miles, just after making a delightful crossing of Basin Brook, the light-colored forest of beech and birch trunks is suddenly flushed with beautiful dark green wisps of young hemlock. Much of this area was at one time thick with mighty hemlock, but these were removed in great quantities by lumbermen during the nineteenth century for their tannin-rich bark, used in the tanning of leather. Approximately 0.1 mile, just past this last stream crossing, is a small side trail marked by a sign that says Hermit Falls Loop Trail. We'll climb along this path for another 0.1 mile to our turnaround point at the base of Hermit Falls. On the way look for a couple of fine clusters of polypody fern. The roots of polypodies contain a licorice-flavored substance many times sweeter than sugar, which even before Roman times was valued as a remedy for coughs and chest congestion. Don't be alarmed if you hear strange noises in the woods around these plants—footsteps, twigs crackling, even voices—without seeing anyone. Some cultures, you see, believed that carrying the ripe spores of polypody would make them invisible.

Though not spectacular, this is certainly a wonderful spot to linger—a cool, shaded ravine thick with hemlock, spruce, and striped maple. The falls themselves consist of a thin veil of water plunging headlong over the rock, touching down in the midst of a patchwork of soft green moss.

Maine

STEP FALLS

Distance: 1.2 miles
Location: Follow combined routes U.S. 2 East and Maine 26 North out of the town of Bethel, to the point where these routes split. Follow Route 26 for 8 miles, to a small grassy parking area on the right side of the road, just before a bridge crossing Wight Brook. The path leaves from the north side of the parking area.

One thing is certain. This stream is definitely not just another pretty face tumbling down from the high country bound for the Gulf of Maine. Against one exceptionally beautiful, carefully sculpted flow of granite laced with glimmering intrusions of quartz, mica, and feldspar, Wight Brook has worked its magic, transforming the upper reaches of this ravine into one of the most comely marriages of rock and water I have ever seen. If it's true, as Richard Franck claimed three centuries ago, that art imitates nature, there could surely be no finer source of inspiration than this area.

Established in 1964 as the first preserve of the Maine chapter of the Nature Conservancy, Step Falls is cradled on the lower slopes by groves of spruce, fir, and hemlock, with the higher, more open areas a lovely mix of beech, white and yellow birch, and sugar and striped maple. There are nice wildflowers and ground covers along this pathway as well, including Canada mayflower, partridgeberry, trillium, blueberry, wood sorrel, bunchberry, Indian cucumber, hob-

259

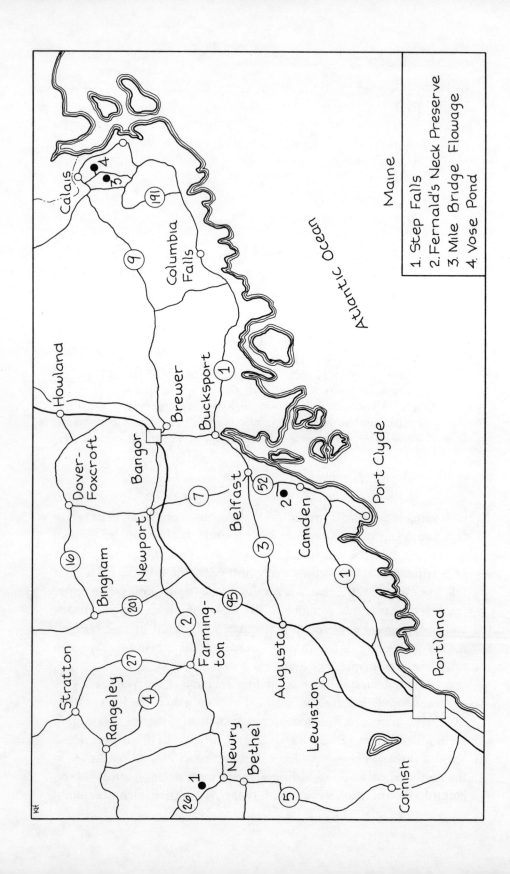

Maine

1. Step Falls
2. Fernald's Neck Preserve
3. Mile Bridge Flowage
4. Vose Pond

blebush, and goldthread. This latter plant of the cool woods—sporting shiny, strawberrylike leaves and delicate white flowers—was named for its shallow braid of yellow, threadlike roots. Many a colonist used this bitter rhizome as a treatment for fever blisters and canker sores, as well as to make a mouthwash from it to alleviate the pain of sore throats. The active substance in the roots of goldthread is a gentle alkaloid painkiller known as berberine.

Shortly after reaching an enchanting grove of white birch at 0.5 mile, you may wish to work your way up and across the granite rock flows that form the bed for Step Falls. (Be very careful, however, since these can be slippery.) The cooling of this granite from its molten state caused parallel fractures to develop in the rock. The waters of Wight Brook found these weak joints, along with splits that occurred from later upthrustings of the land, and probed, gouged, and polished the gorge into the striking collage of falls and plunge pools you see before you today.

When you reach the center portion of the rock flow, brace yourself, and turn around for a dizzy, breathtaking view of the high, forested peaks on the south side of Bear River. Standing on this high perch, it's easy to believe John Muir's claim that "the great poets, philosophers, prophets, able men whose thought and deeds have moved the world, have come down from the mountains." If greatness was indeed within them, what better stimulus to its flowering than to bask in these soaring, rocky realms of the gods?

FERNALD'S NECK PRESERVE

Distance: 2.75 miles
Location: From U.S. Highway 1 in the town of Camden, turn north onto Maine Highway 52. Just past the village of Youngtown Corner, you'll see the Fernald's Neck Road taking off to the left. Follow this road for 1 mile, keeping to the left at the one fork. The parking area is in a field on the right side of the road, adjacent to a small opening in the forest.

Viewed from any of several high perches nearby, Fernald's Neck, at the northeast corner of Lake Megunticook, appears as a patchwork of green forest and cool, blue water. This place is very quiet and rather subdued, a spot where upland streams gather and pause before toss-ing themselves headlong into the waiting arms of the Atlantic. Though not spectacular, this Nature Conservancy Preserve is most certainly an engaging place. The laughing of loons still rolls across the lake and into the thick of the balsam and birch. Feathery fern gardens can be found here, as well as huddles of red pine, hemlocks, and northern red oak. Slow down when walking these trails. You may see moose, white-tailed deer, or any of nearly six dozen species of nesting birds.

Our trail begins at the edge of an open, grassy swell, but immediately plunges into a woodland filled with the sweet, spicy smell of balsam. In less than 0.2 mile is the official entrance point for the 315-acre preserve, where you'll find a blue trail taking off to the right, and our path—an orange-blazed route—taking off to the left. Along the first few hundred yards you'll rub ankles with mats of huckleberry, whorled wood aster, clubmoss, ground cedar, and bracken and hayscented fern, as well as with some very nice stands of red pine.

Shortly after a fork in the trail, where our orange route takes off to the left, you'll arrive at the edge of Great Bog. Look here for pitcher plants, busy garnering nitrogen for themselves by breaking down the bodies of unlucky insects who have drowned in pools of water held by their tight weave of leaves.

You'll also be able to find nice clumps of blue-flag iris here. True to their name, which is taken from Iris, the Greek goddess of the rainbow, these beautiful blossoms are banners of pure, rich color, particularly striking when held against the bog's dull mat of greens and browns. It was the regal yellow-flag iris, incidentally, that once adorned the staffs of French kings, the three-part bloom representing courage, faith, and wisdom. The reason you most often see iris growing in clusters is because the flowers sprout directly out of the root rhizome, which, growing just beneath the surface of the soil, each year thickens and splits into branches. Though toxic, these rhizomes were for centuries used by Indians of the Northeast as a diuretic, a blood purifier, and a poultice for treating bruises.

There is a certain ethereal quality to this bog, made all the more dramatic if coastal fog has tiptoed in during the night. As you walk along its perimeter watch for clumps of beech, witch-hazel, red maple, and oak mixed in among the conifers, and listen for the chatter of red squirrels as they boldly announce their squatters' rights from the shaggy canopies overhead. Go right at a split in the trail at 0.7 mile, which in another 0.15 mile will deliver you to the shore of Lake Megunticook. This Indian name, by the way, is thought to have meant "big mountain harbor," and originally referred only to the quiet waters of Camden Harbor. As often happened, though, European settlers either didn't care or were too confused to understand what the boundaries of the highly descriptive native names really were, so today Megunticook also labels a river, a mountain, and a lake.

Lake Megunticook is where you may spot the common loon, which in summer wears a black and white checkerboard jacket with a striking zebra-striped necklace around its black-feathered head. The large webbed feet of the loon are set well back on the body, an arrangement that provides the bird with a great deal of kicking power in the water, but proves more than a little cumbersome when it comes time to navigate on land (which these birds seldom do). Loons are tremendous divers, and have actually been caught in fishermen's nets at depths of over two hundred feet!

Even if you never actually see a loon, just hearing its call can

Red Squirrel

Common Loon

be an unforgettable experience. Besides the unharnessed laughing for which loons are famous, they also emit a rather mournful yodel—a sound that some Maine Indian tribes believed foretold the coming of the wind. Henry David Thoreau wrote of the pleasures of listening to loons, especially after having been serenaded by them on the shores of Maine's Chamberlain Lake. "I could lie awake for hours listening to it, it is so thrilling," he said. In *The Maine Woods*, published two years after his death in 1862, Thoreau tells how he used to lay quietly in the middle of the night and try to decipher the sounds of the woodland's inhabitants. "I had listened to hear some words or syllables of their language but it chanced that I listened in vain until I heard the cry of the loon."

The trail continues around the deeply scalloped edges of Lake Megunticook, past northern red oaks, balsam, spruce, birch, and red maple, with pond lilies, arrowhead, and bur reed growing in the quieter stretches of the lake. At just over 2 miles you'll complete the loop portion of the path, after which you'll retrace your steps for 0.7 mile back to the parking area.

An old political saying that originated in the late 1800s claims, "As Maine goes, so goes the nation." I can't help but wish that the nation could have also followed a bit more closely the breadth of nature preserved in the Pine Tree State. It's indeed a pleasure to see this wild fabric still woven into so much of the land.

MILE BRIDGE FLOWAGE

Distance: 1 mile

Location: Moosehorn National Wildlife Refuge. From downtown Calais, Maine, head north on U.S. 1 for approximately 3.5
miles to Charlotte Road, and turn left. (You should see a sign for
Moosehorn National Wildlife Refuge at this intersection.) Continue south on Charlotte Road for approximately 5 miles, to a
small, gated roadway on the right named Mile Bridge Road. Park
here (though not in such a manner as to block the gate), and
begin walking northwest along Mile Bridge Road.

This short trek will take you to a fine wetlands area set in a wild,
woody lowland just east of the Moosehorn Wilderness. This land is
abundant in waterfowl and raptors, from black ducks and Canada
geese to bald eagles and osprey. Mile Bridge Flowage, which is
reached just 0.45 mile from the parking area, should be approached
as quietly as possible in order to have the best chance of sighting one
of these feathered beauties.

Our walk begins in a forest of black and white spruce, white
pine, birch, and balsam fir, with an occasional tamarack lending a
light, feathery touch to the scene. The airy structure of tamarack
branches allows modest amounts of sunlight to drip to the forest floor
below. Thus, if soil conditions are right, you will sometimes find
more ground covers and wildflowers doing business at the feet of
tamaracks than would otherwise be found in, say, a forest of spruce or
balsam fir.

But what makes the tamarack (also known as American larch)
truly different is the fact that it's deciduous. Late each autumn its
needles turn yellow and fall to the ground, to be replaced the following spring by an entirely new crop. Tamaracks do not do well in
shade, and hence are soon replaced by conifers whose young can
better survive having grown-ups continually blocking the sun. The
tamaracks' trump card, if you will, is that they have a very high
tolerance for acid soils, making them and black spruce nearly the sole
heirs to bogs and peatlands.

A short distance past a clearing on the right filled with raspberries, purple vetch, flat-topped white asters, and orange hawk-
weeds is a sizable stand of dead spruce. These unfortunate fellows
are victims of spruce budworm, an invasion by the larvae of a small
moth that feed on the buds of both spruce and fir. Spruce budworm

infestations can be devastating, and tend to run in cycles of about sixty to eighty years. The last major outbreak in Maine occurred in the late 1970s and early 1980s.

At 0.45 mile is the eastern edge of Mile Bridge Flowage, a long, sinewy water pocket fringed with cattails, sedges, and alder. Along the road here are evening primrose, orange hawkweed, goldenrod, and jewelweed, the most famous natural remedy for the itch of poison ivy or stinging nettle. Jewelweed is also known as spotted touch-me-not, and during late summer and early fall it produces fruits that explode at the slightest touch, sending a battery of tiny seeds in every direction. On sweltering summer days you may see the leaves of the jewelweed drooped and wilted. This condition is temporary, thought to be a means of conserving water.

Approximately forty yards to the west of where our walking road first joins Mile Bridge Flowage is an osprey nest in the top of a dead snag. One of the greatest thrills of all of nature is to watch one of these magnificent "fish hawks" hovering above a lake or pond, and then suddenly making a fast, silent plunge to the surface to grab a fish with its strong, spiny feet, carrying it headfirst back to its nest or treetop feeding roost. This method of hunting depends entirely on the osprey being able to see its prey clearly. Therefore, you'll find these birds along quiet waters, where the surface is not often broken by large waves. When young osprey are in the nest during early

Osprey

summer, only the male will be hunting, making dive after dive in order to supply his mate and her hungry brood with food. (Osprey eat only fish.) By mid-August, the youngsters will be hanging from the summer skies as well, each trying to master the delicate art of aerial spear fishing.

The high ridge visible ahead and slightly to the left is the eastern boundary of the Moosehorn Wilderness. If you have binoculars, scan the skies along this highline for a glimpse of the bald eagles, which have been nesting in the area on a fairly regular basis. These great birds of prey often make use of their imposing strength and size (6-foot wing spans are common) by stealing fish from neighboring osprey.

As you walk along Mile Bridge Flowage, you may wonder why there's a thick blanket of coniferous trees on the right, while the pond side of the road is covered predominantly with aspen and a few red maple. What has happened is that wildlife managers have burned the left side in order to encourage the growth of hardwoods, which provide better forage for wildlife. If left alone, the more shade-tolerant members of the coniferous forest will soon begin reclaiming their lost territory.

VOSE POND

Distance: 3 miles

Location: Moosehorn National Wildlife Refuge. From U.S. Highway 1 west of the town of Calais, turn south at the sign for Moosehorn National Wildlife Refuge. Follow this road south for several miles. Our walk is reached by turning left (east) on a small dirt road directly opposite the road that leads to the refuge headquarters. You'll reach a fork in the road 0.1 mile after turning off the pavement. Both branches have been gated. Park here, and begin your walk along the left fork.

Although Moosehorn is not a particularly dramatic place, it is nonetheless a beautiful one. Contained in this north unit of the refuge is a fine collection of lush, quiet nooks filled with a myriad of waterfowl, as well as a list of wildlife ranging from bear to beaver, moose to muskrat. Most of the treks here are along gentle roadways closed to motor vehicles, the perfect kind of track for easy, rhythmic walking.

Sometimes the images of Moosehorn are gentle ones—the wake line of a muskrat as it swims across a glassy pond, the waddle of a porcupine disappearing into the cover of a spruce grove. But the sights can also be dramatic, even startling. If you come here in the spring you may be treated to the striking aerial spirals and high-speed plummets of the male woodcock's courtship ritual. And in many places in the fall, you'll have a good chance of coming upon the rather surprising spectacle of a fat black bear dining in the high reaches of an apple tree.

Up the road 0.1 mile on the right is Tyler Flowage, one of more than fifty water-control areas in the refuge built beginning in the 1950s in order to increase habitat for waterfowl. You may spot mergansers, ring-necked and black ducks, as well as an occasional loon on these waters. Beside the culvert that runs beneath the road at Tyler Flowage are the remains of a beaver dam. "No matter what level we keep the water at," muses refuge manager Doug Mullen, "the beaver feel obligated to alter it." Aspen and birch serve as food as well as materials for the beaver building department, and are in good supply around the perimeter of the pond.

Continue up the road past a fairly young forest of black and white spruce, white and gray birch, red maple, and white pine. Along the fringes of the road are nice clusters of wild sarsaparilla,

Orange Hawkweed

Raccoon

bunchberry, whorled wood aster, Canada mayflower, purple vetch, and orange hawkweed. Hawkweed, by the way, takes its name from an old belief that hawks ripped apart these plants and bathed their eyes in the juices to sharpen their vision. It has long been given by herbalists for the relief of diarrhea and respiratory disorders.

In 0.4 mile the road will split; stay right. Just past this inter-section, in the forest on the right, are several narrow, cleared areas. These are strip cuts, harvested on a 50-year cycle in order to create the type of early successional vegetation preferred by many forms of wildlife, including the American woodcock. From the trailhead 1 mile, after passing collections of wintergreen, bracken, mead-owsweet, and sheep laurel, you'll come to Upper and Lower Goodall Heath flowages—large, wild-looking waters cradling both sides of the road. Here you'll find beaver, osprey, and marsh hawks. At the next road split continue bearing to the right, and at 1.5 miles you'll reach Vose Pond.

Vose Pond is an especially lovely place in the fall, when the surrounding canopies of birch, aspen, and maple catch fire with reds, oranges, and yellows. Very soon the woodcocks will be leaving for some faraway river or stream in the forests of the Carolinas. Black bear continue to fatten themselves on apples, berries, mice, and maybe even an occasional porcupine, one day to drag their bloated bellies into some hollow log or rocky den just one step ahead of the cold slap of winter. The geese are restless now, rising and falling from the open water in a clatter of honks and a rush of wings. "Days decrease," wrote Robert Browning. "And autumn grows, autumn in everything."